LENYA

THE LEGEND

THE LEGEND

A Pictorial Autobiography

Compiled and
edited by
David Farneth

THE OVERLOOK PRESS

WOODSTOCK & NEW YORK

First published in the United States in 1998 by
The Overlook Press, Peter Mayer Publishers, Inc.
Lewis Hollow Road
Woodstock, New York 12498

Text and compilation copyright © 1998 Kurt Weill Foundation for Music, Inc.

Library of Congress Cataloging-in-Publication Data

Lenya, the legend : A pictorial autobiography / edited with
an introduction by David Farneth.
p.   cm.
Includes bibliographical references and index.
1. Lenya, Lotte—Portraits. 2. Lenya, Lotte. 3. Actors—Germany—Biography.
4. Singers—Germany—Biography.   I. Farneth, David.
PN2658.L39L46   1998   792'.028'092—dc21 [B]   98-10625

Book design and type formatting by Bernard Schleifer

Manufactured in the United States of America

ISBN 0-87951-825-1
First Edition
1 3 5 7 9 8 6 4 2

Preceding page: One of the most famous images from
The Threepenny Opera: *Lenya singing "Pirate Jenny."*
Theater de Lys, 1954. Photo: Neil Fujita

PHOTO CREDITS: Al Hirschfeld/Margo Feiden Galleries, pp. 6, 136 (top), 209; Arbit Blatas, pp.
127, 138; Artists Rights Society (ARS), New York, p. 87; Atlantic Recording Company, p. 169 (top
right); Barron Storey, p. 215; Bertolt-Brecht-Archive/Akademie der Künste, Berlin, pp. 53, 61, 65
(bottom); Bildarchiv Preussischer Kulturbesitz, p. 59 (middle); Bildarchiv und Porträtsammlung
der Österreichischen Nationalbibliothek, p. 78; Corbis-Bettmann, pp. 90, 172; Dover Publications,
p. 169 (bottom left); Estate of Carl Van Vechten, pp. 18, 173; European-American Music Corp.,
pp. 51, 54; George Hoyningen-Huene/Harvard Theatre Collection, The Houghton Library,
pp. 82, 102; George Platt Lynes, pp. 12, 93; Institut für Theater- Film- und Fernsehwissenschaft,
Universität zu Köln, p. 64 (top), 66 (bottom), 68 (bottom), 113; Lee Snider, p. 208; Lotte Jacobi
Archives/University of New Hampshire, p. 14; Louise Dahl-Wolfe/Staley-Wise Gallery, New
York, pp. 91, 129, 133; Martus Granirer, p. 202 (bottom); Museum of the City of New York,
pp. 92 (bottom), 105; Neil Fujita, jacket and pp. ii, 134 (bottom), 136 (bottom right), 204 (top),
225; New York Public Library, pp. 101 (top and bottom), 124; Opera News, p. 213 (bottom);
Polygram Records, pp. 144, 145 (left), 152 (bottom), 162, 169 (bottom right); Richard Ely,
pp. 89, 168, 206; Sony Records, pp. 145 (right), 148, 149, 153, 160 (top), 175 (bottom),
195 (bottom); Stadtarchiv Zürich, p. 40; Ted Mitchell, pp. 187 (bottom), 196, 197 (top),
198, 214 (top and bottom), 219; Ullstein, p. 70 (top left and top right); Vincent Scarza, p. 19;
Warner-Chappell Music, pp. 96 (bottom), 152 (top); William V. Madison, p. 104.
ALL OTHERS: Weill-Lenya Research Center, Kurt Weill Foundation for Music, New York.

For Henry Marx

*In commemoration of Lotte Lenya's 100th birthday
by the Kurt Weill Foundation for Music*

Contents

Introduction

It's nice being called a legend. If you become a legend you must have made your point somewhere. Perhaps I did something which, if you want to get hifalutin', is recognized as art.

I think the more I write, the easier it will get. Maybe not, because it gets more difficult when you discover the danger of trying to make up stories. So "schtick" to the truth Kid— it's bad enough. — LOTTE LENYA (1898-1981)

"Mack the Knife." "Surabaya Johnny." "Alabama Song." With a shock of red hair shrouded in cigarette smoke, Lotte Lenya showed generations of Americans and Europeans alike "the way to the next whisky bar."

Some remember Lenya as the foremost interpreter of songs by Kurt Weill and Bertolt Brecht, or as the optimistic Fräulein Schneider in the Broadway version of *Cabaret,* or as the devious Rosa Klebb in *From Russia With Love* trying to take down James Bond with a knife concealed in her shoe. Others see her as a latter-day icon of Weimar Berlin, through whom they can experience the highly romanticized excitement and self-indulgence of that spirited and disorderly time. Still others praise her tireless efforts to introduce the public to the entire scope of Kurt Weill's music. Those who knew Lenya intimately remember a complex personality: warm but dispassionate, proud but unpretentious, tough but vulnerable, fun-loving with a streetwise sense of humor, frugal to a fault. But everyone who admires her art finds a special quality of honesty, directness, and true-to-life emotion in her performances. Lenya remains the personification of a bygone era, and, in many ways, a survivor.

A performing artist's one hundredth birthday offers a good vantage point from which to survey an entire career and the historical context in which it was achieved. Because the work of an actor or singer tends to be

Opposite: Al Hirschfeld's caricatures of the principal cast members of Cabaret, 1966. *From top: Joel Grey (Emcee), Bert Convy (Clifford Bradshaw), Jill Haworth (Sally Bowles), Jack Gilford (Herr Schultz), and Lenya (Fräulein Schneider).*
© Al Hirschfeld. Art reproduced by special arrangement with Hirschfeld's exclusive representative, The Margo Feiden Galleries Ltd. New York

ephemeral, captured primarily by audio recordings, stills, or moving images, it is the memory of live performances and the stories of behind-the-scenes maneuvers that provide the makings of a rich folklore. This collection, therefore, celebrates Lotte Lenya's centenary by presenting photographs, documents, and reminiscences from a life that paralleled the first eighty years of the twentieth century.

As a master weaver of myths, Lenya helped to create the multi-colored cloak of her public persona, but the stories that made her a legend in her own time were almost wholly designed and "accessorized" by her literary and media-savvy second husband, George Davis, a respected fiction editor for several New York-based magazines. He also wrote all of the magazine articles and record liner notes in the 1950s that appeared under her name. More importantly, Davis crafted the image of Lenya as the foremost interpreter of Weill's music and codified the embellishments to her story that she retold word-for-word, in interview after interview, long after he died. For the rest of her life, Lenya never deviated in public from her well-rehearsed stories about life in Weimar Berlin, her German career, and especially about how she met Weill, how he heard his music in her voice, how they supposedly escaped Nazi Germany together, and, by implication, the happiness of their relationship. (The fascinating tale of this truly "modern" and troubled union is revealed in their complete correspondence published by the University of California Press in 1996.) Lenya never was able to complete her autobiography beyond making some brief notes about her childhood. Even though she made a greater effort late in life to "stick to the facts," she could never bring herself to confide the whole truth, even to her closest friends.

Lenya's story begins in Vienna, telling of the abuse she suffered from her alcoholic father, the hope instilled by caring teachers, and the love of a mother who helped her escape a life of poverty. Practically on her own at age fifteen in Zurich, she recalls training in dancing and acting, her ascent from walk-on parts in operettas to roles in plays, the flush life in "neutral" Switzerland during World War I, and how she gradually came to enjoy gifts from her many male admirers. Following her mentor, Richard Révy, to Berlin, Lenya had difficulty finding work as an actress until she married Kurt Weill and secured a part in *The Threepenny Opera*. Her success in the role of Jenny led to steady employment in Berlin's theaters and several early recordings of Weill's music. Stifled in Berlin and confident in her new-found fame, Lenya tells how she left Weill for a tenor named Otto Pasetti, and demonstrates that she never knew the details of Weill's flight from Nazi persecution in Germany and his emigration to France. (In all her public interviews, she never discusses her divorce from Weill and their subsequent remarriage.) Weill, in his fashion, remained loyal to Lenya and even helped her and Pasetti with money and jobs. Eventually leaving Pasetti, Lenya came to the United States with Weill in 1935 and did not return to Europe until a decade after the war.

She had great difficulty establishing a career in America, resulting in a fifteen-year period of frustration. Devastated by Kurt Weill's death in 1950, she relied on George Davis to give her life meaning and to help her establish a new career as the keeper of Weill's flame. Thus began the Weill renaissance of the 1950s, during which she traveled back and forth between Germany and New York making recordings, giving concerts, and appearing in the famous off-Broadway production of *The Threepenny Opera* in New York's Greenwich Village. After Davis's death, Lenya, for the first time in twenty years, felt liberated enough to accept acting roles unrelated to Weill's work. She triumphed on stage in *Brecht on Brecht* and *Cabaret*, and made memorable appearances in a number of movies. Until her last days she remained steadfast in her mission to promote and protect Kurt Weill's music.

This book presents excerpts from Lenya's writings culled from personal and business letters, interviews conducted for newspapers, magazines, radio, and television, and the rudimentary notes she made about her life in Vienna, Zurich, and Berlin. Often these writings simply recount consciously prepared myths about her career; other times—especially in personal letters and informal interviews conducted late in her life (most notably one with Gottfried Wagner, the great-grandson of composer Richard Wagner)—they reveal more fully the qualities that make Lenya fascinating as a performing artist, and, in the process, debunk many of the legends that she herself propagated.

Lenya's life story is told in five chapters organized chronologically by the obvious periods of demarcation in her personal and creative life: childhood poverty in Vienna and freewheeling teenage years in Zurich; fame as a bona fide actress in Berlin; failure to establish a career in America; transformation into a singer, international recording artist, and keeper of Kurt Weill's artistic legacy; a return at age sixty-one to her first love: acting on stage and in films. This concocted "narration" is, by necessity, a patchwork of reminiscences, some made close to the events as they happened (as in letters) and others recalled years, even decades, after the fact. Many of the excerpts were chosen specifically to comment upon the photographs, which consist of production photos, headshots, posters, sheet music, news clippings, programs, and record jackets. Because the texts were selected only from Lenya's extant writings and interviews, several important moments in her career receive only sketchy treatment and many details are omitted entirely. For a complete and accurate outline of Lenya's life and career, the reader should rely on the chronology (pages 233-44) and the information provided in photo captions.

Framing the five main chapters are two thematic sections: a prologue, illustrated by photos spanning five decades of Lenya in performance, presents her views on acting and singing; an epilogue features Lenya's musings on life and art, illustrated by informal snapshots from her private life. A third section—an "interlude" about her life with Kurt Weill—falls between chapters three and four to mark the transition period between the "old" and "new" Lenyas.

Lenya's stories are edited for clarity and readability but with an effort to retain her syntax and speech patterns. English translations of writings or interviews that originally appeared in German are by Lys Symonette. Most German words or expressions that appear in English texts are also translated. In some instances, two accounts of a story are conflated into one; in others, the text may present two conflicting accounts of the same event. The editor's annotations are purposely brief and intended to provide historical background only when it is lacking in Lenya's narration. The identification of people, places, and titles of literary and musical works is minimal. Corrections of small details of fact are made without editorial comment. Because they are readily available elsewhere, letters to Weill are included only when needed to fill gaps in the narrative.

In the end, it is probably Lenya's private writings that provide the most distinct insights into those aspects of her personality not apparent in her public persona, for instance, her complex relationships with men. She summarized her feelings on this topic quite succinctly, "It's so nice to be dependent on a man. I can't think of anything nicer. Besides, I was born free and remain that way." Although she denied ever being a "heap of sensuality," the facts of Lenya's life may contradict her modesty. Still, intelligence was the trait she admired most in people. Possessing only an eighth-grade education, she took unstated but evident pride in moving comfortably among some of the brightest creative minds of the century.

Here, then, in celebration of her 100th birthday, is Lenya's story—in her own words.

Legends: On Singing and Acting

Caricature by Hesto Hesterberg of Lenya in the role of Jenny in **Aufstieg und Fall der Stadt Mahagonny,** *produced at the Theater am Schiffbauerdamm in Berlin, 1931.*

Although her singing may not be to everyone's taste, there is no doubt that in her own line Lotte Lenya is incomparable. Some may object to the raspy quality of her voice; but, after all, there is no such thing as intrinsically "good tone" in singing . . . . Lenya can infuse the word "baloney" with a wealth of knowingness that makes Mae West seem positively ingenue.

Lotte Lenya transports us to the Rue Sans Joie. The effect might perhaps be not so potent did one not recall her superb entrance dressed in a dirty blazer, stockings rolled beneath the knees, the flowers in her hair half concealed by a straw boater, inquiring the way to the "next whisky bar."[43]

— CONSTANT LAMBERT, composer, conductor, and critic

Rehearsing for a concert at Lewisohn Stadium, New York, July 1958.

An early U.S. publicity photo, New York, 1937. Photo: George Platt Lynes

I never took a singing lesson. Any Viennese can sing, you know? Really, it's in their blood.[70]

I love singing with an orchestra. Like a fish in water. Like on the ocean, being carried on a wave of marvelous sound. It's a happy loneliness when I approach a microphone to begin a performance. There is just the microphone and you, and it's almost like being on top of Mt. Everest. No one can touch you. It's a strange and wonderful feeling.[31]

I never sang in cabarets. At that time, in Berlin, cabaret was at its peak, and everyone sang in cabarets. I was approached many times to sing in cabarets, but I never could. I need distance, an orchestra in between, a pit. You see, I can't be so close—that's why I can't entertain at parties, for instance.[66]

Maria Callas is *the* dream singer of my time, because she is also an actress—a tremendous actress. If she wouldn't have had that voice—which so many people say is not that beautiful—I

think it's such a wonderful voice! But, do you think there's so much difference between the way she sings her aria in *Traviata* and the way I sing "Pirate Jenny"? She sings with the same understanding of what she wants to express, without losing herself, without completely swooping away into a trance, you know? Sure, Callas has a voice—she has to. Where I use five horse powers, she uses fifty-five, because her material is so much bigger than mine. But the effect is the same. Maybe this is very presumptuous of me to say, but they have called me so many times now, Callas of the Songs.[8]

No, no, no. No, I never will be a prima donna, and never was. Prima donnas are very stupid anyway, otherwise they wouldn't be prima donnas. My attitude in the theater is that you just step in and step out of your performance. If someone asked me a question in the middle of singing "Pirate Jenny," I could stop, answer the question, and pick up singing right where I left off, because I don't need to create a mood. I don't have to get into a trance to do what I do. I'm like a ditch digger, digging the ditch. He can stop, drink his coffee, and keep on digging until the ditch is finished. There's no difference.[8]

I learned music very fast. Weill would play it and sing it for me once or twice, and then I had it. When I sang for Brecht, he didn't correct it, you know? He let it go. For them it was the right way.[72]

The notion that singing "against the music" represents some sort of Marxist dialectic is the most nonsense I've ever heard. Brecht said it is very effective, at certain times when it's necessary, to speak against the music. I do that all the time. And it's very effective, but it doesn't mean you shouldn't sing the music at all. That's not what he meant. That is a misunderstood theory. Listen to my records carefully, because I really sing. I sing the melody. Sometimes I speak in between, when the emotion needs it, but every note is there, even if I speak.[52]

When I'm on stage I never try for anything special. I do just what's handed to me. If it's a poem by Brecht or a song by Weill I sing it the way it is written. I try to understand what they are trying to say, and I do that with utmost sincerity. That's all I can do. Whether the way I present it becomes a personal style, that is

A classic pose from Mahagonny, *autographed to Kurt Weill: "Für mein Kurti von seiner Jenny, Berlin d. 29.5.1932." Photo: Elli Marcus*

14

Berlin, ca. 1930.
Photo: Lotte Jacobi,
Lotte Jacobi Archives,
University of
New Hampshire

something else again. But you will always know what I am singing about. It is clear, crystal clear. The idea is to feel it. No trick involved. As honest as you can be.[34]

Look, everyone gets older, and that means your voice also slides down a few notes. But my style has not changed a bit. I don't think of the Brecht-Weill songs as my material exclusively. I'm sure of what I'm doing, but the agony of doing it is always there. I get so angry when people say, "But you have sung it so many times." I say, no, it's always new, don't you understand? It's never the same. The structure is the same, but I think this fear and agony which I go through brings an intensity which is always fresh and always new. That's something one should never lose.[73]

Acting. I preferred it to singing, at least to singing alone. I played such beautiful things in Zurich—plays by Wedekind, Kaiser, Tolstoi—all those things. Singing came too easy for me. That was no big deal. But acting was a challenge.[72]

The role I liked best of any was Anna I in Weill's *Seven Deadly Sins.* It's total theater—singing, dancing, acting—they are one.[9]

Young American actors have to resort to acting studios to learn their craft. When they do get a job, and let's say the play is a hit, then they are stuck for two or three years in one part and have no chance to develop. In Berlin we worked in repertory companies, which meant that you play Shakespeare, Schiller, Molière, Wedekind, Brecht all in one week. That gives you a great variety. American audiences are used to the star system; they'd have to be taught to appreciate the repertory system.[52]

I never get bored with playing a part that I like. I'm enthusiastic from the first day until the end. If you don't give whatever you can to the audience, I think it's cheating them. I don't want to do that. I love the part, so I play it the best I can. And it shows, you know?[70]

My quality on stage, besides being humorous, is a little sad, and that's what makes it a bit special. You can't talk about it; you have to show it. When I'm on stage, I can show it. This quality of being funny and sad at the same time is very hard to talk about.[34]

Top: Preparing to sing "with utmost sincerity," Berlin, 1929.

Bottom: In the role of Ilse in Frank Wedekind's play Frühlings Erwachen (Spring's Awakening), *Berlin, 1929. Lenya co-starred with Peter Lorre.*

Left: As Rosa Klebb in the James Bond film From Russia with Love *(1963). "My most famous role." Photo: United Artists*

Below: Plucking a chicken in Bertolt Brecht's play Mutter Courage, *Ruhrfestspiele in Recklinghausen, 1965 Photo: Manfred Pauls*

Left: As the luxuriantly wicked Contessa Magda Terribili-Gonzalez in The Roman Spring of Mrs. Stone *(1961), based on a novel by Tennessee Williams. Photo: Warner Bros.*

Opposite page: A concert in Munich during Lenya's second European career, 1960. Photo: Werner Neumeister

Portrait by Carl Van Vechten, New York, 1962.
Photo reproduced courtesy Joseph Solomon,
Executor of the Estate of Carl Van Vechten

They should let me pay to be in movies. In a film, it's only my reputation at stake. But when it comes to Kurt Weill, I feel a great responsibility to do the best. It's ten times harder than when I'm on my own.[28]

Like a friend of mine said, "I love that voice of Lenya, it's one octave below laryngitis."[8]

Walking a Tightrope 1898-1921

Lotte Blamauer, who also was from Vienna, had been engaged at the theater in Zurich at the same time I was. . . . Blamauer always sat next to me in the only dressing room for ladies. We were also practically the same age. She was terribly interesting to me. She was always seen with officers and picked up by officers—always different ones—and the gossip about her naughtiness was enormous. The nicest thing about her was that she was always in a good mood. Also, she had an air about her of something taboo, therefore very interesting.[10]

—ELISABETH BERGNER, actress

I was born October 18th, 1898. Karoline Wilhelmine Charlotte Blamauer are all the right names . . .[49]

My father, Franz Blamauer, came from Anzbach. He was already a coachman when my mother, Johanna Teuschl, fell madly in love with him. He was not just a driver for hire, but drove the finest horses of a rich factory owner who lived in central Vienna and was the final authority on anything that concerned horses. That made him adored by the neighbors, so handsome and such a son-of-a-bitch: tall, slim hips, high polished boots, reddish sideburns and moustache, blue hound's eyes,

Jenny, as painted by third husband Russell Detwiler. From the collection of Vincent Scarza.

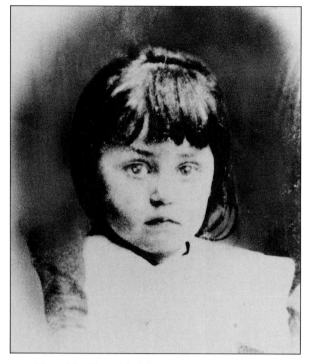

*Above: Karoline Wilhelmine Charlotte Blamauer
(Lotte Lenya) at age three.*

*Below: Group photo of children in the Penzing district of Vienna
(1901 or 1902). Lenya, front row, third from left. Lenya's
older brother, Franz Blamauer, at age four, sixth from left.*

sharp thin nose, and wonderful white teeth that he ground in a terrible way when he was drunk, which was most of the time.[45]

My mother, a tiny, well-rounded woman with high Slavic cheekbones, wonderfully alive and searching gray eyes, and thick chestnut hair pulled tight back into a knot, came from Ottenschlag, a village near Melk. Her mother was a hard-working, hard-hitting woman with no tenderness for the children, but her father was a gentle man who sang in church on Sundays. My mother had three sisters, all the same height—five feet—and one brother. All the girls came to Vienna to work. Aunt Julie was extremely smart. She married a gardener, and together they took care of a villa that belonged to the Brauns, a wealthy industrial family. I think she stole quite a fortune! Aunt Wetti would do almost anything too. My mother was much more honest—stupidly honest, you know? Her nature was basically gay, stalwart, intrepid, with a horror of all fake sentiment. It was also deeply and resourcefully female, with a quietly operating magnetism that attracted all men within reach. The neighbors used to say, "Frau Blamauer has only to see pants on a clothsline and she's pregnant," to which my father added his own pretty saying, "As many dumplings as there are in the soup, that many must come

out." All of which added up to a seemingly endless succession of miscarriages, stillborn babies, and others that died soon after birth. Of the four that came out intact, my brother Franz preceded me by a year, Max was two years younger than I, and my sister Maria (or Mariedl) eight years younger.

I was the third child born. The first one died when she was four years old, and I was given her name, "Karoline"—"Linnerl" for short in Viennese. It was an unfortunate choice, this name, because my father, who adored the first child and took to heavy drinking after she died, could never look at me without resentment. I had to stay out of his way as much as I could in that crowded one room and kitchen we lived in until I left home for good.

My father had no love for me and showed it whenever he could. He used to come home drunk in the middle of the night and lift me out of my bed so I could sing for him the most stupid song he knew from his youth, *Wenn der Auerhahn balzt und das Rotkehlchen schnalzt* ["When the grouse clucks and the red robin keeps time"]. The worst thing was the way he lifted me out of my bed. It was just a wooden box, this bed of mine, with a straw mattress and a pillow, and during the day it was used as an ironing board, or a bench for people to sit, or the place where my mother made noodles. He placed his two big hands around my neck like a strangler would do. There I stood with my eyes full of sleep and tried to please him, tried to be as good as the first one was, tried desperately to turn my head the other way so I didn't have to smell his sour breath, until I was pushed back to bed to hear him say, "She's a cathead," whatever that meant. There I would lie trembling with fear. But my mother, whom I loved, came to my rescue, putting the wooden board over my bed so that he would forget about me.

Other nights my father would grab the kitchen knife, and I would run down one floor to the concierge to hide under her bed until morning. One night I escaped near death. He was dreadfully drunk and after the usual procedure of lifting me out of bed, he got so furious at me for not remembering all the lines of the song that he picked up the oil lamp and threw it at me as I stood trembling in the corner. From the force of his throw the flame went out, and I was saved from burning to death when the lamp crashed into the wall. I was shaking for the next ten days and was kept out of school. The next day my father came home from his

Above: Mother, Johanna Teuschl Blamauer, ca. 1915

Below: Father, Franz Blamauer, a coach driver, ca. 1900.

job three times during the day to bring me things to eat, which I refused without saying a word. I simply turned away from him. He was frightened that my mother would report him to the police. When he got so wild at times and hit her, she only had to say, "I'll let the police take you away," and he immediately calmed down and went to sleep.

Tucked away in my box (which had a square hole cut in it for breathing), I was safe from my father when he got up in the morning, screaming for his boots, which he had taken off on his way home and my brother had to search for in the little field behind the house. From our kitchen window we could see across the field to the tavern where he spent most of his meager salary. When my father finally slammed the door to go to work, my mother took the board off the bed and gently said, "Linnerl, you can get up now." And then I crawled out and went down to the basement to help my mother wash the laundry of her different clients until it was time to go to school. I loved those washdays, where I would be alone with her and could watch her across the steam-filled room, with her strong peasant face, her beautiful gray eyes, and her incredibly delicate hands wrestling with those big sheets. And once in a while she would look across what she was washing and say, "Linnerl, try to make a better life for yourself," and I would say, "Yes, Mother, I will." And the woman in the other corner of the room, washing the laundry of her thirteen

Josef Englehart's painting "A Dance at the Drying Grounds," 1896, depicts the spirit of Viennese laundry women.

children, looked up and said in a strident, bitter voice, "Why do you think she is something better than my children? She'll never get out of this house, just like the others." And I would look back at my mother and smile, and only my eyes would give her the promise to fulfill her wish for a better life for me. Then it was time for me to leave for school. Before I said good-bye to my mother, she gave me two little pieces of lump sugar she saved for me from my father's coffee.

I used to say to my mother, "Why weren't we born rich? Why did you have to marry that man? He can't be my father! Think, Mother, couldn't I have another father?" She would only smile, but never answered.

Lenya's childhood tenement building at 38 Ameisgasse in the Penzing district of Vienna, as it looked in 1993. Photo: David Farneth

Below: Apartment door and staircase at 38 Ameisgasse. Photos: Lys Symonette

All I remember from our first house on Linzerstrasse is one cherished possession: a small box filled with bits of ribbon. At about age three, we moved to a tiny, two-room apartment on a courtyard, ground floor, and very damp. At the end of the alley was a wooden shed where a butcher slaughtered calves and pigs. We used to go and watch him suspend them by their hind legs and slit their throats, absolutely fascinated, to the disgust of my mother.

Then we moved into a large tenement building located in Penzing, the 14th district of Vienna, and a vast improvement from the previous place. There were three houses on each side of the street called Ameisgasse. The houses all looked alike, and you could only tell them apart by their numbers. There were forty-one families living on its three floors. A huge painting of Christ hung in the entrance hall. Every so often, when in a hurry for school, I forgot to make the sign of the cross and usually ran back to do so. My mother and sister lived there for the rest of their lives.[45, 72]

The building was literally on the wrong side of the tracks, only a stone's throw from Hietzing, a very elegant quarter. Years later, when I visited my sister in the same apartment house where we grew up, I was overwhelmed by the terrible proletarian smell of the building. My life-long fear of poverty made my heart pound! My sister's little apartment was immaculately clean, but the smell of the house still crept through the door.[22, 45]

The nice thing about the house was, being at the corner, our bedroom window faced the park. There were big fields between the factories and our joy was a little hill called Flea Mountain, where we spent our winters sliding down hills on our homemade sleighs. The fields were full of thistles in summer, and we developed a technique to catch butterflies while they were resting on the buttercups or cornflowers. Then we pinned them on pieces of cardboard and brought them to school for drawing material. (I did not like to pin them and left that to my brothers.) From our bedroom window one could also see the golden roof of the insane asylum called Steinhof. My father's sister was interned there, having been picked up in the streets of Vienna naked. My mother took us there one Sunday afternoon for a visit; she had also baked a cake for her. My aunt came with a warden, smiling, and telling us how much she liked it there, and the only thing that bothered her was that they kept pouring water on her head during the night. My mother gave her the cake. When she broke off a piece and handed it to me, I went screaming into a corner refusing to eat it out of fear I would become crazy too. Shortly after that visit, she died.

From the kitchen window sill we could see the Emperor's summer palace, Schönbrunn, and the two circus wagons stationed in the field throughout the year. The circus was run by a large family. In the early spring they set up their source of income for the long winter months by building a stage twenty feet long and twenty feet wide, a little balustrade for the four musicians, and bleachers for about 100 people. A wooden fence framed the stage and the bleachers; the people on the outside of the fence paid a nickel, and those on the inside, controlled by a little box office, paid a dime for the privilege of sitting on hard wooden benches. The entertainment consisted of dancing, acrobats, tightrope, and clowns. The clowns were the saddest part of the evening. Their jokes were feeble, and that audience of laborers was hard to please. Among the people outside the bleachers was a five-year-old wide-eyed girl, who never was asked for a nickel but was asked whether she would like to learn to dance and walk the tightrope. Having watched from my kitchen window for two years since the age of three, I was only too willing. My father could not have cared less, and my mother was happy for me, knowing how crazy I was to be in the "Theater." They dressed me in a Hungarian peasant dress with lots of ribbons flying

Lenya could see Schloss Schönbrunn from the bedroom window of her family's two-room apartment.
This photo, taken in the 1950s, shows Lenya's sister Maria and her husband Peperl.

around my head, a tambourine in my hand, and there I was, dancing to the tune of, I think it was Brahms (nobody ever could recognize it the way those three or four musicians played it). I learned to stand on my head; I had practiced that long before with my brother. But the more difficult task was learning to walk the tightrope. It did not matter how high the wire was placed; it still worked on the same principle, which is balance. A wire was put up four feet above the ground, a little Japanese paper umbrella was placed in my hands for balance, and off I went. I fell many times, but I eventually learned it, and I was a success with the audience, mostly consisting of neighbors. One night they hired a sensational attraction: a woman who slid down on a wire drenched in pink light, wearing a dress that opened like wings of a butterfly, hundreds of pleats. It was breathtaking. I went home, and the next morning after everybody had left the house, I took my father's suspenders, placed them on the hook my mother put up in the doorframe for drying her laundry during the winter months, got up on a kitchen stool, placed the suspenders in my mouth, and flew, with the result of losing two baby teeth. For the time being, this was the end of my theatrical career. A few years later, their license for the field was not renewed and the circus moved away; the field was taken over by a huge company that sold coal and wood. My kitchen window lost its attraction for me, but I shall never forget that little company that gave me the first opportunity for *"Die Bretter, die die Welt bedeuten"* ("The stage, which means the world to many people").

I was born with an allergy for which no doctor could find the cause. In a way, that was a blessing for me. I could enter the hospital, which was within walking distance from the house on the Ameisgasse, at the first sign of swelling, which usually appeared at my lips, eyes, and neck. (This harmless stigma gave me great trouble later on when I was a student at the ballet school in Zurich.) The doctors at the hospital knew every member of the Blamauer family. My brothers were there constantly with either broken arms or cuts on their feet from walking through brooks in the Halderbach, near Hütteldorf, where people carelessly threw beer bottles at the end of their picnics.

My mother did not bother to go with us whenever we had to go to the hospital, for she knew that we would be treated nicely, and I was especially treated nicely because the doctors liked me. I recited little poems for them during their lunch hour, and for that I was allowed to pick strawberries in their garden, to the envy of the rest of their patients. The moment I checked in, I was put to bed and put on a diet consisting of rice and applesauce. I loved both. Once I was lying in the ward with grown-up patients and children. Right across from me, a servant maid was brought in one afternoon. She had tried to kill herself with Lysol (the most popular way of committing suicide at that time). Since I was lying directly across from her, I could watch the nuns taking the innumerable hairpins from her jet-black hair, cursing her as much as their Catholic religion allowed them to do, and finally slapping her face with cold towels to revive her. Her skin was marble-white and showed no sign of life after hours of trying. Finally a screen was put up around her, and our beloved priest appeared to give her the last rites. I felt a strange curiosity; I wanted to see her, wanted to see once more that alabaster face now gone forever. But the screen was not removed and the body was taken during the night to the chapel. When I woke up in the morning, a clean bed was waiting for the next patient.

As soon as the hives disappeared, they sent me home. After being released for a few days, I prayed that my hives would soon show up again. The hospital is now a home for the aged and located across the railroad tracks which divided Penzing (the workers' district) from the elegant Hietzing, where the emperor

Church near Lenya's childhood home as it appeared in the 1980s. Photo: Lys Symonette

Left: Brother Franz at age 19 (1917). "Franz was the first surviving child. My father never looked at him."

Below: Brother Max, two years younger than Lenya, became an ambulance driver during World War I.

Franz Josef got off the train at the Penziger-Bahnhof station to be driven to Schönbrunn, with us schoolchildren throwing little bouquets of flowers at his open carriage. Next to the hospital was a church, where my brother and I rang the bell every evening and morning. You had to pull hard on the rope to make the bell ring. I did not do so well. I was too light. But my brother managed, and I was glad when they took the job away from me.

My brothers and I used to get bread that the soldiers tossed down to us from the barracks, and sometimes we got wonderful food—like goulash—from the kitchen of the Hopfner Hotel in Hietzing, that the cooks put in the little pots we brought.

At six I started at an elementary school off the Linzerstrasse and soon was transferred to another overcrowded school (35 pupils) in the Diensterweg Gasse. I was 9 years old when I was placed in the fashionable school in Hietzing am Platz with only 15 pupils in the classroom. Miss Schwarz, the teacher, became the love of my childhood. She was no more than 5 feet tall, black hair with here and there a thread of silver running through, eyes like black cherries, kind and lovable. Her hunchback, which made her seem even smaller than she actually was, made her look like everything she had to carry was too heavy for her fragile shoulders. She was wonderful with the three poor children in the class, never patronizing us. I still can hear her gentle voice asking me, "Blamauer, why don't you answer me? That's the second time I called you to the blackboard." I did not hear her. I was occupied with my feet, which were icy cold. I tried to squeeze out the water which came through the torn soles of my shoes. I started walking towards the blackboard, and all the kids giggled because my shoes made a squeaking sound. When I arrived at her desk, tears were running down my face, partly from shame, partly from the cold. She saw me stepping from one foot to the other, leaving a little puddle of water under my feet. Lovingly she looked at me, made me take off my shoes, and wrapped my feet in newspaper for the rest of the hour. My shoes were put on the radiator to dry them out. Then she asked the girls (most of them came from well-to-do families, some of them very rich) to bring shoes and clothes for me the next day. Then she arranged for me to get a certificate for "community shoes." I hated those shoes with a passion. They were so stiff, as if made for eternity, with thick soles, much too big; they gave me blisters the first day I wore them, and on days when it was not raining or snowing, I went right back to my old shoes in spite of all the holes. Some sunny days she took me for a walk in the Schönbrunn next to the school, the emperor's summer residence, where no child was allowed to pass through the gate unless accompanied by a grown-up. I carried her books and she took me to the Palm Garden, teaching me the names of all the beautiful tropical plants. Those were my happiest days.

Every now and then, some of the kids brought Miss Schwarz fruit from their own gardens. And she would share with me delicious candy from her father's store on the way home. She even bought me a white dress for my first communion. At Christmas I made her bookmarks, which she loved. I painted on them some of the flowers whose names she had taught me on our walks in the Palm Garden. Her kindness never faded through the three years I was her pupil. She gave me excellent marks, which I needed in order to get into the *Bürgerschule*, or middle school. Many times after I left her school, I waited outside for her, again to carry her books and tell her all about my progress in the new school. She smiled proudly when I showed her my first good report. After all, she was part of it.[45]

The first time I went to a theater was in school. They took us to a theater in Vienna, but we sat so far up that we couldn't see or hear anything. So it left no impression on me whatsoever.[17]

Both my parents were absolutely unable to carry a tune, but all of their children were musical. My older brother taught himself to play the piano, and my sister sang like a nightingale. My mother's father was musical, so I guess the talent skipped a generation. School helped to develop my talent, because I was always asked to recite poems. Music was my favorite subject, it was so easy for me, but teachers didn't push me to learn to read music because I could sing all the songs right away. I wish I could have learned an instrument. I loved history and geography with a passion. All the rich kids got to sit in the front, and I was stuck somewhere near the back. So I pretended to be nearsighted and teacher put me in the front row. That still wasn't good enough for me—that front row! I almost ruined my eyes by pretending to read everything up close.[72]

One day during my school vacation, my father took me to his sister, Aunt Marie, who had visited us many times, always bringing cookies and chocolate from her little store in Ottakring in the 17th district in Vienna. The walk was a very long one, crossing an enormous garbage dump. My aunt needed help to distribute the milk and rolls she sold, among other dairy products. I had to get up at six o'clock in the morning, fill ten tin cans with milk, one pint each, stuff two rolls in a bag, and off I went to place the milk and the rolls in front of the door where people found them before going to work. It took me about an hour before I returned to the store. I loved this little dairy store and after a while I even grew very fond of my aunt. She used to take an afternoon nap right after lunch, and that was the time when people looked in the window and came in when they saw me alone, knowing that I always gave them more than the scale indicated.

I was with my aunt for about a month when the whole picture changed. She made the acquaintance of a man, and he moved in pretty soon after. I could not sleep in the bed with her any more, but was put on a couch, which I should not have minded after sleeping on a straw sack at home. But I was hurt at being shoved around on account of this stranger. What made me dislike him even more was that when I sometimes had to cross the living room in order to get to the store when the bell was ringing, I saw my aunt putting some bandages around his privates, which frightened me. I never did find out what he had, and when I told it to my mother, she brushed me off by saying, "He

Lenya with her sister Maria (left) and a friend, ca. 1913.

Sister Maria as a child. Photo: F.K. Adler

is a sick man and you would not understand it even if I would tell you." I grew more and more homesick; nobody from my family came to see me. One noon, when he got *Wienerschnitzel* for lunch and I got a pair of frankfurters, my pride was so hurt that I took a nickel from the cash register and ran to the streetcar—which was very close by—and went home. I was not received enthusiastically at home, and my father greeted me with his usual love for me, hitting me as hard as he could. My mother quickly shoved me into the bedroom so my presence would not aggravate him further. I did not cry; I was happy to be home.

Miss Freyer made a hissing sound when she addressed me as "Sie" (the formal word for "you") instead of the familiar "Du" used in elementary school. She was not lovely to look at, yet she had the impertinence (or so I thought) to braid her hair in the style of the beautiful Empress Elisabeth. Beneath her coal-black beady eyes was a nose that seemed larger than it really was—first because there was almost no chin to balance it, and secondly because her stiff white collar was therefore free to ride up over her mailbox slit of a mouth and emphasize the flare of her nostrils.

When I was called to her desk to hear her criticize my drawings it sounded like "Sie" was spelled with six S's instead of one. "*Blamauer, SSSSSSie nehmen sich zuviel Freiheiten heraus in Ihren Zeichnungen* [You're taking too many liberties with your drawings]. The carrot I gave you to draw had wilted green on top; yours is fresh green. Go back and change it." Since she evidently did not like me, I got nothing but vegetables to immortalize. Miss Freyer's two "pets" sat next to me. Greta had a lovely, lemon-colored butterfly, pinned to a small wooden block, and Paula a bunch of snowdrops, to my great envy. They had no talent whatsoever but got an A mark, and my carrot, criticized by Miss Freyer, drew a meager C. I never managed to get an A throughout the semester. I also never got an object which interested me; she saw to that. The second year we had a male teacher, and I was in heaven with the things he gave me to paint. While under the thumb of Miss Freyer, I swore to myself that when I was out of school I would, if I should meet her, turn my head, showing her my dislike. Well, the last school day came and I got my revenge (which was a childish one but felt good).

It so happened that she always passed my house on her way home. After my last day at school, I was (as usual) sweeping the sidewalk, a job for which I was paid a nickel a week—which I invested immediately in a *Punchkrapferl*, a cake no bigger than an egg, covered with pink icing, dipped in rum. I saw her familiar figure approaching. Even from a distance she was unmistakable, because of her peculiar gait—with thighs kept close together as if to protect her virginity, although, in fact, it was never in the slightest danger. I leaned on the broom and watched her. As she passed me, I ostentatiously spat in the gutter, and then continued sweeping.[45]

The day I finished public school, at age fourteen, my mother took me to begin a four-year apprenticeship at the Ita hat factory, a stone's throw from where we lived in Penzing. I had to learn to trim and decorate men's hats. All kinds of hats: soft hats, top hats, derbies, wide brimmed and rounded, low crown, etc. It was very delicate work: little ribbons attached to sweatbands, satin pleating, piping around the brims. I learned very fast, but I hated when they gave me those shiny cardinal's hats to do. My fingers were so sore at night that my mother had to wrap compresses on them.

In those days we never heard of a lunch break or coffee break. Everyone worked right through lunch, eating a little something while they worked. Whenever one of us left for the washroom, the supervisor would pointedly glare at the clock so as to warn us that every absence was strictly timed. Unfortunately she would always ask me to stay late to help her prepare for the next day. Some days I didn't get out until eight o'clock. There was no garment workers union in those days to protect a fourteen-year-old apprentice.

Actually, I was treated very kindly. Mrs. Ita, who distributed the wages to the regular employees, liked me and sometimes used to slip me a Krone (worth about 50 cents) when no one was looking. Of course, apprentices weren't paid. The best part was when the owners gave me the key to their luxury apartment when they went away on vacation so that I could feed the parrots. I'll never forget walking barefoot on their thick Persian rugs. Sometimes I had to make deliveries to the retail store on Am Graben, a very fashionable street in the central section. I'd take the tram into the center, make the delivery, and then walk through the parks, St. Stephen's cathedral, or through the arcades of the Hofburg. This is when I realized that I had a keen interest in beautiful things.[45, 72]

Anton Kreuzer, a soccer player, was Lenya's first boyfriend in Vienna.

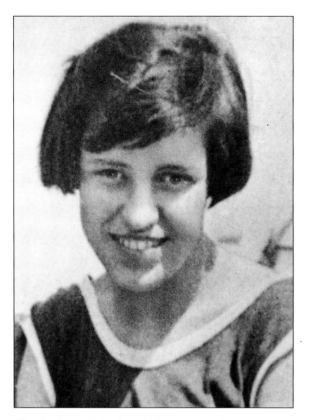

Shortly after arriving in Zurich, 1913, age 15.

Little did I know, when my Aunt Sophie, who lived in Zurich as a housekeeper and companion to an old retired Swiss doctor, invited me to visit her in the summer of 1913, that I was to stay there and become a dancer, "The Dream" of my childhood ever since I can remember. Aunt Sophie was my mother's older sister and looked quite like her. She too had first come to Vienna to work as a maid, but then married in rapid succession three well-to-do but sickly men; after the death of the last one, she mysteriously landed up in Zurich. I will never forget the shock my aunt got when she picked me up at the station. I don't know what she expected—she knew how poor my parents were. My aunt was a tiny woman, like my mother, but my mother was wonderfully quiet and humorous, and I still saw her smiling face when she said good-bye to me at the train station, handing me the little bundle of my belongings and saying, "Be smart, Linnerl, and don't come back if you can." Mother always hoped I would get out of the slums we lived in. This was my chance and I was determined to use it. So there I stood, still clinging to my bundle. "Where's your hat?" was the first question my aunt asked me, after she saw I had no suitcase. Well, before she took me home to introduce me to "The Dr.", as she always called that old stingy guy, we rushed to a department store and I got my first straw hat, with a bunch of red poppies wrapped around it. I felt weird with that big hat, but she thought I looked presentable.

After a couple of weeks with my aunt, she arranged for me to stay with friends, a photographer and his wife named Ehrenzweig. They were a sweet, elderly couple, with no children, and seemed delighted to take me in. Herr Ehrenzweig specialized in theatrical portraits, and did well at it, photographing not only all the resident singers, dancers, and actors but many of the visiting celebrities. He arranged for me to be accepted as a student of Steffi Herzeg, the ballet mistress at the Stadttheater. The lessons cost five dollars a month—a sum that made my head spin, but Aunt Sophie agreed to pay a part and the Ehrenzweigs the rest. In return I was to prepare breakfast and clean the studio before my morning class, hurry back to help with lunch, and return in the afternoon after my lessons to do whatever chores needed to be done. For Aunt Sophie's part, all I had to do was stay out of sight of the Doctor.

I have never known a moment of purer exaltation than when I tied on my first pair of ballet slippers. Unhappily, it didn't last. Of the twelve girls in the class—eight from the Stadttheater ballet and four students—I was, and remained, among the least talented when dancing on my toes. I was always hanging on to the other dancers! My feet, body, and entire nature were against all the attitudes of formal ballet. Instinctively I seized upon pantomime, improvisation, free movement; in these I found myself. However, I was fiercely determined to learn everything; I never missed a class, and at night I watched every performance at the theater. Soon I was given my first walk-on part, as a vaguely weaving Blessed Spirit, far upstage, in Gluck's *Orpheus*. It was in German, of course, "Ach ich habe sie verloren, all mein Glück ist nun dahin" ["What will I do without my Euridice?"].

Since I could sing a little bit, and act, evidently better than the other ballet kids, I was always given small parts in straight plays. So, I learned to sing, I learned to dance, I learned Shakespeare, Molière, Wedekind, Georg Kaiser, you name it. Russians, all the Russians. That's what I did, little parts in Zurich.[45]

In the first season I was a page in *Lohengrin*, I helped carry the Holy Grail across the stage in *Parsifal*, I saw Mary of Scotland's head chopped off, I looked out of Mistress Overdone's whorehouse as one of her girls in Shakespeare's *Measure for Measure*, I carried the gold of the Rhine on my shoulders as a dwarf in *Das Rheingold*, I danced to *The Blue Danube*, and I was a gypsy dancer in *Mignon*. In *Mignon*, I came out out of the dressing room with shoes on, and when the director saw them and asked me to take them off, I said innocently, "I can't, my feet are dirty." He laughed and said, "That's just fine for a gypsy," and pushed me onstage.

I almost got fired because of what happened in *Parsifal*. In the last scene I had to pull back a blanket at a certain musical cue to expose the dead body of Titurel. Well, we were using a dummy for the body, and I accidentally grabbed the beard on this dummy along with blanket. Timed perfectly with the whoosh of the orchestra, I threw off the blanket, and Titurel's head went flying into the orchestra pit! They docked me quite a bit of salary as punishment for that one.[68]

So, I was busy all of the time while I was studying little parts, and this is why I got all my training as a dancer—not a singer because I wasn't trained as a singer. But I sang with my natural voice. It always surprised Kurt Weill when I sang snatches from those operas. And he said, "My god, how do you know all this?" So, that was an everlasting delight for Kurt Weill, my knowledge of opera, which is a very thorough one because I know all of the Wagner operas inside out.[8]

Above: Three ballet students at the Zurich Schauspielhaus. Lenya is to the far right. Below: Ballet students, Lenya is at left. The photos were taken by Herr Ehrenzweig, Lenya's landlord.

Aspiring actresses in the Zurich Schauspielhaus.
Lenya is second from right.

By the end of the first season, I was a little homesick. My aunt thought that I should go back home. I didn't know that she hoped I wouldn't come back. So she got me money for the trip through the Austrian consul, pretending that she couldn't afford to send me home. I came home at a bad time. The whole country was in state of terror over a possible war. My mother wasn't too happy to see me back, and nothing had changed while I was gone except that she had separated from my father and had taken in two boarders in order to be able to support her children. She had taken up with one of them, Rudolf, who had tuberculosis and only a few months to live. (I never saw my father again; my sister wrote me in 1928 that he had died of acute alcoholism.) We had only one bedroom and a kitchen, and the place was crowded. I hadn't minded it before I left, but now I had gotten a glimpse of a better life and felt unhappy and full of fear that I couldn't get back to Switzerland. I was supposed to be back by the first of September. Weeks and weeks passed and I didn't hear from my aunt. Finally, she wrote me that she thought it would be better for me if I stayed home and gave up the idea about the theater. And she couldn't help me any more, either. I cried my eyes out, but my mother promised to get the money for my ticket. She took on more laundry to wash, and I helped her as much as I could. But then, the terrible thing everybody was afraid of happened, and war was declared on the third of August, 1914. In order to get a passport, I had to get a contract from the theater. I wrote a desperate letter to the director to send me one (I was entitled to one only after three years of studying). Thank God, he was very kind to me that first season, and he understood my problem and I got my passport. By the time I could leave the trains were full of soldiers and people who were leaving the country. I rode four days on that train, for what was normally an overnight trip. When I crossed the border into Switzerland, I laughed and cried at the same time. From the border to Zurich is only a few hours. My heart was jumping when I saw the lake and knew I had finally arrived.

I went straight to the theater (I was already two weeks late) to let them know that I was back. Then I went to see my aunt. She opened the door and I never saw a more surprised face in all my life, before or since. She rushed me right into her room, and whispered that I couldn't possibly stay with her. She would lose her job. I had no intention of staying. I was tired of being shoved under a bed every time she heard a door opening. But I arrived without a cent and I needed a little money to get me through the first month. She did let me stay overnight, and the next day I went back to the Ehrenzweigs, the family I had stayed with sometimes the previous year, to start my old routine. The second season was already much better. I made about thirty francs playing at the theater, and the fee for the ballet lessons was reduced to fifteen francs. But it still wasn't enough to get a room so I could live by myself. So when my aunt asked me whether I would help a friend of hers who ran a little store selling postcards, I was only too glad to go there every weekend and whenever else I had time. I didn't know then that Emil, who ran the store, was my aunt's boyfriend. He was a nice man, about fifty, and had a passion for catching flies. There he sat with his big cigar, catching the flies, putting them under a glass, blowing the smoke into the glass, and watching them get dizzy. I never found out what he finally did with them. I couldn't look. I kept myself busy looking at those beautiful colored postcards. It was like traveling through all of Switzerland. Emil loved the hours I spent in the store. I sold more cards in an hour than he could in a day, and when I was there, he could devote his time to his passion, the flies.[45]

During this season Richard Révy, a director of the theater, offered to take me as his private pupil. That's where my real study began. I was extremely lucky to have him as a mentor. He nourished my talent, even teaching me to read the whole of Dostoyevsky. Needless to say that we slept together, too, but that was my way of paying him, you know? I loved him. Yes, I did.[16, 72]

I saved every penny I made and after a few months, I could accept the offer of Greta, one of the dancers, to move into her mother's big apartment. She rented out rooms, but only to people in the theater. She was enormously fat, very Semitic looking in spite of her pretty blond hair, with a golden cross dangling from a black velvet ribbon which rested on her big bosom like a landmark. "It's been in the family for centuries," she insisted. Her husband was a shy little man with thick glasses, who was shut up by her before he could even say good morning. We all had breakfast together, which Mrs. Edelmann announced by running her fat fingers in a glissando over the piano, her prize possession. Greta was more like her father. She had none of her mother's brassiness. But she had a passion for men. She had a boyfriend, called a fiancé by her mother, who insisted that her daughter remain a virgin (which she wasn't) until the day she got married. The boyfriend was a Serb, a dreary guy, who was very proud of his country which I knew nothing about, except that the archduke Franz Ferdinand was shot there, which is what started the

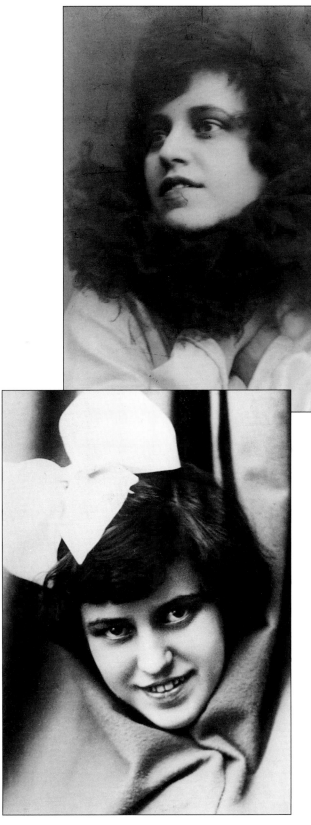

In Zurich. Top: ca. 1915. Bottom: 1916

In Zurich, 1916. Photo: Ehrenzweig

In Der lebende Leichnam (The Living Corpse)
by Leo Tolstoy. In Zurich, 1917.

war. I never liked him. Greta was constantly in trouble, getting pregnant practically every month. But it wasn't always his doing. He just happened to be her steady.

Zurich was a very international city during those years of war, with students from all over the world and hotels filled with rich foreigners waiting for the war to end. The nightclubs were crowded with rich war profiteers and their lavishly dressed girlfriends. It was a rich and elegant city. I never saw a sign of a poor Swiss anywhere, not before and not after the war. Even the girls who occupied the red-light district, Niederdorf, looked prosperous and well-fed.

The theater was wonderful at that time. I remember the first rehearsal with Richard Strauss conducting his *Salome* with the famous diva Maria Gutheil-Schoder. He was an extremely elegant-looking man. The orchestra had a tough time with him. They weren't used to such a controlled way of conducting. He hardly raised his baton, and when the musicians couldn't get the right sound for the chopping of Jochanaan's head, Strauss stopped and said in his gentle Bavarian accent, "My dear gentlemen, it's very simple, simple like *Lohengrin.*"

The beginning of the third season, we got a new ballet mistress. She was a Jacques-Dalcroze pupil and didn't care much for toe dancing. Thank God, I didn't have to suffer through that any more and could dance in my bare feet. Our prima ballerina didn't like the new regime and left soon after. But I was in heaven. Now I could use all the acting I had learned in the meantime and combine it with this new way of dancing.

Finally I got my first contract as a full-fledged member of the ballet with a sixty dollar salary. During the summer months, when our theater was closed, my friend Greta and I worked at the Corso Theatre, where they played nothing but operettas. She did the choreography, and I danced and sang whatever part I got. No big parts. On the top floor of the theater was a nightclub, and there I sat one night with Greta and her Frenchman, looking at a rather good-looking young man with heavy dark glasses, surrounded by a noisy crowd of his guests. I saw the star of the program rushing to his table, throwing her arms around him, and I wondered who he was. He was Czechoslovakian and one of the richest men in town. Greta's boyfriend knew him, and after a while he left his table and sat with us. He seemed bored with his company and

Performing in a dance recital, 1916 or 1917.

After three years as an apprentice, Lenya became a full-fledged, salaried member of the ballet.

In the corps de ballet, 1916.

enjoyed every remark I made about his loud, heavily drinking friends. Next day, I got my first flowers, the first big ones at the theater. I was rather embarrassed. After the show, I met him at the nightclub, thanked him for the flowers, and asked him not to send any more. And here starts the old, familiar rich man-poor girl story. He didn't stop sending me presents, and he asked me to move to his villa on the lake, which I did—it was too tempting. I wanted to know how it feels to have everything, to be driven to the theater by the chauffeur, to have beautiful jewelry and not a worry any more. I almost fainted when I discovered the secret of his heavy dark glasses. He suffered from thyroid and his eyes stuck out like two bubbles on a stick that children blow with soap water. But I got used to them, like I got used to the sudden wealth. But soon I started to miss Mrs. Edelmann's glissando for breakfast, missed my walks along the lake to the theater, and I felt lonely. I didn't like the way I left him—sneaking out at night without explanation. He was so good to me, but there was nothing I could say. He sent me all my things I left behind, and a year later, he asked me for the last time to come back to him. I wished him luck and stayed at Mrs. Edelmann's. Greta never could understand what got over me to make such a foolish decision—as she put it.

Lenya's mother with her second husband, Ernst Heinisch, ca. 1918

In 1916, my mother started working in a war hospital in Meidling, where she met Ernst Heinisch. My sister, then ten, remembers my mother coming home one day, putting on her Sunday best, and cooking *Palatschinken*, a Viennese variety of crepes Suzette. Where she got all the ingredients at a time of terrible shortages, nobody knew and mother didn't tell. When my sister asked what the occasion was, my mother answered, "A gentleman is coming to visit, and very likely he will stay here for good." Soon there was a knock at the door and Ernst walked in. Mariedl took one look at him and ran in horror down to her girlfriend's, who had already seen him come into the building. Mariedl told her friend, "I will never call him father," and she never did. Ernst ate up all the rations, and there was nothing left for the two children. After school Mariedl would go to the hospital to see mother, where she got scraps. Ernst knocked her around constantly and mother seemed not to notice, she was so infatuated.

A few months before the war ended I went back to Vienna for a short visit, this time sure of my return fare. Coming from sleekly prosperous Zurich, I was shocked by the gaunt and care-ridden faces. I had been sending packages of food and clothing, and what money I could, but that was little enough when stretched among so many.

Back in Zurich, I was busier than ever. There were nights when I rushed back and forth between theaters: first the Stadttheater at seven o'clock, to be a strolling maid in Act I of *Die Meistersinger*, then dash by taxi to the Schauspielhaus for a frenzied change of costume and make-up to play a Hindu girl in Tagore's *Das Postamt*, then back to the Stadttheater by ten o'clock to play a boy apprentice in the Wagner. I began getting solo parts in full evenings of dance, even though my contract was only for the corps.

"Here I am seventeen years old, with a rich boyfriend. That's why I have all that sable around my neck!"

Opposite: Playing a Hindu girl in Das Postamt (Post Office) *by Rabindranath Tagore at the Zurich Schauspielhaus, 1918*

Sculptor Mario Petrucci, Lenya's first serious lover, in Zurich, ca. 1918.

Program for a production of Frank Wedekind's Lulu *at the Pfauen-Theater in Zurich, 27 January 1921. Lenya (listed as Caroline Blamauer), played the role of Hugenberg, a student. The production was directed by her acting teacher, Richard Révy.*
Photo: Stadtarchiv Zürich

My boyfriend at the time, a sculptor named Mario Petrucci, had to go to Vienna. I got him to arrange for a passport for my sister Maria and put her on a train to Zurich for a visit. She stayed for about four months, spending the first two with me in the Pension Griese and the next two in a rest home in the mountains run by nuns.

When the war ended, I got restless. I didn't know what I wanted, but I had heard of Berlin, I had seen some wonderful productions by Max Reinhardt, and I felt kind of at a standstill with what I was doing. I had played good parts by then; I knew how to act, I knew how to dance. I had never given up studying with Révy, and when he told me he was thinking of going to Berlin, my mind was made up. He said he would do whatever he could to help me, if I decided to go. So Greta and I started to work on a ballet evening, which we hoped would take Berlin by storm when we got there. All that summer we spent every spare minute in a little rehearsal room, with the accompanist banging away at the piano. Révy's wife made our costumes, and we made up our own choreography. In one number I was a faun and Greta a nymph, in another I was Pierrot and Greta a Columbine; we were Scotch lassies in another; Greta danced a Hungarian czardas, and I did the Blue Danube as a solo à la Greta Wiesenthal. All in all, a corny mishmash of ballet, Dalcroze, Isadora, and the Sakharoffs. We were certain we would take Berlin by storm. Mama Edelmann was rather less sure, convinced that if anything was stormed, it would be Greta's virginity. Our preparations didn't go as fast as we thought, but by the fall of 1921 we were ready to leave Zurich.[45]

CHAPTER 2

Hoppla!
1921-1935

Silhouette by Lotte Reiniger made during rehearsals of **Die Dreigroschenoper** (**Threepenny Opera**), *Berlin, 1928.*

Madame Lenya sings, or rather croons, with an impeccable diction that reaches the farthest corner of any hall and with an intensity of dramatization and a sincerity of will that are very moving. She is, moreover, beautiful in a new way, a way that nobody has vulgarized so far. . . . It will not be long, I imagine, before some movie gang gets hold of her and stuffs her down our throats like Garbo.[61]

—Virgil Thomson, American composer and critic

Richard Révy was living in a boarding house in Berlin while looking for work, and his wife had taken their two children to live at her family's country place near Munich. When Greta and I arrived in Berlin in the early fall of 1921, Révy met us at the train station. He took me to his rooming house in the Lützowstrasse and Greta went to live with a relative of her mother. When I walked into that gloomy-looking room with that one light bulb, I felt rather depressed. Zurich was such a clean city, and here was poverty-stricken Berlin with inflation rising daily. I had great trouble understanding the ever-changing money, and the food was almost inedible.

So when we got to Berlin, Révy was looking for a job and I was looking for a job. But nothing happened. There we sat.

In costume for her ballet evening in Berlin, early 1920's. Photo: Louise Hartung

We couldn't get an agent interested in our ballet evening, so our trunks full of costumes stood in one corner of my room, a constant reminder of what we came to Berlin for. We could get single jobs dancing a number or two in obscure nightclubs. But neither one of us liked the idea. Greta was a dancer only and not interested in anything else. I couldn't make her go and see plays. She didn't want to walk around and get the smell of the city. When she finally got an offer as a choreographer in Elberfeld, a small German city, I didn't have to urge her to accept it. I still had enough to live on. I still had my jewelry I could sell.

By that time I had lost faith in our project and was glad when she left. Now I didn't have to run daily from one stupid agent to another, and I was free to see all the great actors at that time. I had a passion for the Scala, the greatest variety theater in Berlin, where I saw the great juggler Barbette and the Fratellinis swinging way out in the audience. It was my passion until I left Berlin in 1933. I saw my first wrestling matches in a Biergarten in Friedenau—mostly Polish wrestlers, walking in a long line through the garden toward the ring, accompanied by an incredible brass band playing the "March of the Gladiators." I loved to walk on Saturdays up to the corner of Tauentzienstrasse and the KDW, a big department store where you could see girls in the strangest outfits standing at the corner, some with whips in their hands, some with high, shiny boots on, indicating that they were equipped to fulfill every kind

Right: The Scala Girls in front of the Variety Theatre on Lutherstrasse, 1929. Photo: Herbert Hoffmann/Bildarchiv Preussischer Kulturbesitz

of human passion. It's a funny thing the way people think of Berlin those days as a sexual paradise, or hell. But besides the famous corner of the KDW and the well-walked pavements of the Friedrichstrasse, there were other places and other occupations. People did go to work in the morning and come home in the evening. They did—some of them—fight for the things that matter.[45]

I came to Berlin from Zurich, which was a land of milk and honey. The only thing rationed there during the First World War was sugar: five pounds a week. So, I went to Berlin in 1921, and in 1921, '22, inflation wasn't that bad. You still could get food. But inflation was at its peak in 1923. In those early days, during the inflation, there were lots of little theater groups usually organized by one enthusiastic, idealistic director. We played Shakespeare in the suburbs. This is where I played Juliet, 36 times. I played *As You Like It*. I played Maria in *Much Ado About*

A fifty million mark note, issued by the German government in 1923 at the height of inflation. (This note was signed by Joe Masteroff and presented to Lenya as a souvenir of her performance in Cabaret *in 1966.)*

Advertisement for Zaubernacht, *a children's pantomime by Kurt Weill and Wladimir Boritsch, 1922. Lenya was hired for a part but declined the role when her teacher, Richard Révy, was not engaged to direct.*

Nothing. I have still a little paper from the theater that says Miss Lenya's salary for tonight is 3 billion marks. You had to stuff your money into a suitcase and quickly go shopping, because otherwise an hour later it would have no value. None whatsoever. I always was crazy, I don't know why. I was so delighted because the only thing I could really buy quickly, besides a little food, or whatever—was cactuses. I had a whole collection of cactuses. They were very cheap. Nobody wanted cactus. They wanted food, you know?[8, 16]

So one day Révy found an advertisement in the paper where it says "young dancers, singers" for a ballet by a young composer named Kurt Weill, and it was called *Zaubernacht (Magic Night)*. And so I went and Révy went with me because he was looking for a job, too. So I got to the audition—all those stage mothers with all those little ones, you know? Little ones, bigger ones and so on. It was terrible.[45]

"I think it's you they want." I didn't hear them calling me. I wasn't used to that name, Lotte Lenya, which was only a few days old, a name which I had decided to take instead of my given name, Karoline Blamauer, which seemed too long for a stage career. Then the producer—a Russian man named Boritsch—said go ahead, and I must have looked completely lost until I heard a gentle voice coming from the orchestra pit asking, "What do you want me to play for you, Miss Lenya?" And Boritsch turned around and said, "Oh, this is Mr. Weill, our composer." I hardly saw him; he was half-hidden under the overhang of the orchestra pit. I asked him whether he could play "The Blue Danube," and I heard him say, with a slightly amused voice, "I think so." The moment I started dancing to that tune—that tune I had heard practically from the day I was born—all my fears disappeared. The producer said, "That's enough" after a few minutes, which seemed so short to me. He asked me what else I could show them, and I did an imitation of a circus clown on a tightrope and sang a song as a street singer, this time without music from the pit. I still hadn't seen the composer. I wouldn't see him again until a year later, under quite different circumstances.[45, 59]

I met Germany's famous expressionist playwright Georg Kaiser through Révy. Knowing that I needed work, Kaiser said "Well, Lenya, in the interim, why don't you come and stay with my family? We'd love to have you there." So, for two years I stayed with Georg Kaiser, doing nothing but helping with the children.[70]

Kaiser had a mania for boats. One of the reasons why he was

always in debt was that whenever there was any sign of money coming his way, he bought a new boat. He was the most contradictory man I have ever known. He dreamed of being an English country squire and master of an estate, and yet lived a life which swung like a pendulum between the simple life and Adlon elegance.[46]

There were three Kaiser children: Sybille, Anselm, and Laurenz. Anselm was the beautiful one, Laurenz the proletarian, and Sybille so blonde, blue-eyed, and innocent, just like a drawing by Zille, the poet. Kaiser liked to make jokes about that Zille-child. He used to say to her, "Sing 'Put on your Dirndlkleid [Bavarian peasant dress] from Lake Tegern,'" and she would stand and sing, without an ounce of musicality. It was pathetic how Kaiser made fun of her. He was a rather cruel man. Once when his wife was frustrated with Sybille, Kaiser retorted, "Why don't you step on her and kill her dead once and for all, Margarethe." He said things like that, you know, but of course it is was half in jest.

Kaiser always had mistresses. I particularly remember Blanche Dergan, an untalented beast, horrible, for whom he wrote *The Escape to Venice*. She always had to hold on to something on stage so that she wouldn't fall off it. Kaiser was very impressed with her because she lived in the Hotel Adlon, very elegant. I remember him getting his son all dressed up in his sailor suit, and blonde curls and all, and taking him there to show off—eating cake with Dergan—all very strange.[72]

Leading German playwright Georg Kaiser, ca. 1925.

Attending the three Kaiser children at the beach (left to right: Anselm, Lenya, Sibylle, Laurenz).

*Kurt Weill in a musician's hat, ca. 1929.
Photo: Thiele*

*With Margarethe Kaiser at the Kaisers' estate in
the Berlin suburb of Grünheide, 1923.*

At that time Georg Kaiser was writing a libretto for Kurt Weill's *Der Protagonist*. And one Sunday morning he said to me, "Lenya, I have that young composer. I'm writing a libretto for him. Would you mind picking him up at the station?" I said, "Why not?" And Kaiser's house was right on the lake, so you could either take the rowboat to the station or walk through the woods, which was much longer. So, I said, "I'll take the rowboat." So, I took the rowboat and went to the station. And it wasn't very difficult to recognize Kurt Weill because there was nobody else at that station on Sunday morning, you know? I could spot him like you spot a fly in a milk bottle, wearing a Borsalino hat—musician's hats which at that time were in fashion. And I remember exactly what he had on, a little bow tie, you know, a little blue—like a bar mitzvah suit. I thought, "That's very sweet." Thick, thick glasses, you know? And I said, "Are you Mr. Weill?" And he said, "Yes." And I said, "Well, would you mind entering my transportation here?" And he did. So that's how we met.

Kaiser didn't have a study in his house; indeed nobody actually ever saw him sitting at a desk or writing. Home was something Kaiser kept completely apart from the theater. Probably the most important talks Kurt and Kaiser had were in the afternoons, on their bicycle rides, or in the mornings out in the rowboat—Margarethe and I could see the boat slowly disappearing in the distance as they talked. Or on long walks around the lake Kurt and Kaiser would walk ahead, and their talk and laughter would float back to us. Both men were shy—though with Kurt it was almost entirely a surface shyness—once one knew him, he was the most direct and warm of people, though he rarely discussed with anyone his deeply personal problems. As for Kaiser, you knew as little, or as much, on the first day you met him as on the last; an eternally evasive and enigmatic personality. However, both men had enchanting wit—Kaiser's the more fantastic, Kurt's the drier—and the two men appreciated and respected each other. This was the first time I saw one of Kurt's working methods that survived his whole lifetime. While absorbed in conversation with him, he would seem to be still listening, but suddenly take on the mask of a child, listening with an inner ear. Then with an almost furtive, embarrassed manner, he would find a piece of paper—envelope, corner of a newspaper or paper bag, anything—with the quickest of strokes, only readable to him, sketch the five lines of the staff and a few bars of music, and slip it in his right-hand pocket. All his coat pockets and desk drawers were filled with these notes.[45]

Preceding page: Reminiscing in the tiny bedroom she shared with Weill in the Pension Hassforth, Berlin. Visiting years later, in 1955, she found it "completely unchanged."

One day Weill invited me for tea and played parts of *Der Protagonist*. "Did you really like it?" he asked. I said, "I like it very much" and pointed out a few things that really surprised him. His brothers had hated it, teasing him with their usual name for him, *Dachstubenkomponist* [attic composer].[72]

Soon after we started living together, the Kaisers gave us their apartment on Luisenplatz in Charlottenburg. It was one of those typical Berlin pensions, and they gave us two rooms, reserving one room for themselves, to stay overnight when they came from Grünheide. A very tiny, small bedroom, and we slept together in that tiny bed. When we had to turn around, we had to turn around together, because, you know? Otherwise we would have fallen out of bed.[59]

We had a large circle of friends—there were two girls who were later witnesses at our wedding, one, Caña, a government worker, and Martha Gratenau—many of Busoni's pupils, also his son Rafaello Busoni—who was then married to a Japanese girl and they were always cooking exotic dishes—pianist Walter Kaempfer, who became a priest during the Nazis—Philipp Jarnach, Maurice Abravanel, Heinz Jolles, Claudio Arrau, and of course the Kaisers, with whom we spent practically every weekend. It was during this period that I got a job, through Kaiser, as understudy to Grete Jacobson in the part of Juliet. Kaiser's friend, Emil Lind, was the director, a rather elderly, hard-of-hearing man, but a reliable, conservative director. (Jacobson was so much under the influence of Elisabeth Bergner that she never made it, though she always claimed Bergner was imitating her.) When Jacobson quit, I got to play Juliet for sixty performances. The theater was Das Wallnertheater, in the Wallnerstrasse, near Alexanderplatz, what is called a *Volkstheater*, a popular theater at reduced prices. Kurt brought me to the theater every night, and always with a bottle of May wine that I shared with the cast.[45]

Kurt especially loved the poetry of Zille, he loved Zille more than anybody. And, of course Ludwig Meidner was one of our closest friends. We often went to Paul Hindemith's for dinner; Kurt was always amused by his wife Gertrud.

Once we went to Philipp Jarnach's for dinner. His wife, a real Bavarian, answered the door wearing slippers and she whispered to us, "Shhh, the master is creating for all eternity." We almost peed in our pants laughing when she said that. Not out loud, but inside—both of us.[72]

[Letter from Weill to Lenya, July 1926?]

Just one week ago we sat on the Piazza Signori in Verona and slowly discovered how beautiful it was there. As I think back now, I begin to feel a powerful yearning for you—so no more memories! Anyway I'll be seeing you the day after tomorrow. This very same thing happened to me before: when I feel this longing for you, I most of all think of the sound of your voice, which I love like a very force of nature, like an element. For me all of you is contained within this sound; everything else is only a part of you; and when I envelop myself into your voice, then you are with me in every way. I know every nuance, every vibration of your voice, and I can hear exactly what you would say if you were with me right now—and how you would say it. But suddenly this sound is again entirely alien and new to me, and then it is the greatest joy to realize how affectionately this voice caresses me—it's almost like those first weeks when the mere thought of you seemed outrageously frivolous. The wonderful thing is that today I still have that feeling of reverence toward you as in the very first hour, which makes it seem almost miraculous that you've come to me and all has turned out so beautifully. And now—just as it was on that first day—I'm no longer sad that somewhere else your voice resounds, and I'm not close by.[77]

Above: First page of manuscript letter from Kurt Weill in Berlin to Lenya staying in Leipzig with his family, written about six months after their marriage.

We lived for two years together without being married. The only reason we got married was because of the neighbors, "She's not married." Oops. So, I said "Come on, Kurt, let's get married. What the hell? What difference does it make?" So, we did.[70]

We didn't have a church wedding. Naturally not, because Kurt was Jewish and I wasn't—but that's beside the point. We had a civil ceremony, no family and only two witnesses, the pianist Martha Gratenau and another woman, both lesbians. At the ceremony was the only time I saw any trace of the military in Kurt. When the civil servant asked us all those silly marriage vows, Weill stood at attention, clicked his heels, and said "Jawohl." I think he was completely serious. He meant to take care of me for the rest of his life.[52, 72]

Wedding certificate, dated 28 January 1926. Kurt Julian Weill marries Karoline Wilhelmine Blamauer in the Charlottenburg section of Berlin.

Weill's parents didn't know anything about my childhood—nothing. They only resented that I wasn't Jewish. My first mistake came when I met them for the first time in Leipzig. I pointed to the mezuzah on the doorframe and said, "What is this little earthworm?" Later on I became their favorite daughter-in-law. I don't know how I did it, but what I said was always accepted. They didn't care for the other daughters-in-law very much. I think I loved his mother more than his father. I don't think Kurt was too fond of his father, a rather stubborn man, and I didn't like him either. I found the mother very intelligent and, on a bigger scale, she understood me. I adored his two brothers. Nathan, who is the oldest, was a doctor and emigrated to Israel. Then Hans, and his sister Ruth, who was something of a know-it-all. I think her relationship to Kurt was the strongest. She confided in him when she had problems, and he really played the big brother.

His father was a cantor in the synagogue, but neither Kurt nor his brothers were very religious. They mostly went along with the family tradition of observing the Sabbath, things like that. I don't think religion meant much to him anymore. He was much more interested in his libretti.[72]

"This was our wedding picture. We were quite poor at the time. Kurt was making money by giving music and theory lessons. He has our dinner here in a paper bag, which was some kind of herring and jelly. And I got some autumn leaves from the park in the back, to decorate the table, and this was our wedding dinner." January 1926.

Weill family photo, 15 August 1926. Back row, left to right: Ella (a maid), Albert (Kurt's father), Nathan (Kurt's brother), Kurt. Front row, left to right: Leni (Nathan's wife) holding their daughter Hannelore, Emma (Kurt's mother), and Lenya holding Eva Sohn (daughter of Kurt's sister Ruth).

Der Protagonist seemed atonal then, and it probably was. But if you hear it now, what's hard to understand is Kaiser's language, which is staccato. The new generation of singers doesn't find the music so atonal any more. They don't find Schoenberg so hard to understand now, either.[8]

It was a tremendous success at the Dresden Opera House, conducted by Fritz Busch. Kurt never believed it would be so well received, and after it was over he went straight down to the pit to congratulate the orchestra. But they were looking for him to take a bow. "He's so small, but now he's disappeared altogether!" Well, they finally found him. At the time Weill and Krenek were called the white hopes of Germany, at least as far as music was concerned.[17]

We first met Brecht in 1927, in a restaurant. Kurt made a suggestion that he would like to set some of his poems to music. Brecht said, "Oh, marvelous. This is good." Later, when he came to our apartment for the first time, the landlady took one look at him standing at the door and said to him, "No, no. We can't give anything today." She thought that he was a beggar, you know, and closed the door. Kurt heard his voice and called out, "Wait a minute. Just let him in."[70]

When Brecht and Weill worked together privately, it was a very happy collaboration. Only in public did Brecht become Brecht—a real showoff. Kurt was exactly the opposite, quiet.[72]

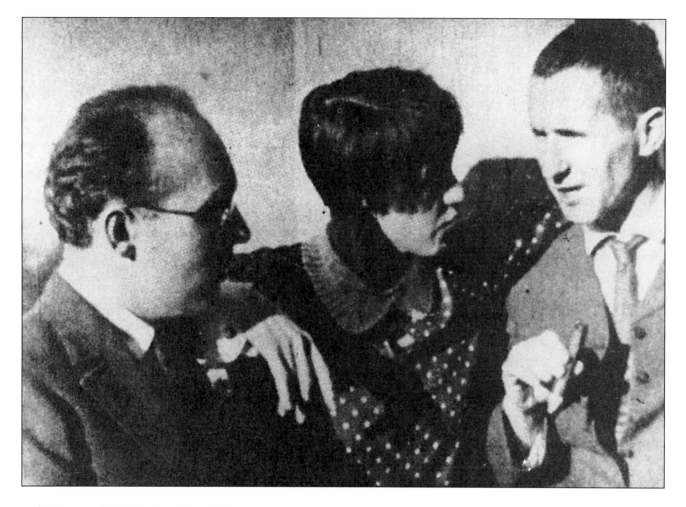

Weill, Lenya, and Brecht during rehearsals for
Die Dreigroschenoper, *1928. Photo: Saeger*

When Brecht became Kurt's collaborator, they worked together in Brecht's studio, an attic studio with a big skylight just off the intersection Am Knie. As always, a guitar in the Wedekind manner, no curtains, no rugs to speak of, a typewriter on the big table, lots of paper flying messily around, smoke clouding the room from Brecht's stogies, a huge couch against the wall, a big iron stove with a pipe because it was a windy corner. As you came up the stairs, there was to the left a tiny bedroom for his secretary, so-called; on the other side of the studio another tiny bedroom for Brecht, a narrow bed under slanting walls. I often went along with Kurt during the writing of *Mahagonny* and *Dreigroschenoper*, and always found Elisabeth Hauptmann there, his secretary, at that time literally his devoted shadow. She still had the neatness of a schoolteacher at that time, despite her conscious effort to be a Brecht-type woman, rosy-cheeked, with slightly popping brown eyes, plumpish with a Rubens-type behind, and the most servile imitation of Brecht's mannerisms of gesture and speech. When possible, Brecht liked to work surrounded by his disciples, getting ideas, reactions, a word here, a thought there, his ear constantly on the alert, freely, ruthlessly, everyone else sitting while Brecht walked leisurely around the room, pausing to question this one and that. On a large easel, which was also standard equipment in a Brecht room, would be the inevitable charcoal drawing by Caspar Neher, Brecht's main designer, with ideas for decor, costume, or character. Brecht often had extremely primitive ideas for a song, a few bars of music which he had previously picked out on his guitar. Kurt always took these with a smile, saying yes, he would try to work them in. Naturally, they were forgotten at once. Often there were complete lyrics waiting for Kurt to take home with him. When it was time for very serious work, the Brecht disciples left, except for Hauptmann,—often I stayed too—and the two men would work steadily, with the most enormous respect for each other's opinions.[45]

I'll never forget, Brecht had a big map of the world on the wall of his studio. Brecht and Weill would play the game "let's find a name" by covering their eyes and pointing to the map. That's how they came up with Surabaya, Alabama, and Bilbao. Of course the sounds of the names were very important.[68]

Brecht with collaborator Elisabeth Hauptmann in his Berlin studio, 1927. "Brecht absolutely killed one woman after another." Photo: Bertolt-Brecht-Archiv, Akademie der Künste, Berlin

A date was set for Brecht to come hear me sing "Alabama Song." Kurt was nervous for me, as usual, but he never got nervous for himself. We had a good-sized living room, with a Swedish tile stove, pitch-black wooden furniture, a grand piano, a big desk, a couch, and an imitation Persian rug on the floor. Large, terrible paintings of a hunt, with ferocious dogs chasing deer, adorned the walls. We called it Grieneisen, after a famous Berlin funeral parlor. So—that's where Weill composed. Brecht came in, very cordial, very gentle, and very patient, as he always was with women and actors. Weill played a little of the music of the *Little Mahagonny* and then asked, "Would you like to listen to Lenya singing 'Alabama Song'?" He said, "Oh, sure. Yea. Can she sing?" So Kurt said, "Well, you decide whether she can or not." I began by walking in rhythm and singing "Oh show me the way to the next whisky bar," looking at the audience but not addressing them. When I reached "Oh moon of Alabama," I stood still with my hands folded behind my back. At this moment Brecht interrupted, "Now let's really work on it." He showed me how to take in the whole audience, asking them to help me find the next whisky bar, because they knew in their hearts why they must not ask why. At the refrain, he told me to forget the audi-

Right: Lenya sitting in Weill's studio at the Pension Hassforth, 1955. The studio had been preserved to look as it did when Weill worked and lived there in the late 1920's.

Below: Cover of sheet music of the "Alabama Song" from Mahagonny, a hit for both Weill and Lenya. Reprinted courtesy European-American Music Corp.

KURT
WEILL

ALABAMA-SONG
AUS „MAHAGONNY"

GESANG UND KLAVIER

UNIVERSAL
EDITION
Nᵒ. 8900

ence and pour out my sorrow to the moon, "We've lost our good old mama ..." and reach toward the moon with my right hand. I did a gesture I had learned for a ballet in *Aïda*. He took my hand and said, "Come on Lenya, not so Egyptian. Just turn your hand around this way." I caught on instantly, and, of course, he liked it very much. That afternoon Brecht set my style of gesture. Kurt gave me the singing style and Brecht gave me the movements. And I sang the role in Baden-Baden without reading a note of music. [45, 59]

Brecht: average height, skinny, with the frailness of a tough herring. Small, white, feminine hands that were invariably grimy with short black fingernails. Moved with a swift elegance, very precise. Shoulders a little stooped, stringy neck, with a tic that went with his talk that started in his jaw, drew in his upper lip, pushed forward the chin, tightened the stringy neck muscles, and set his shoulders alternately twitching. Dull brown hair cropped Russian proletarian style. Dark brown eyes set very close together, deeply sunk in, never still, constantly blinking, always registering reaction. Bushy eyebrows, separated by two deep furrows, a narrow and slightly hooked nose, thin-lipped, with moist brown spittle at the corners from the stogies he smoked all day long. Wretched teeth, many of them black stumps. Stubble on his face. Leather visored cap in winter, linen in summer. Leather jacket, turtleneck sweaters or working-man's shirt with leather tie, never quite clean.

His Bavarian accent gave a softening lilt to his speech, which was not hurried but in the grip of an idea became sharp, strident, and theatrical. Then he would stride back and forth, continuously gesturing, with a great variety of gestures, always translating into terms of theater.

Polite manners, a calculated politeness, a shy social lion who could become a raging one promulgating his own theories of theater. In general, people had to come to him, and he preferred to move within the confines of his own group.

Loved gin rummy, American movies, sometimes played ballads on his guitar (which he played not at all well), and sang agreeably and amateurishly.

Behind all of his posturing and charm was a gnawing concern for his own myth and forever assessing people for what they could contribute to him (and invariably getting it).

Soundless laughter could shake him, with an endearing peasant way of slapping his thin leg, ending in exhausted pants and rubbing his eyes with the back of his hands like a sleepy child, repeating, "Ja, das Leben …"

He drove a Styr, an Austrian car, a cabriolet, with passion and jerkiness. Not a born driver, but even as a driver he could do no wrong.[45]

Photo portrait of Bertolt Brecht, by Konrad Ressler, taken about the time Lenya first met him, 1927.

Mahagonny

Ein Songspiel nach Texten von Bert Brecht
von Kurt Weill

Personen:

Jessie . . . . Lotte Lenja
Bessie . . . . Irene Eden
Charlie . . . . Erik Wirl
Billy . . . . Georg Ripperger
Bobby . . . . Karl Giebel
Jimmy . . . . Gerhard Pechner

Dirigent: Ernst Mehlich
Regie: Bert Brecht
Bühnenbilder: Caspar Neher
Kostüme entworfen von Caspar Neher, ausgeführt von Emilie Walut-Franz Droll
Musik. Einstudierung: Otto Besag
Orchesterbesetzung: 2 Violinen, 2 Klar., 2 Tromp. Saxophon, Posaune,
Klavier, Schlagzeug.
Kurt Weill, geb. 2.3.1900 in Dessau, badischer Abstammung. 1918 Hochschule in Berlin. 1919—1920 Theaterkapellmeister. 1921 Schüler Busonis. Weill lebt in Berlin. Werke u. a. Streichquartett op.8. Quodlibet op. 9. Frauentanz Op. 10. „Recordare" (a capella-Chorwerk) op. 11. Violinkonzert op. 12. „Der neue Orpheus" op 15. Opern: „Der Protagonist," „Royal Palace."
In seinen neueren Werken bewegt sich Weill in der Richtung jener Künstler aller Kunstgebiete, die die Liquidation der gesellschaftlichen Künste voraussagen. Das kleine epische Stück „Mahagonny" zieht lediglich die Konsequenz aus dem unaufhaltsamen Verfall der bestehenden Gesellschaftsschichten Er wendet sich bereits an ein Publikum, das im Theater naiv seinen Spass verlangt.

"I think the meanest character I met in my life was Brecht. I'll never forget him telling me after Weill's big success in Baden-Baden, 'Weill has to get used to the fact that his name will not appear on the program.' That's Brecht."

Right: On the beach in the south of France, 1928, where Brecht and Weill worked on Die Dreigroschenoper.

theater, and Klemperer came in and said, "Is here no telephone" and gave me a slap on my back. I almost fell off my chair, because he understood.

In 1928 a young producer, Ernst Josef Aufricht, was looking for a play. And so Brecht said, "Well, I have a little sketch of a play, based on John Gay's *The Beggar's Opera*, if you want to read it." So, Aufricht was enthusiastic about it. He said, "Oh, that's marvelous. Yes, I would love to do it." Brecht suggested Weill to write the music, but Aufricht, who only knew Weill's atonal music from *Royal Palace* and *Protagonist*, said, "Oh, no, no. He wouldn't be the right composer for that." But Brecht, of course, insisted that Kurt write it. And Aufricht, going behind Kurt's back, engaged a little Kapellmeister to arrange Johann Pepusch's original music for it, just in case. But when he heard Weill's first songs, he shut up. And the rest is history.

Weill and Brecht decided to go on a writing vacation to the French Riviera. Brecht drove ahead of us—he had a real passion for cars. Brecht didn't like water very much, and I'll never forget the picture of him standing in the Mediterranean, with his seersucker pants rolled up and a cigar in his mouth. He never got wet, he just stood there. Both Weill and I were passionate swimmers.[70]

The dress rehearsal for *Threepenny Opera* lasted until four in the morning. It was almost four o'clock when I came out to rehearse "Solomon Song" and they yelled, "No, no, that's out! That's out!" I was heartbroken because it was such a nice song for me, but I had to succumb.[17]

Kurt was furious when he discovered that my name was left off the program for opening night. That was the first time I heard his voice—that he had a voice, a loud voice. He was so mad. He said, "I won't let you go on." I said, "Kurt, please. I've waited so long to appear in Berlin on an opening night. Even if they don't know me now, tomorrow they will know who I am." And they did, because that very famous critic, Alfred Kerr—he was as famous as Walter Kerr or Brooks Atkinson were in New York—he wrote, "There was one among those girls—she was good. She was more than good. Watch her. She will be very soon in the front row." That did it. And that's in all books. That's not a story invented by me.[59, 70]

During rehearsals all those wise guys said it would not work. On opening night there was absolute silence until it came to the "Cannon Song." Then there was bedlam.[18]

You can't connect the song "Pirate Jenny" to the character of Jenny in the *Threepenny Opera*. The two have nothing to do with each other. Jenny sings "Pirate Jenny" only in the Blitzstein version. In the original version, Brecht's version, Jenny doesn't sing it, Polly does. Polly sings "Pirate Jenny" in the stable scene when Macheath asks, "Isn't there any entertainment?" Yes, I know it's become my song, but that's because of the records of it I made in 1930. But originally Polly sings it as a piece of entertainment in a stable scene. She says, "If nobody else will do anything, I'll sing you a song about a girl in a little waterfront dive. Of course, I've never been there." "Pirate Jenny" has nothing whatsoever to do with Jenny's revenge. I think we should just leave Jenny alone—she's done well over those years. Don't try to pluck it like a chicken, you know? Until nothing is left.[8]

Nobody really believed that *The Threepenny Opera* would become the success it became later, because it got very mixed notices at the the opening. It wasn't a smash hit; it was a very controversial evening. The next day the recording session was set, and the woman who played Mrs. Peachum didn't appear. So I said I'd sing her part just an octave lower, to differentiate it from my part. On the records, there are only three people from the original cast: Kurt Gerron, Erich Ponto, and myself. The rest were all understudies. So when people talk about the original *Threepenny Opera* recordings, they're not original at all. It's not the original cast. The original cast was Harald Paulsen, Rosa Valetti, Kurt Gerron, Kate Kühl, and myself.[79]

Plain irony is boring, but when it's subtle you really have something unusual and interesting. It's the subtlety underneath the obviousness that gives the strength to *The Threepenny Opera*.[34]

The Threepenny Opera will last for a long time because it deals with corruption and poverty. Corruption, we know, has quite a future, and, Lord knows, what a past![17]

Caspar Neher was the one who really invented the Brecht style, as far as staging is concerned. The posters in Brecht's handwriting, the sparseness of the stage, the costumes and make-up, the little line curtain halfway across the stage, and innumerable

The brothel scene in Die Dreigroschenoper. *Lenya, as Jenny, stands in the center. After one of the performances, actress Elisabeth Bergner recalled meeting Lenya again for the first time since they worked together in Zurich: "I had to look at this Lenya over and over—she had been so fantastic as Pirate Jenny. And she must have noticed that I kept looking at her, and so finally she said to me, 'Yes, yes, it's me. You are not wrong. I am Blamauer!' I was speechless."*

Lenya, as Lucy, and Hilde Körber, as Polly, in the original production of Die Dreigroschenoper. *Photo: Willy Saeger, Bildarchiv Preussischer Kulturbesitz*

Label of Telefunken recording of Die Dreigroschenoper *from 1930. This recording featured only three members of the original cast: Erich Ponto, Kurt Gerron, and Lenya. Theo Mackeben conducted the Lewis Ruth Band.*

Silhouette artist Lotte Reiniger captured the spirit of the final scene of Die Dreigroschenoper.

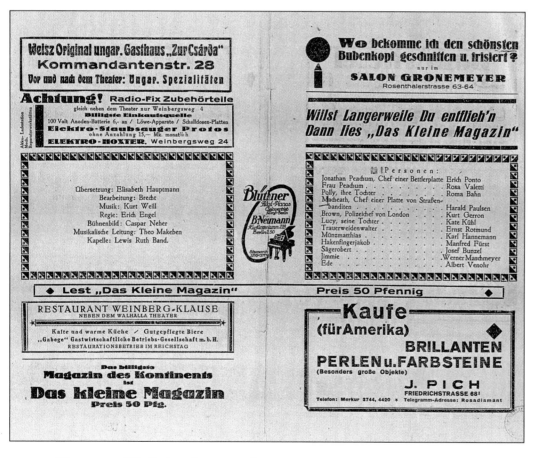

The program of Die Dreigroschenoper *at the Theater am Schiffbauerdamm in Berlin. The production ran several years in Berlin at various theaters. This program, from opening night, did not include Lenya's name. Photo: Universal Edition, Vienna*

other things were all Neher's. Not that Brecht wasn't a genius himself, but Neher was a very important part of the collaboration. I was goddamned lucky to get into that gang and survive and make my little contribution.[79]

A "Threepenny Fever" had swept Berlin and it brought Lenya featured roles playing opposite Hilde Körber and Peter Lorre in works by playwrights such as Frank Wedekind, Georg Büchner, Marieluise Fleisser, Paul Kornfeld, and Valentin Katayev at the Berliner Staatstheater, the Theater am Schiffbauerdamm, the Volksbühne, and the Theater am Kurfürstendamm. G.W. Pabst's film of Die Dreigroschenoper *spread the image of Lenya's aloof and mysterious Jenny throughout Germany, as did her recordings of Weill's songs; preserving her quavering, child-like voice, the records were then widely broadcast on the new medium of radio. Weill bought a sporty new Fiat, and he and Lenya moved to a new apartment on the Bayernallee in Berlin-Westend. It remains unclear how long Lenya lived there before they separated.*

Portrait of Lenya by the famous German photographer Lotte Jacobi. Berlin, ca. 1930.

Caspar Neher's set design for the Finale of **Die Dreigroschenoper.**

Preceding page: Caspar Neher's poster for the original production of **Die Dreigroschenoper.** *Photo: Bertolt-Brecht Archiv, Akademie der Künste, Berlin*

After *Threepenny* we had a little bit more money, and, of course, that made a difference. We could go to the opera more often and sit in better seats, but our life didn't change very much.[17]

Strangely enough, I had a reputation in Berlin for being a fascinating heap of sensuality. You know, singing the "Barbara Song." But privately I'm not sexy at all. Oh sure, I played the part of a vamp for all the pictures, but that was just being an actress. Sex didn't mean much to me. I could live without it, you know? At that time I couldn't live without the theater—it was my life.

I was in *Danton's Death* with Peter Lorre. I played Lucille, the one who sits under the guillotine and goes crazy. And I did *Spring's Awakening* by Wedekind. That was with Lorre too, after the *Threepenny* success. You see, in Berlin we didn't stick for years to the same thing. We went to another theater. I played the repertory for a while, then went back to *Threepenny.* But when I went

As Charmian Peruchacha in Lion Feuchtwanger's satirical play,
Die Petroleuminseln (The Oil Islands), *Berlin, Staatstheater,*
1928. Weill wrote incidental music for the play, including the
popular song, "Das Lied von den braunen Inseln."

Eugen Klöpfer and Lenya in Die Petroleuminseln.
Photo: Institut für Theater- Film- und
Fernsehwissenschaft, Universität zu Köln

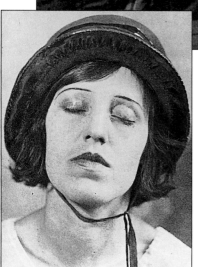

back I didn't play Jenny again. I played Lucy, you see? So, we switched. Brecht switched back and forth, you know?[70]

It's really appalling what Hollywood did to Peter Lorre, he was such a good actor. Once in New York I asked him, "Peter, will they ever give you anything other than 'Mr. Moto Goes to China' or whatever it was he was doing. And he said, "No. All I do is talk with a nasal voice and make faces."[52]

My mother came to see me in a lovely production of *Pioniere in Ingolstadt* by Marieluise Fleisser. She sat in the seat of honor—the Kaiser's box. Backstage afterwards she said, "Haven't you had enough of playing the clown for these people?" But she still came three times. She pretended to dismiss the theater, but she was still proud of me. And she certainly understood the story of the play, which is about a servant girl.[72]

I played Ilsa in *Spring's Awakening*. Afterwards I learned that Max Reinhardt made all his pupils go to see me so that they could see how the part should be played.[17]

I couldn't go to the opening night of *Happy End* because I was playing in another theater. Kurt said that after the second act, people in the audience said it was going to be a bigger success than *Threepenny Opera*. Then came the third act. In the middle, Helene Weigel, Brecht's mistress and future wife, pulled out a pamphlet which nobody ever saw before, and read it. The pamphlet was an attack on the audience, purely a political document. It shocked the

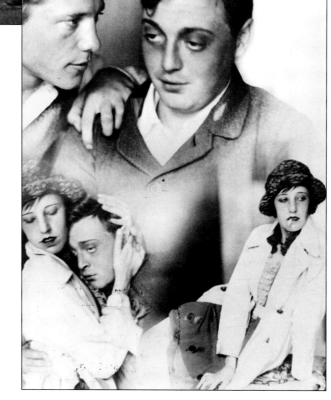

From top to bottom:
Magazine photo of Eleanora von Mendelssohn (Antigone), Fritz Kortner (Oedipus), and Lenya (Ismene) in Leopold Jessner's staging of Oedipus at Colonus, *Berlin, Staatstheater, 1929. Photo: Zander & Lebleck/Institut für Theater- Film- und Fernsehwissenschaft, Universität zu Köln*

Left to right: Franz Weilhammer, Lenya (Alma), Heinrich Mathies, and Ludwig Stössel in Marieluise Fleisser's play Pioniere in Inglostadt (Pioneers in Ingolstadt), *Berlin, Theater am Schiffbauerdamm, 1929.*

Lenya as Lucille in Georg Büchner's play Dantons Tod (Danton's Death), *Berlin, Volksbühne, 1930.*

Publicity collage featuring Lenya and Peter Lorre for the production of Frank Wedekind's play Frühlings Erwachen (Spring's Awakening), *Berlin, Volksbühne, 1929.*

audience beyond belief, because they didn't come to be attacked on that level. So it was a disaster, and that was the end of *Happy End*.[79]

By the time Brecht and Kurt wrote *Happy End* their working relationship came to a temporary dead end, and both needed a rest from each other. Brecht had become more and more involved in politics, and all his ideas were now tinged with his political beliefs; he became increasingly opinionated and dictatorial. All this had an unfortunate influence on *Happy End*. Also the struggle between Carola Neher, who played Lilian Holiday, and Weigel produced unhappy results—Neher's voice was thin and sharp, but she was very musical, and her songs, "Surabaya Johnny" and "Und das Meer ist blau," were vigorously applauded. But Brecht had insisted on a song for Weigel too, in the second act, and she was practically tone-deaf; Kurt wrote a kind of patter song for her, and the audience gave her only polite applause. (I saw this at a performance for actors, because I wasn't in the show.)

Carola Neher, Brecht's mistress at the time, and Helene Weigel, his steady mistress and the mother of his son Stefan, were both in the cast. So three of Brecht's women, including Elisabeth Hauptmann, were present at the rehearsals. The atmosphere seethed with jealousy, and Brecht presided over it with superb tact. He was careful to see that both mistresses had equal roles in the play. They were of course completely different types. Carola Neher was vivacious, eyes like black cherries, auburn hair bobbed, wavy tilted nose, the perfect soubrette type, extremely talented. She always had a banker in the background to surround her with great luxury, an apartment with Persian rugs, bamboo walls, ottomans with satin pillows, very modish, in the Bayernplatz, a stone's throw from where Kurt and I lived. She had a Packard convertible, considered the elegant car at the time, which she drove in a typically fidgety manner. She was middle class, from Munich, had studied to be a pianist, had married a poet named Klabund, who was shy, quiet, always dying of TB. A typical actress, very jealous, she accused me of imitating her style. Many years later, she disappeared into Russia.

Helene Weigel was the daughter of a Galician peddler, small and slender, strong horse face, big teeth that she showed, two deep sunken dimples in her cheeks that appeared when she smiled, always looked much older than she actually was because of the severity of her appearance, hair pulled straight back, no makeup or nail polish. Extremely good-hearted, a born mother without looking like one, willing to knock herself out to help anyone, sincerely

Carola Neher (no relation to Caspar Neher) played Lilian Holliday in the original production of Happy End, *Berlin, Theater am Schiffbauerdamm, 1929. Weill did not write a part for Lenya in the show. Photo: Schmidt, Berlin*

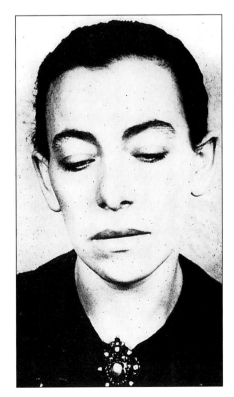

Brecht's second wife, Helene Weigel, ca. 1933. Photo: Bertolt-Brecht-Archiv, Akademie der Künste, Berlin

Lenya attended the opening of Aufstieg und Fall der Stadt Mahagonny, *Leipzig, Neues Theater, 9 March 1930. Again she did not have a part because the work is written for opera singers.*

Below: Cast members in Ferdinand Reyher's play Harte Bandagen (Hard Boxing Gloves), *Berlin, Staatstheater, 1930. Photo: Institut für Theater- Film- und Fernsehwissenchaft, Universität zu Köln*

Opposite: Lenya and Hermann Speelmans in blackface, in Michael Gold's revue Das Lied von Hoboken, *Berlin, Volksbühne, 1930.*

devoted to friends, straight and direct. I never considered her a born actress, but with her great stamina and determination, and with Brecht's great help, she has become a competent actress in her own style, intelligent, controlled, with inexhaustible energy. There were the three women: Hauptmann the shadow, Neher sexy and talented, which unquestionably fascinated Brecht, and Weigel, deeply in love with Brecht, knowing him better than anyone ever has, or ever will, determined to wait her turn. And indeed, when Neher flew to London with one of her bankers, Brecht married Weigel, and then she was secure. At heart Brecht is a family man, with *two* trees at Christmastime. Brecht's close friends, even his children (but not Kurt), called him Bidi.[45]

Brecht absolutely killed one woman after another. He really did. I sincerely believe that he killed Ruth Berlau. He surely killed Hauptmann, in the end he killed Weigel, Isot Kilian, and a few that are still remaining. Many of the affairs were short, but the one with Hauptmann lasted over twenty years, you know?

Everyone had enormous fun working with Brecht. He took everybody in, anyone who had an idea to contribute to him. For instance, he asked me, "Lenya, what does one of *those* girls say to her customer when she meets him." I told him, "Do you like me to wear panties under my dress." He took it right away. Stretches of dialogue came from different people. He always had a lot of people sitting around—pupils, mistresses, or whatever.

The Rise and Fall of the City of Mahagonny opened in Leipzig, which is about three hours from Berlin. And when the curtain went up, everything went fine. But in the middle of it a tremendous riot broke loose because there were already lots of Nazis in the audience. I was sitting in the audience, and the man next to me, in that turmoil, began applauding and whistling at the same time! But whistling meant disapproval, like booing. Everyone was so confused, you know, they didn't know what the hell had hit them. And so then a big fistfight broke loose. The next day they had to leave all the lights on during the performance, and each exit was guarded by the police. And outside the Nazis were parading and picketing the opera.[16, 79]

You cannot apply Brecht's theory to opera. It was anti-opera, you know? I love opera, and—as much as I love Brecht—I hope and I know that opera will survive in spite of his theory.

Kurt Weill was very close to Hindemith in Germany. We were all in the same age group. We saw him quite often, and it

Top: Hilde Körber and Lenya (Frau Götz) in Paul Kornfeld's play Jud Süss (The Jew Süss), *Berlin, Theater am Schiffbauerdamm, 1930. Photo: Elli Marcus*

Bottom: Peter Lorre and Lenya (Tanja) in Valentin Katayev's play Die Quadratur des Kreises (Squaring the Circle), *Berlin, Theater am Schiffbauerdamm, 1930. Photo: Institut für Theater- Film- und Fernsehwissenschaft, Universität zu Köln*

was real friendship, which then—after the immigration, you see—by no fault of anybody, you know—it just broke up. They just went in different directions. Quite understandably so. Everybody had to make a living. Wherever they found it they had to go.[8]

We did a play by an American author, I have forgotten his name, *The Song of Hoboken*. It was very funny, because it was a play about Negroes, and I played a half-Negro, a mulatto. And when we came to this country—in 1935—we went to Hoboken, Kurt Weill and myself, because we wanted to see the Negroes. And they said, "Well, you're in the wrong city. You mean Harlem." And then that's when we knew how wrong *that* play was. Nobody ever knew at the time that the name had been mistranslated.[17]

I first met Marlene Dietrich when she came to audition for Jenny in the Pabst film of *Threepenny Opera*. Her legs were much too beautiful, and she was tall. Brecht's women characters are all very small and fragile, so they didn't take her.[71]

The *Threepenny* film was a big mess because they had a lawsuit. They changed Brecht's text, and they cut a lot of Weill's music. Weill won the lawsuit and Brecht lost: the violation of Brecht's script was not as drastic as the violation of the music. It was a great, great film, that Pabst film, enormous. But it was a very peculiar situation for me, with them suing the producers and me playing Jenny, you know? It wasn't, no, it wasn't very pleasant.[8, 70]

I saw the film again twenty-five years later, with my second husband George Davis, during my first trip back to Berlin. It was strange to see myself some twenty-five years younger. Very slender, very soft-spoken. And the audience listened as attentively as before. George grabbed my hand and was very moved by the whole thing. I wasn't. I looked at it too critically.[21]

One day the stage and film director Erwin Piscator called, his thin voice pitched even higher than usual with excitement. Would I play in a film that he had been invited to make in Russia? It would be based on the novel by Anna Seghers, *The Revolt of the Fishermen of Santa Barbara*; there would be a Russian and a German version, and I would play Maria, the sailor's whore, in the German version. The German cast and crew would all go to Moscow, where Piscator would get the script approved and hire Russian actors and crew members; the film would be shot in

Advertising collage for Pabst's Dreigroschenoper. *Photo: Casparius*

DIE 3 GROSCHEN-OPER

Cover of a 1931 issue of Illustrierte Film-Kurier featuring a scene from the opening of G.W. Pabst's film of Die Dreigroschenoper. *Ernst Busch, as the Street Singer, sings "Mack the Knife" while pointing to painted panels illustrating Macheath's crimes.*

DIE 3 GROSCHEN-OPER

Frei nach Brecht / Musik von Weill

Manuskript:
Lania, Vajda, Balazs
Regie: G. W. Pabst

Gesamtleitung: S. Nebenzahl
Bild: F. A. Wagner
Bauten: Andrej Andrejew
Musikalische Leitung:
Theo Mackeben
Ton: Adolf Jansen
Tonmontage: Hans Oser

Tonsystem:
Tobis-Klangfilm
*

Mackie Messer . . . . . . Rudolf Forster
Polly . . . . Carola Neher
Tiger-Brown . . . . . Reinhold Schünzel
Peachum . . . . Fritz Rasp
Frau Peachum . . . . Valeska Gert
Jenny . . . . Lotte Lenja
Der Pfarrer . . . . Hermann Thimig
Der Straßensänger . . . . . Ernst Busch
Smith . . . . Wladimir Sokolow
                        Paul Kemp
                        Gustav Püttjer
Mackie Messers Platte   Oscar Höcker
                        Kraft Raschig
Filch . . . . Herbert Grünbaum

EIN TONFILM DER TOBIS-WARNER-PRODUKTION

TOBIS   NATIONAL   WARNER BROS.

Left: Original program for Pabst's Dreigroschenoper *film, produced by the German company Tobis and the American company Warner Bros. Left, top to bottom: Rudolf Forster (Macheath), Carola Neher (Polly), Fritz Rasp (Peachum). Right, top to bottom: Reinhold Schünzel (Tiger Brown), Valeska Gert (Mrs. Peachum), Lenya (Jenny).*

Below: Lenya singing "Seeräuberjenny" in the Pabst film.

Odessa. I told him Kurt and I would talk it over and give him a quick answer. I was dubious, having no great love for travel, nor any strong political beliefs. Only while reading Dostoyevsky have I been a passionate Slavophile. I thought Kurt would scoff at the whole idea and give me a firm and sensible no.

But Kurt surprised me with a somewhat qualified yes. This was Piscator's first film. It might make history, it might flop; but that was my kind of gamble, wasn't it? And my kind of part. Not a starring role, but one that could be done with a few—the *right* few—bold, incisive strokes. I might be gone a long time, but I would have a wonderful chance to see Russia, especially Russian theater and films, close up.

We talked to Piscator in his luxurious, modern apartment. He looked faintly apologetic in all this Hollywood-type grandeur. He was not physically impressive, but great authority came from him and he talked with persuasive fervor. The Seghers novel had the right politics, but it was thin, no more than a point of departure. Maria was allied instinctively with the working class, and she would be no less important than any other character in this collective drama. Piscator made it sound better and better. Before Kurt and I left, we had agreed that I must play Maria.

Reproduction of magazine photo, 1929.
Photo: Ullstein

Berlin, ca. 1930. Photo: Ullstein

Berlin, 1931. Photo: Gerty Simon

Berlin, ca. 1928.

Berlin, 1928. Photo: Gerty Simon

Vienna, 1931. Photo: Feldscharek

Opposite: Portrait of Lenya, 1928.
Photo: Elli Marcus

Berlin, ca. 1930.

Before I left, Kurt insisted that I must have a car in Russia, and we bought a second-hand Buick convertible in Hamburg. It was supposed to arrive in Russia right after I did. That accomplished, I was ready to go to Russia. When we left, an entire sleeping car was reserved for our party of actors, technicians, and Piscator's entourage. We settled down to a dull and seemingly endless journey. No games, no cards: theater talk, work on the script, discussions of our parts. We were *German* actors, after all!

We were met in Moscow by people from the film company Mezhrabpom and taken to our lodgings. I wound up in a small, sleazy hotel across from the large, luxurious Metropole. My room looked decent, but the chair collapsed under the weight of my bags, the faucet broke off in my hand, and the foot of the bed hit the floor when I lay down. My spirits, which had been sagging from fatigue, lifted high: "Dostoyevsky, I have come!" The first two weeks we were in Moscow, I was thrilled. My only Moscow tram ride was a nightmare, but I walked the dirty streets for hours at a time, trying to identify with the grim-faced, shoddily dressed people. I waited with weeping peasant women in a long line to see Lenin's body. I saw a remarkable production of Georg Kaiser's *Kolportage*, with the scene in the senile aristocrat's castle played in slow motion. All the other plays I saw were new, violently anti-capitalist, quite absurd, magnificently acted and produced, and so crowded that spectators sat in the aisles.

We were in Moscow for five weeks. We rarely saw Piscator, who remained calm in spite of bureaucratic inertia and obstacles. Once we went swimming in the Moskva, surrounded by naked Russians, but the water was filthy and full of used contraceptives. I thought it might brighten my spirits if I went to see the Romanov treasures—the gold-encrusted coaches, the splendid robes, the fabulous jewels. "Why don't you sell all that?" I said to the guard who spoke German. "We might," he answered coolly. "We didn't have the Revolution so you could come here and boss us around!"

Then we traveled to the spot in Odessa chosen for the village scenes. For a brief while it looked like business. Piscator had us scrambling up and down the rocks, cameras catching us every which way. But construction proceeded with almost droll slowness on the houses on the set, a sill here, a window there. As the days passed, in withering heat, all the green turned brown in the hotel garden, and we made that jaunt less and less often.

I studied Russian with a thin, fortyish schoolteacher; she seemed scared out of her wits, I think because if I learned Russian too rapidly she might be subjected to official questioning. So I was dumb, and learned only the most innocuous words, and she seemed relieved. Kurt wrote faithfully, and sent packages of ginger, Roman plums, and Toblerone chocolate. He and Caspar Neher were deep into writing *Die Bürgschaft*. The most popular evening pastime was Russian billiards, played on an immense table in the game room; Wedekind had taught me the game years before in Zurich, and it astonished everyone how well I played.

One night a member of our crew stopped me when I was playing billiards to tell me that a young tovarich had asked him to ask me if I would walk with him some time soon. I answered yes, maybe, but only if the man spoke some German. I knew who it was; night after night he had been there watching me—bony, prematurely ravaged, with the look of an Asian holy man. He said to expect him in about two weeks. When he came, we walked down to the harbor, then through a weird tangle of streets in pitch darkness. He must have known every step of the way, because we never stumbled. He spoke German, heavily accented, with much thought; he must have learned it while he was away. He told me that he knew I was married to a composer named Kurt Weill. He asked if I intended to remain in Russia. I told him that I would go back to Berlin soon, but that I might be back. He fell into silence, while up and up we climbed, surrounded on all sides by an appalling stench of excrement. At last he spoke: "I don't understand how any intelligent person would willingly become a Communist." He may have been sincere, or he may have been an agent; we Germans were constantly watched, that we knew.

My last week in Odessa, the Buick arrived. The explanation for the delay was that the tires had been stolen en route and had to be replaced. The next morning, needing the car for a last trip to the studio, I couldn't find it anywhere, so I took the tram. Halfway out, the car passed us, crammed with Russian studio workers, waving wildly to me when they saw me. I did manage to get the car for myself for a day, and I took Piscator out to a deserted country road to teach him to drive. He learned in two hours. He seemed in indestructible good spirits and was remaining in Russia, sure that he would finish his film in a blaze of glory. Then, as always, I liked and admired him.

Back to Moscow, seven in the morning, a cold gray October drizzle. There was no room at the hotel where I had stayed before. With the crowds pouring into the capital for Red Army Day, things would be as bad at any hotel. I was told to keep trying. It was not until one in the morning that I finally staggered up to a tiny room under the roof, dragging two heavy bags. It

Weill's and Lenya's last dwelling in Berlin, at 7 Wissmannstrasse (now Käthe-Kollwitz-Strasse), in Klein-Machnow, located in the western suburbs of Berlin. Weill bought the house in 1931 as a present for Lenya, but she may never have used it a permanent residence. Weill first occupied the house in February 1932. Lenya sold it in November 1933, eight months after Weill had fled Germany.

contained a cot, a table, and a small basin. I put on my pajamas and took out a couple of chocolate bars, then fell onto the cot and went dead asleep. I woke up to see an enormous rat devouring the chocolate; I threw a slipper, which did not budge the rat, and blotted out again. I woke again to a loud pounding on the door: time to vacate. No chocolate, or even tinfoil, left on the table.

Red Army Day. Those of us who had passes from Mezhrabpom were in Red Square by six-thirty. A Russian director had our German contingent in tow, and we found our places not far from the lofty reviewing stand where Stalin and the Soviet dignitaries would be. The whole square was enveloped in fog, which lifted like a gigantic curtain, slowly revealing first the feet in the towering portrait of Lenin, gradually all of him. The endless battalions of soldiers began to march, tanks rolled past, planes roared overhead. At one moment, when clenched fists shot up from the vast crowd, I saw many among us Germans lifting high their clenched fists. I was embarrassed for them.

Kurt had written that he would telephone on my birthday. Miraculously, the call came through promptly, his voice as clear as though he were in the next room: "Darling, I have bought you a house for your birthday!" The moment was so wonderful, and so unreal, that I kept croaking, "Yes . . . yes . . . where is it?" Kurt told me that it was in Kleinmachnow, a modern house with a little garden, then: "Lenya, the house number is seven! Seven! Our lucky number!" He waited for me to speak, then said, "Lenya, are you unhappy about the house?" I heard myself answering, stuffily, "I don't think anybody has a right to own a house." Kurt laughed, and said, "Oh, you'll change your mind when you get home."

It was harder to leave Russia than to enter it. For several weeks we had been paid in Russian currency, which we could not take out of the country. I was advised to put what I had left in the bank; I still have the bankbook.

Our train arrived in Berlin late afternoon of a brilliant November day. I was shaking with fever. We went at once to our apartment, and it was two weeks before I could bring myself to see the new house.

Only the Russian version of the film, *The Fishermen's Revolt*, was ever completed. Piscator hung on, and in 1934, it was finally released. I never saw it, but the criticism from Russia was interesting. Piscator's new stunts, his devices that would revolutionize Soviet film, failed to impress; what he had done, Russian directors had done better. But high praise was heaped on two female performers: Yudif Glizer as a stoical fisherwoman, and an actress named Janukowa as the waterfront whore.[45]

That period in Russia had a very strong influence on me. I was just as red as I could be at that time. But all that changed very quickly when I got back.[52]

In December 1931 when I played Jenny in *Mahagonny*, in Berlin, strangely enough the audience was normal. Nothing happened. No riots, whistles, or disturbances at all. There it was done by that marvelous producer Ernst Josef Aufricht, who did the *Threepenny Opera* and was the producer and owner of the theater where the Berliner Ensemble now plays, Schiffbauerdamm. It was a beautiful production. Harald Paulsen sang the lead, and the very famous Alexander Zemlinsky conducted. In Berlin it went without the audience blinking an eyelash. That was a year after the opera caused riots in Leipzig, and politically everything was already leaning much, much more toward the Nazis. Still, there was no riot.[16, 79]

Caricature by Linne[?], published in 12-Uhr-Blatt, *of the cast of* Aufstieg und Fall der Stadt Mahagonny, *Berlin, Kurfürstendamm-Theater, 1931. On the left: Lenya as Jenny, Harald Paulsen as Jimmy.*

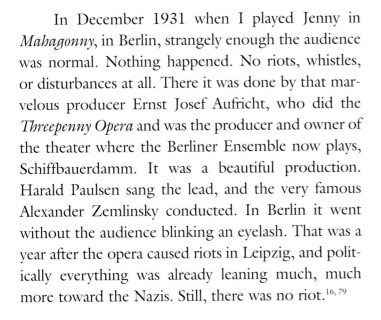

I never can do much in a rehearsal, you know? Especially not with those opera singers listening to me. Zemlinsky always said, "Sing out! Do you ever sing out in the rehearsals?" I said, "Never." He said, "Well, I have to hear you." That was in a rehearsal room. I said, "I can't do anything here, you know? I'll show you. Let me get on stage and you will see what I can do." And then the first rehearsal on stage, while all those trained opera singers fluffed, I went straight through the score, of course, without the slightest mistake. And then he looked at me, and said, "Okay, I know now what you are doing." And from then on he left me in peace.[8]

I never had a problem with Brecht. Sometimes he showed me extraordinary things. Like when we were rehearsing the big *Mahagonny* in Berlin. There was a line drawn across the stage for me to walk as I sang "Denn wie man sich bettet" ["As you make your bed"]. And then came the reprise and Brecht showed me something, just one simple movement of the hand, that made all the difference. We understood each other immediately, no discussion. Brecht hated actors who talked. He'd say, "Don't talk, show me. If it's good, I'll take it." He never listened to an actor—it bored him. But he was great with actors, even the dumbest ones. He had incredible patience.[72]

In 1932, when I did *Mahagonny* in Vienna for a limited engagement, after the opening the publisher gave a little party. Kurt Weill couldn't come because he was working on his new show in Berlin, so I sat next to the composer Ernst Krenek, but he didn't say anything. I said, "Well, you evidently didn't like it." He said, "No, I hated it. I'm sorry, Lenya. I loved you, but I hate that work. I think it's raw and vicious." Then in 1937, when we saw him in New York, he said, "Lenya, do you remember that evening after *Mahagonny*? After the opening?" I said, "Yes." He said, "Now I understand. Having lived in this country, now, for two years—now, all of a sudden, I understand *Mahagonny* much better than I did then." And still it has nothing to do with America. This is the funny thing. *Mahagonny*'s not about America. It's about capitalism at that time. It has much less to do with America than it has with the man dying in the electric chair because he can't pay for his whisky. They used an electric chair because, at the time they wrote *Mahagonny*, the first woman to be executed was named Snyder—so the electric chair made a terrific impression on them. Brecht, as flexible as he is, took that event immediately and used it, you see? You might think it's about America, but it's not at all. It can be about China, too.[8]

When I sang Jenny in Berlin, my voice wasn't high enough to sing the music for "Havana Song," and Kurt didn't want to transpose it. So he said, "I'll write you something else. I'll write you a different 'Havana Song' and the chorus can just sing what they already have." That's how one of the loveliest songs he ever wrote got into *Mahagonny*.[68]

Anti-Semitism always existed in Germany, but I personally wasn't very aware of it at first, because when you are young and dream of being a success in the theater you aren't so aware of the political situation. But, of course, I wasn't blind to it either, especially after *Mahagonny*. I remember walking down the street on a Sunday afternoon with the artist Lotte Reiniger and her husband Karl Koch, neither of whom were Jewish. A bunch of young Nazis were walking behind us and one of them hit Karl in the neck with an apple core. Another time I remember going to an afternoon movie with Kurt and overheard some typical German housewives telling some Jewish people there, "If you don't like it here, why don't you just go back to Palestine?" The Jews just ignored them, because they didn't want to cause a riot.[17]

It was Kurt's idea that Caspar Neher write a libretto for an opera. At the time I was in Russia making a movie with Piscator. Kurt was of course a tremendous reader, and he and Neher searched diligently for a subject. They found a fable by Herder and turned it into *Die Bürgschaft*. By this time we were very friendly with the Nehers; both Kurt and I really liked Erika, and their young son Georg, the image of his father, adored Kurt and called me "*Zwiebel*" [Onion]. By the time I came back from Russia I found that Kurt and Neher had a passion for cocoa made with water, which Erika made for them by the gallon. Neher himself

Cast members Maris Wetra, Harald Paulsen, Trude Hesterberg, and Lenya of the 1931 Berlin production of Mahagonny *read the reviews. This photo first appeared in the Berlin newspaper* 12-Uhr-Blatt.

Promotional record for the Berlin Mahagonny, 1931. The recording featured dance arrangements of "Alabama Song" and "Wie man sich bettet" by Emil Roosz und sein Künstler-Orchester. The disc was made of laminated cardboard and printed in color on both sides.

Alabama Song
Slow-Fox
Emil Roosz
und sein Künstler-Orchester
BIEM
"1002"
Musik. Leitung v. Zemlinsky, Insz. Neher
Hauptdarsteller:
Trude Hesterberg, Harald Paulsen, Lotte Lenja

Aufstieg und Fall der Stadt Mahagonny Oper von Brecht und Weill

Gastspiel der Ernst Josef Aufricht Produktion im Kurfürstendamm Theater

Sketch by Caspar Neher for Die Bürgschaft, *the opera written by Kurt Weill to a libretto by Neher while Lenya was in Russia. The opera premiered at the Städtische Oper in Berlin, 10 March 1932.*

Below: Publicity photo for the Vienna production of Aufstieg und Fall der Stadt Mahagonny, *Raimundtheater, 1932. This is the only known photo of Lenya with her lover Otto Pasetti. Pasetti, a tenor, played the role of Jimmy. Photo: Dietrich/Bildarchiv und Porträtsammlung der Österreichischen Nationalbibliothek*

would say that Kurt was really a collaborator on the text. There were no shenanigans of speaking over a tune; Neher had a deep love of opera (which Brecht detested) and wrote big arias and choruses, for which Kurt composed soaring melodies and intricate chorus parts. Brecht never came to rehearsals but sent his spies, among them Hanns Eisler, servile, a born bootlicker, with a drooling lisp, who rushed back to Brecht with a report that this was more a *Spiessbürgerschaft* [bunch of philistines] than *Bürgschaft*, greeted with roars of laughter by Brecht and his disciples. Kurt and Neher worked on the opera with great joy, and Kurt found it so wonderful to expand into the realm of opera. Of course Neher's sets for the opera were extraordinary.[45]

I think the fact that Weill never talked about Germany after leaving, that he never wanted to speak German, and that he didn't want to go back to Germany, even for a day, showed me how deeply hurt he was by having his career broken up. He was so happy writing *Die Bürgschaft*, he said, "Finally I can just make music again!" He was so tired of singing actors, no matter how good they were, holding back his forces all the time. He really wanted to write operas.[72]

Feeling claustrophobic in Berlin, Lenya accepted an offer in April 1932 to play Jenny for eleven performances at Vienna's Raimund Theater. She played opposite tenor Otto Pasetti, who became her first serious relationship, apparently, since Weill. Weill, feeling intense pressure from the rise in Nazi popularity, kept expecting Lenya to return to Berlin, but instead she stayed in Vienna with Pasetti. That summer Lenya proposed to Weill a divorce; he agreed and both hired lawyers in Berlin. In December 1932, Weill arranged for Lenya and Pasetti to appear in a concert version of an expanded Mahagonny Songspiel *in Paris, after which both returned to Vienna. On 30 January 1933, Adolf Hitler became chancellor of Germany. Lenya joined Weill for the premiere of his opera* Der Silbersee *on 18 February 1933 in Leipzig; all performances were officially forbidden as of 4 March. It is difficult to know Lenya's travels in detail between 1932 and 1935, because those pages in her passport have been carefully cut out, apparently by Lenya herself.*

Weill was very jealous and always so goddamned understanding about whatever I did. In 1931 when I lived with that guy Otto Pasetti in Vienna, he understood. I wasn't even in love with that stupid tenor. I don't know what it was. Maybe I was tired of the whole Berlin scene and needed to get out. Whatever it was, he understood.[72]

Kurt's last work in Germany was *Der Silbersee*, which he wrote with Georg Kaiser. It opened simultaneously in three theaters. There is a ballad in it, "Caesar's Ballad," which is obviously meant to portray Hitler. The very next day Goebbels forbade any more performances.[79]

Lenya never stopped telling interviewers the legend of how she and Weill escaped from Germany together. Only late in her life did she confide some of the details to Gottfried Wagner (great-grandson of Richard Wagner) of why she wasn't with Weill when he left, and even then she had to be prodded to deviate from her well-rehearsed script. In truth, Hans Fallada, who had already been arrested, warned Weill through an intermediary to leave Berlin and wait for the election results in Munich. While Weill waited at a Berlin cafe, Lenya and photographer Louise Hartung apparently gathered together some items from the house in Kleinmachnow; together they drove to Munich.

In March 1933, Kurt and I left Berlin in order to go to Munich, where all the refugees went to wait for the elections of Hitler, because they thought he would just be defeated. They all sat at that famous Hotel *Vier Jahreszeiten*, waiting until the votes came out. Pretty soon they knew the outcome. Then I went to Vienna to say goodbye to my mother and to my sister. This crazy Kurt went back once more to Berlin to get some material out and then Caspar Neher drove him to the French border and to Paris, but he hardly took anything with him. He could have been caught then. I returned to Berlin later to try to sell the house and take things out. We got a divorce so that I could get the money out. After that he never talked about Germany. He never wanted to go back, not even for a day.[72]

Caspar and Erika Neher drove Weill over the German border on 22 March 1933, two days before the Reichstag passed the so-called Enabling Act, which transferred a wide range of powers from the legislature to the Reich Cabinet. Photo: Reimann

A letter to Caspar Neher written in the early 1950s confirms that Lenya had no idea what happened to Weill after he left Munich; apparently it was a topic they never discussed later.

In 1933, Kurt and I went by car to Munich.

When? In Spring?
You had given us a thermos bottle with coffee. I went on to Vienna, and Kurt went back to Berlin. What happened after that?

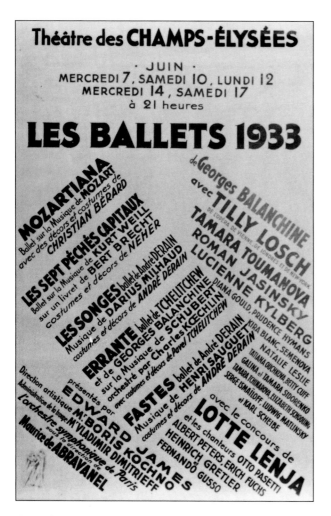

Poster for "Les Ballets 1933," including the premiere of Weill
and Brecht's Die sieben Todsünden (Seven Deadly Sins),
a ballet with songs in which Lenya sang the part of Anna I.
The production opened in Paris and traveled to London.
Arts patron Edward James sponsored the short-lived company
that provided the springboard for George Balanchine to come
to the U.S.

Opposite: Tilly Losch (dancing Anna II) and
Lenya (singing Anna I) in Die sieben Todsünden,
Paris, Théâtre des Champs-Élysées, 1933.
Photo: Studio-Iris, Paris

Did he go back to the house in Kleinmachnow?
When did he decide to leave Germany?
Who had advised him to do that?
Did he *have* to leave?
What were his thoughts when he left?
What did he take with him?
What did he wear?
What route did he take?
Where did he cross the border?
Were you with him?

In case you were with him: what was discussed during
the trip?

Was he depressed or was he confident about his future?

How about that story when he crossed the border, when
children drew a swastika into the dust on his car and the man
at the border said that it should be wiped off because those over
there (which country, Italy or France?) don't like this emblem.

Where did he go after he crossed the border?

How long did the trip last?

Did he take books and music with him?

Cas, I'm just giving you some clues. You probably can
remember much more. Everything is enormously important.
Don't leave out anything. Good or bad.[50]

*Weill immediately began pursuing work in Paris, where he landed a commission
from Edward James to compose* Die sieben Todsüden (The Seven Deadly Sins).
*He persuaded Brecht to write the libretto, Neher to design sets and costumes, and
invited Lenya and Pasetti to perform. After playing in Paris, the production
moved to London for a two-week engagement.*

Weill had had a big success with *Mahagonny Songspiel* and
Der Jasager in Paris a year before, but coming back as a refugee
was much harder. George Balanchine and Lincoln Kirstein
formed a company to do a dance series in Paris called "Les Ballets
1933." Balanchine wanted to do *The Seven Deadly Sins*, which
was very courageous of him, I must say. A very famous dancer,
Tilly Losch, played opposite me. Rehearsals were very funny
because Balanchine didn't speak French very well and didn't
know a word of German. He didn't understand what the goddamn thing was all about. So everything was translated for him:
from German into French, then from French into Russian. Still,
he did a beautiful job. The story is this: Anna I—that was me—

Fashion photographer Hoyningen-Huene photographed Lenya as Anna I for Paris Vogue. *Lenya reported to Weill, "*Vogue *has taken pictures of me, and I just showed them to [Edward] James. He was so enthusiastic that he ordered three big ones for the lobby. . . . Besides, the pictures are very beautiful. Very Parisian. But good." Photo: George Hoyningen-Huene*

guides her little sister through all the seven deadly sins. Their family in Louisiana sends them into the big world to earn money so that they can build a house. Every time little Anna commits a crime, you see the house getting bigger. Finally, after the seventh sin, the house has a roof. The girls come home, completely destroyed, but the family is happy with their house. The French didn't like it, probably because it was sung in German. At the time they were very chauvinistic.[17]

> *[Letter to Weill, 8 May 1933]*
> I think the contract with Edward James sounds really good. Just now I wrote him a few lines and asked him for the contract. I'm all for treating these contractual matters purely as business. I'm really very happy to earn this money, plus I'm so very much looking forward to this work. Pasetti is very glad to be in it too. It's also very good for him to sing a little bit again.
>
> I've already thought about a beautiful costume for the practical girl from Louisiana [Anna I]. Won't it be wonderful to stir things up a bit again? I'll sing like a songbird. But how all this is going to turn out without Helene Weigel and Brecht is sure a mystery to me. Have you heard anything from him? I hope not. Sometimes I really do miss Cäschen [Caspar Neher]. He's always the same nice Cas. I wonder what he's doing—whether a little national flag is already fluttering from his Hanomag [a forerunner of the Volkswagen].
>
> P.S. I've dropped the Lotte from my name and want to write it instead like this: L. Marie Lenja. Isn't that better? The Lotte is so like a Kraut.[77]

Neher was really underhanded—not quite kosher. When Kurt got him the job to design *The Seven Deadly Sins*, he met Weill in Paris and said to him, "You know, Kurt, it's really quite nice now to go along the Kurfürstendamm and not see any Jews there anymore." And do you think Kurt said anything to him? No, he just looked at him. And Neher continued, "The Kurfürstendamm now is so *pure*, you know what I mean, Kurt?" Maybe he meant it half-jokingly, but it's a true story. Maybe he said it to hurt Kurt a bit, who knows? On one hand he was tremendously open and honest, and yet there was a kind of vicious streak in him saying things like that. I am almost sure he didn't 100 percent mean it. Brecht used to say about Neher, "Oh he's an ox, he doesn't understand anything."[72]

[Letter to Weill, 23 June 1933]

Again there were lots of people at the *Mahagonny* performance. Only Marie-Laure [Vicomtesse de Noailles, one of Weill's patrons in Paris] was missing. (I think I'll make a stink about that one.) I think it's much more likely that you yourself are the eighth deadly sin. As for me, the Duchess of Clermont Tonnerre attended the performance, and this no longer entirely youthful lady was so enthusiastic about *Mahagonny* and me that she came into the dressing room and absolutely demanded to see me. Already the next morning she called, and in the afternoon I went over to have tea with her. All alone, and no company. She was really charming. She wants to write an article about me. Then she showed me her house (which is in the Rue du Raynard.) In the music parlor she confessed to me that she plays "the flute." Hee, hee, I almost said, like old Fritz [Frederick the Great] and probably as poorly, too. But I kept hold of myself. She asked what she could do for me in England. Today she sent me two letters for different ladies in London. I should go there. Well, in a word: I've been at a Duchess's. I really fancied myself like Eliza Doolittle in *Pygmalion*. There's something of that in this whole thing. But people were crazy for *Mahagonny* again. That's much more fun than anything else.

After London I'll go to Kleinmachnow for sure. I also think it's the right thing to do. But Weillchen, don't *you* even think of going back to Germany. Don't let yourself be enticed by Cas. It would be terrible. I haven't heard anything about the divorce. I'll call Strauss before I leave. We can meet you at the end of August, and then we'll fix you up an apartment in Paris. Everything is OK with the house.

You were absolutely right to leave immediately after the premiere, because I find the clique here much worse even than the one in Berlin. In Berlin at least once in a while somebody spoke the truth. But here everything is encrusted in this slime-pile "*merveilleuse*" ["Wonderful!"].[77]

We did the piece again in London, in a terrible translation by Edward James, who had initially commissioned the piece for his wife Tilly Losch. They were separated at the time, but he hoped that this would bring them back together. It didn't, of course. We did it at the theater in the Savoy Hotel, and it failed bitterly there too, worse than in Paris.[17]

*In late August 1933, Lenya returned to Berlin to pack her and Weill's belongings
and sell her house in Kleinmachnow. Their divorce was finalized on 18 September.
If a letter Lenya sent to Pasetti on 20 October is to be believed, she planned to stay
in Berlin. (This is the only extant correspondence between Lenya and Pasetti; the
letter was found in Lenya's house in New City after her death in 1981, hidden
under her mattress.)*

[Letter to Pasetti, 20 October 1933, from Berlin]
I received your letter and I'm wondering how in all seriousness
it's possible to write that kind of nonsense. It's really a joke to
make the statement that a city like Berlin has nothing to offer
intellectually. A city like this with that kind of future. If that's
your opinion, o.k.—but don't try with your endless letters to
force your opinion upon me. I think it's somewhat presumptuous
to talk about my poor soul that's been torn to pieces.

I believe that you miss me by being with that Conti group—
but honestly, I'm not in the least inclined to take that into consideration. I feel so infinitely free here, having escaped all that
loathesomeness, and up to now I haven't the slightest intention of
coming back. As far as your letters are concerned, I can do very
well without that tenderness and love you profess for my poor soul
when you write to me like a high school student who is searching
for a subject for his essay. If you can't write anything more intelligent, then you better forget about it altogether. I think I can do
very well without your good advice. You are asking me for logic?
You don't seem to have understood the meaning of this word
when you have the gall to write me such letters. I will take the fact
that you may still change your mind into consideration. I'd like to
write you some more and tell you about this city's plentiful, won-
drous and interesting things—this city which has nothing to offer
intellectually—but your letters really make it impossible for me.[53]

When I left Berlin for good in October (I think it was
October) I gave a suitcase stuffed with music and newspaper
clippings, pictures, etc. to the wife of Manfred Fuerst for safe-
keeping. Of course, I don't know whether she is still alive and
where she is. I rather doubt that among this total destruction one
single suitcase has survived in some cellar in Berlin. That would
be a miracle and since I have stopped believing in miracles I
wouldn't know how I could find out whether it—the suitcase—
by yet another miracle still exists.[50]

I got as much paper money as I could, in very large bills,
and folded it into the palm of a glove. I took the car, having
already made up my mind to go to Monte Carlo. I had every cent
that I could lay my hands on in this one glove. When I arrived at

the border, I was determined, if the guards made any trouble, to gun the car and force my way through. Fortunately nothing happened. My papers were examined, and I was waved through. And off I went to the casino.[2]

Beginning in late November 1933, Lenya spent six months with Pasetti at the casinos in San Remo in a failed attempt to make their fortune by experimenting with various gambling systems. In June 1934, Pasetti traveled to Vienna and reported to Lenya on "passport difficulties" and his unsuccessful efforts to smuggle Weill's money out of Austria. It is doubtful that Lenya ever saw him again.

[Letter to Weill, 26 June 1934]
Now once again I've waited an entire day. Nothing. Yesterday there was an express letter from Pasetti, which was mailed Sunday morning. He has been reported to the police anonymously because of "political machinations," and they've taken away his passport as a result. He can tell me about this only in person. He thinks that it may take days to get his passport back, and he has to be glad that they let him run around loose. Which pig turned him in like that can't be determined for the time being. He thinks that *he* must make a report in San Remo, since the money was deposited in the bank there under his name and the transactions were also under his name. He writes that if the accounts are gone, we won't get anything anymore; if they're still there, there's still some hope. Also that then they will wait for a while to do something with that money. He's absolutely desperate. He suggests that I come to Vienna if he can't get away any more this week, in order to make a written complaint to San Remo, and then to stay in Vienna until the fall, to live off the sale of the antiques, which he has had appraised, and for which one can get approximately 2,000 schillings, and then go to Paris and sell the stamp collection in Paris. We could surely get the money out through Peresleny, but it will take some time. In no case do I want to go to Vienna. That would be terrible for me. I sent him a telegram yesterday that I'm anxiously awaiting him here [in San Remo]. I do so hope that he'll arrive here in the next few days. I don't want to lose my nerve now, although this waiting is awful. I'll write to you immediately when I hear something from him. If you didn't exist, I really wouldn't know what I could possibly do now. But this bad luck has to stop soon. I accompanied Robert Vambery [librettist for *A Kingdom for a Cow*] up to St. Mark's, then went back again. I've canceled the cabin, as I don't need one just for myself. I hope you had a good trip and arrived safely. If only you have some luck in London. Now I'll go mail this letter. If only something would arrive tomorrow.

Now farewell my Weilili. When I think about you, the tears always come to my eyes, because you're so good to me. If only I could pay you back for all of this some day. I'll write you as soon as I hear something.[77]

Lenya took a job at the Corso Theater in Zurich playing in Lieber reich aber glücklich *until October, when she went to Paris and began a brief affair with artist Max Ernst. In April 1935 Lenya joined Weill in London, presumably to study English, while he completed the score for a new operetta,* A Kingdom for a Cow. *After he returned to Paris in July, he sent Lenya letters in care of Gerty Simon, a photographer friend from their Berlin days.*

[Letter to Weill, 23 January 1935]
Yesterday at 5 p.m. I took your car to Louveciennes. At the Étoile the bumper fell off, and I managed to tie it back on with the belt of your raincoat, which was lying in the backseat. When we got out there—Moni[?], M. Ernst and I—Berthon [caretaker of Weill's house] was busy repairing all the chairs. M.E. will definitely leave tomorrow. Last night we were at Paul Strecker's (the painter) with Mrs. Sternheim and Mops. He was quite delighted. Had been in Germany. I wanted to pump him a little about Hindemith, but he was very careful. Furtwängler is said to be acting quite stupidly, humbling himself before the cross. How disgusting all this is! Your *Dreigroschenoper* music is being played quite openly everywhere, Strecker says. Nobody uses "Heil Hitler" as a greeting anymore.

Advertisement for Lenya's last pre-war stage appearance in Europe, at the Corso Theater in Zurich, 1934. The comic operetta, Lieber reich aber glücklich, *had music by Walter Kollo.*

Right: Production photo from Lieber reich aber glücklich.

But he also thinks that all this doesn't help much. He was very nice, that's that. Nothing more has happened. Today I sent 200 francs to my old lady. So I'm done with that. Think of your Linerl on the 28th, the day you married the little one with a heel-clicking "Jawohl." Many little kisses for you.[77]

[Letter from Max Ernst to Lotte Lenya, 1934?]
Each time is a beautiful moment when a letter from you arrives in this lonely desert in which I now live. I think of myself almost as the old Beethoven with his "distant Beloved." Please do write me often, even if there is nothing to report; so much more is happening there than here, where one sometimes can walk 10 kilometers without meeting a living being.

Too bad that you aren't here now, where the sun is shining brilliantly, whereas at night stones and bones are freezing. Unfortunately the water pipes have also frozen, which will make a fine deluge when the warm weather comes. Please do not fear for my poor "sensuousness," because I "sublimate" so much. I think you are exaggerating. . . .[29]

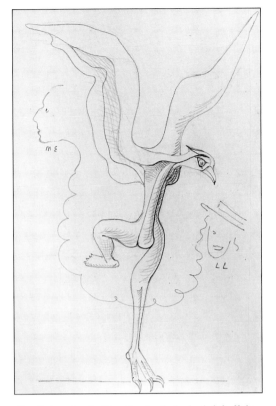

Pencil drawing by Max Ernst, who had a brief affair with Lenya, 1934-35. He depicts himself to the left of the bird, Lenya to the right. Reproduced courtesy Artists Rights Society (ARS), New York/ADAGP, Paris

First page of a handwritten letter from Lenya in Paris to Weill in London, 10 February 1935. Weill was in London to promote his operetta Der Kuhhandel, *text by Robert Vambery. The operetta was staged in London in the summer of 1935 under the title* A Kingdom for a Cow. *Lenya comments on a disastrous British radio broadcast of* Die Dreigroschenoper, *which was panned nearly unanimously by the English critics. © Kurt Weill Foundation for Music 1998*

[Letter to Weill, 10 February 1935]
Your sweet long letter arrived just now. It's simply dreadful that now we've reached the point where they [the British press] have to tear *Die Dreigroschenoper* to pieces. I'm very depressed. My poor Weili. It seems that they're still clinging to their old *Beggar's Opera*, as far as *Die Dreigroschenoper* is concerned. But maybe the way I sing the songs could really help matters along. It would be one way to get the people to understand them better. Only one needs to be very careful that the piece is presented in the right way. Otherwise it will be very difficult for me to get myself out of a flop again. Cabaret is not quite as dangerous. I'm dying to play Polly. I'm much better suited for theater than for cabaret. I'm sure that I'd be successful. Up to now it's always worked out.[77]

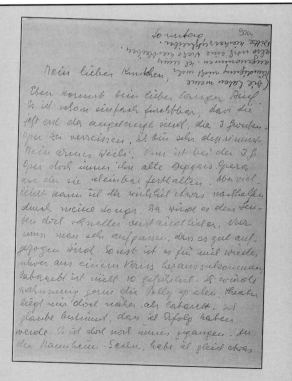

London, 1934. Photo: Gerty Simon

[Letter to Weill, 11 February 1935]
Perhaps, Weilchen, you should consider moving to England altogether. We could arrange to live there very inexpensively. As I told you before, I'm game for anything. It'll be so easy to do that little bit of housework. And you can be completely independent. I won't disturb you at all. But you know that anyway. I'm reading six plays in English: "Famous Plays of 1934." One worse than the other. Unbelievable trash. I can read it almost as if it were a German play. You see, Weili, your Kleene [baby] looks ditzy, but really isn't. I'm so looking forward to seeing you. My residence permit hasn't come yet. I think they must have forgotten about it. Now farewell, my Weilchen, many little kisses.[77]

Lenya's passport, stamped by the German embassy in London, 30 August 1935, just five days before she set sail to the U.S. with Weill on the SS Majestic.

Against the advice of several friends, Weill invited Lenya to go with him to New York, where he was to prepare the premiere of The Eternal Road, *a huge Biblical spectacle directed by Max Reinhardt. He even secured a small part for Lenya in the show. Lenya joined Weill in Paris on 2 September, just in time for her to obtain a temporary American visa before they sailed on the SS Majestic on 4 September and arrived in New York Harbor on 10 September as Mr. and Mrs. Kurt Weill.*

CHAPTER 3

Sing Me Not a Ballad
1935-1951

The quality possessed by Lenya, and by all singers of extraordinary ability, is that of taking a song at its utmost seriousness. They sense its ultimate scope, and they yield to it wholly and unguardedly, and with the effect, finally, of bringing something new to the song itself. It is scarcely an exaggeration to say that each song ever sung by these performers becomes her own — her rendition is definitive, and all previous versions merely its framework, and all subsequent ones its reminiscence.[64] —TERRY SOUTHERN, in *Glamour* magazine

A favorite portrait by Richard Ely.

Weill hoped that American theater and film would provide a livelihood and a venue for his music. Lenya hoped for a better reception in the United States than she had received in France and England. They arrived enthusiastic, sat together for their first publicity photos, and represented themselves as a married couple. The League of Composers welcomed Weill with a special concert of his music in which Lenya performed songs from The Threepenny Opera, Mahagonny, *and* Marie Galante. *Composer Marc Blitzstein, reviewing the concert in* Modern Music, *found Lenya "too special a talent for a wide American appeal; but she has magnetism and a raw lovely voice like a boy soprano. Her stylized gestures seem strange because of her natural warmth; but in the strangeness lies the slight enigma which is her charm."*

We always had a nostalgia for America because we saw all the movies. We knew them all. So, when we finally came in 1935 and saw that famous skyline of New York, it was like coming home, because we had seen it in the movies. We had read all of the American literature. The first thing we did when we stepped

*Weill and Lenya arrive in New York Harbor on 10 September
1935 with Francesco and Eleanora von Mendelssohn, and Meyer
Weisgal. Photo: UPI/Corbis-Bettmann*

off the gangplank was pick up our suitcases and go to the St.
Moritz Hotel. It was very exciting to go up in the elevator to the
twenty-second floor, you know, because we didn't have any skyscrapers at that time in Berlin. It was like going to the top of Mt.
Everest, it was so high! So we just dropped our bags and went
straight down to Broadway. And it was really like walking down
the Kurfürstendamm in Berlin, it looked so familiar. And we went
to the movies and saw *The Dark Angel*.[16, 68]

When I came to the U.S., I had to relearn English because
I hardly understood what anyone was saying. I was so proud of
my accumulated English, I thought, until I hit New York. I
remember going into Saks Fifth Avenue one day to buy a sweater.
I asked the salesman, "Will you please rape it for me?" And he
said, "Sorry, madam, but she's not my type."[8, 17]

It was hard in the beginning, for sure. For about a year
producers would say, "How do you spell your name? What is it?

First publicity photo of Weill and Lenya in America, 1935. Photo: Louise Dahl-Wolfe/Staley-Wise Gallery, New York

W-E-E . . . Wheel? Wheel?" For all the actors and writers who came here, it was enormously difficult because they had to learn a new language. Weill never looked back, spoke German only very rarely, didn't cry about his past, probably because he was so deeply hurt. That's why he was successful.[36]

Production difficulties delayed the opening of The Eternal Road *a full year, and Lenya's small role received scant critical attention. Having to support a cast of 200 and an almost equal number of stage technicians, the show closed after 153 performances with huge financial losses. While waiting for* The Eternal Road *to open, Weill wrote* Johnny Johnson *with Paul Green for the Group Theatre and began networking with everyone he had known or met in Germany, including George and Ira Gershwin.*

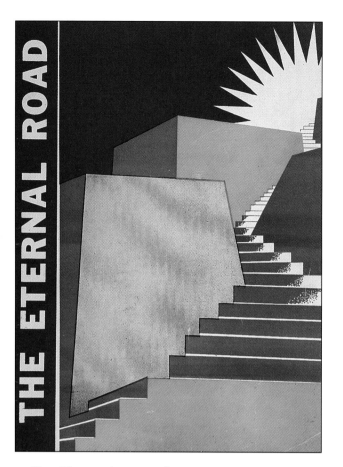

Kurt had composed large parts of *The Eternal Road* somewhere between Paris, London, and Salzburg. I didn't meet Franz Werfel until we came to America. Werfel did not look like a writer to me, he looked like a composer. He was short, flabby, terrible teeth, a drooling mouth, always wet, thin straggly hair, greasy looking, ready to burst into tears at the drop of a hat, a Viennese buttery voice, the sorrows of humanity on his shoulders and in his voice. I think most of this was an act. Mrs. Werfel still had the remnants of her famous beauty, tall, blonde, blue eyes, voluptuous, very much like the opera singer Maria Jeritza. She had been Mrs. Gustav Mahler. Always snapping at Werfel, I always felt at heart that she was deeply anti-Semitic from her remarks, even reactionary (she talked about having champagne after the workers were mowed down in Vienna). She even started breakfast with champagne, a heavy drinker.[45]

Max Reinhardt, Franz Werfel, and Kurt Weill all came here for the production of *The Eternal Road*. The piece was finished except for the changes that always take place in rehearsals. It took place at the Manhattan Opera House. The stage wasn't big enough for the grandeur of Reinhardt's directing style, so he had all the rigging torn out and widened the stage. Then when it

Above: The souvenir program for The Eternal Road, *an immense Biblical spectacle directed by Max Reinhardt, with music by Weill and libretto by Franz Werfel. The show opened on 7 January 1937 at the Manhattan Opera House on West 34th Street.*

Right: The slaves revolt in Egypt, Act 2, Scene 1 of The Eternal Road. *Photo: Lucas Pritchard/ The Lucas-Monroe Collection, Museum of the City of New York*

Opposite: Photographer George Platt Lynes took a series of publicity photos for Lenya at the time of The Eternal Road, *when she was trying to establish an American career.*

Weill secured for Lenya the small parts of Miriam and the Witch of Endor in The Eternal Road.

came time to install the sets, new rigging had to be built. And then, one day, four huge columns arrived. When they put them on the stage, they were so heavy that they sank to the basement. So they left them there. So that went on and on, and they spent an enormous amount of money. The show broke down about three times before it finally got on the stage and was actually produced. It was an enormous prestige success, you see, but it couldn't possibly run, because of 300 people on stage. You'd have to be a Vanderbilt to keep that kind of show going.[79]

We saw *Porgy and Bess* very soon after coming to New York, and I think Kurt was almost heartbroken to see and hear it, because that's what he so much wanted to do. He didn't want to hold back the strength of his music because of having to work with singing actors, myself included. He said, "Now I really have to write an opera." Later I remember being at George Gershwin's house, and Kurt wanted me to sing something for him. So I sang "Pirate Jenny," which of course was very much removed from what George did. He listened and said, "You know, Kurt, she has this—she sings like a hillbilly." At that time I didn't know what a hillbilly was, but Kurt said "Oh, really?" So we dropped it. We didn't get any further than the hillbilly stage.[17]

Rehearsal for The Eternal Road *captured by German cartoonist B.F. Dolbin. Foreground, left to right: Franz Werfel, Meyer Weisgal, and Kurt Weill. Background, center: Lotte Lenya.*

The meeting between Kurt and Paul Green was arranged by Cheryl Crawford, who was at that time one of the directors of the Group Theatre. She and Kurt had many discussions about the possibility for a show, and Kurt had something in mind like an American version of the *Good Soldier Schweyk*. Cheryl thought that the ideal collaborator might be Paul Green, who had done *In Abraham's Bosom* for the Group. Cheryl and Kurt went down to Chapel Hill to Green's home, and down there began discussing what became *Johnny Johnson*. This started in the spring of 1936 and that summer Kurt, Cheryl, Dorothy Patten, and I took a house in Trumbull near the summer camp of the Group Theatre. Paul Green came up many times during the summer, stayed with us, while the work progressed under the close supervision of Cheryl. This was my first real encounter with a Southern accent, and I found it very hard to understand. Green was tall, stalwart, with chestnut curls, with blue, evasive eyes, soft Southern voice, strong farmer's hands, something of a gentleman farmer, as opposed to Clifford Odets (so unmistakably my idea of the type of intellectual who might have been a steady at the Romanisches Café in Berlin). Green was sometimes a little slow for Kurt's terrific speed, and Green sometimes had difficulty with lyrics, which his wife Elizabeth helped him with. Kurt called him *hinterfortzig* [Bavarian-Austrian for clumsy and inept], shifty, not outspoken, said he was like a Tyrolean, but on the whole worked well with him. The scene of the Catholic and Protestant chaplains saying their prayers over the battlefield was Kurt's idea. The subject of the play was close to Kurt's heart, and he produced one of his best scores. Green was an excellent tennis player. When summer was over, we shared an apartment with Cheryl in the East Fifties overlooking the East River. Green would come up from Chapel Hill and stay at the Hotel Bristol. Kurt had to push, drive, to make Green see things, the way he did with most of his collaborators. Here Cheryl was a great help, with her sensitivity and understanding of writers. She was one of the first Americans to appreciate Kurt's music.[45]

"Hillbilly" Lenya smoking a pipe in the hills above Santa Monica, 1939.

Before we remarried here in the U.S., I asked him, "Kurt, did you ever doubt that we would get together again?" He said, "No, never." And he said it so quietly, "No, I never doubted it." So it wasn't always an easy marriage, but it was fundamentally so right, you know?[72]

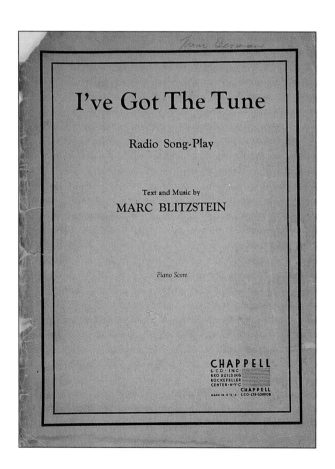

Certificate of remarriage to Kurt Weill, 19 January 1937, North Castle, New York.

The piano-vocal score for Marc Blitzstein's radio song-play I've Got the Tune. *Lenya sang the role of The Suicide. Reprinted courtesy Warner-Chappell Music. Lyrics reprinted with the permission of the Estate of Marc Blitzstein.*

A week after reciting the marriage vows again, Weill made his first trip to Hollywood to follow up on film prospects; he stayed for six months. Lenya remained in New York where she appeared in The Eternal Road *until it closed in May. Lenya thought she should have her teeth fixed so that she would be more marketable in Hollywood, but Weill cautioned her to wait until something definite comes along, "Regardless of the movies, I don't even know whether it would be right for your face, because your teeth lend character to your face just as they are and certainly enhance your personality on stage." At the end of May Lenya made an impromptu trip to Texas with her current love interest, Bill Jones.*

With money Weill had earned in Hollywood, he and Lenya moved out of the rooms provided them by producer Cheryl Crawford and into their own duplex apartment on East 62nd Street. Apparently Marc Blitzstein found Lenya's "magnetism and raw lovely voice" enticing enough to cast her in his song-play for radio, I've Got the Tune, *which aired on CBS in October 1937. Lenya played the role of The Suicide, a young lady who sings a mocking torch song before jumping to her death from a rooftop.*

Still trying to establish a career in America, Lenya tried her hand at performing in a nightclub. She landed a booking at the newly opened Le Ruban Bleu at 4 East 56th Street, a place owned by Herbert Jacoby which Harper's Bazaar *described as "tremendously popular with the same international crowd that patronized the* boîte *with the same name in Paris." In her act she sang a varying program of songs mostly written by Weill, including "Cannon Song," "Pirate Jenny," "Surabaya Johnny," "Barbara Song," "Bilbao Song," and the "The Right Guy," which Weill had recently composed for his latest film project,* You and Me. *Apparently the audience especially appreciated a song written by Marc Blitzstein for her act, "Few Little English," which not only pokes fun at her German accent and lack of perfect English, but also parodies Weill's music. An early draft of the lyrics survives under the title "Jimmy's Moll." [first verse only]:*

> when I first came over
> on a boat from Dover
> I was just a rover
> but I knew every trick
> on the boat it was funny
> strangers called me honey
> then they gave me money
> I was rich in a week.
> Then I meet Jimmy
> and Jimmy said gimmie
> and I gave him all I had
> that was Chicago
> and you know Chicago
> Well-Jimmy is a Chicago lad
> Jimmy is not in business
> not exactly business
> kind of irregular business
> but he makes lots of cash
> and I always like that
> then he is suddenly flat
> and we have to eat hash
> I meet the landlord
> and that's where my tricks come in
> Plizz, I no good speak English
> I speak only few little English
> Since I am in this land
> I no understand.[11]

[Letter to Weill, 19 April 1938]

I got a nice write-up in the *Times* (Sunday): engaging <u>young</u> Lady (I don't put much value on the "Lady" part). Jacoby was in seventh heaven. Yesterday it was so crowded again that you couldn't breathe. I'm really good now (after Charlie Alan read me the riot act on Sunday about everything I was doing wrong, and he was right, too). I sing "The Right Guy" very softly now, and it's a big success every time.

The club again was packed to the last seat. Meyer Weisgal was there. Enjoyed himself and was as proud as if he had given birth to me. It now seems very strange how it's beginning to crystallize and people are simply going along with whatever I do. They love the German songs. The "Kanonen Song" is always a big success, during the "Pirate Ballad" they're as quiet as little mice. Actually, all of it goes well. They're really showing off with me now.

You won't believe what kind of people are coming and requesting songs. Yesterday someone wanted to hear the opening song from *Anna-Anna* [*The Seven Deadly Sins*]. I'm enjoying myself now, and I'm glad I accepted this gig. I'm learning a great deal from it. I know how to grab an audience now.

Last night Marlene Dietrich suddenly showed up! She looked marvelous and was unbelievably nice to me. When Jacoby announced me, she said quite loudly, "How wonderful," and applauded like crazy (which, of course, made an impression on everyone, including Jacoby). I sang "The Right Guy," "Surabaya Johnny" (I sang that one for her), and "Pirate Ballad." She brought me over to her table. Well, you should have seen all the others turn green with envy. But I thought the way she acted toward me was awfully nice. And tonight Cole Porter was there. He sat with Horst, the photographer from *Vogue*. I was the only one they invited to their table, which again was good. Cole Porter liked me a lot. He said I had wonderful diction. It really is all the same to me, but showing off to people is important.[77]

I am feeling fine since I finished the night club job. I had a hell of a time every night to cheer up the drunkards (me included).[37]

After her nightclub act closed in May 1938, Lenya did not perform for three years. None of the efforts she had made could overcome the fact that, in America, she was seen as a curiosity whose talents were not appreciated by mainstream audiences. She knew that her accent (and a German one at that) would limit her to playing small character parts at best, and Hollywood showed no interest in using her.

BEGINNING THURSDAY APRIL 7th

LOTTE LENYA

WILL APPEAR NIGHTLY IN A REPERTOIRE

of **KURT WEILL SONGS**

at **LE RUBAN BLEU**

4 EAST 56th STREET   ELdorado 5-9787

Lenya tried to establish a career in America with a nightclub act at Le Ruban Bleu in New York City, opening 7 April 1938.

When Weill and Lenya became friendly with the playwright Maxwell Anderson, his wife Mab, and Burgess Meredith, all of whom lived just north of Manhattan in Rockland County, they moved to a rented cottage in the same area. Anderson agreed to write Knickerbocker Holiday *with Weill, which opened in October 1938. Weill continued developing film and stage projects including* Railroads on Parade *for the 1939 New York World's Fair,* Ulysses Africanus *and* Ballad of Magna Carta *with Anderson, incidental music for plays by Sidney Howard and Elmer Rice, and making his first Broadway hit with* Lady in the Dark *(book by Moss Hart and lyrics by Ira Gershwin). With Weill's name so often in the lights, Lenya surely felt like she was the real lady in the dark. With money from the sale of film rights for the show the Weills purchased Brook House, the home on South Mountain Road in New City which Lenya would keep for the rest of her life. Here she tried to find happiness keeping house and acceptance in a gossipy social circle of women married to creative men.*

At that time, hardly anyone here had heard of Pirate Jenny and *The Threepenny Opera*. There wasn't really anything for me to do—except help my husband the best way I could. I stayed home and kept house for him so he could work. And oh, how he worked.[26]

The first serious play we saw in New York was Maxwell Anderson's *Winterset*, which made an enormous impression on Kurt. Helen Deutsch, the press agent, introduced us to Anderson at a cocktail party she gave for him and Mab. Kurt had looked forward eagerly to meeting Max, having seen not only *Winterset* but also *What Price Glory?* in Berlin, and felt that in person he fitted the man we had imagined—big, eyes that were piercingly direct, quiet, standing away from the crowd but the weightiest person there. The next time we met Max, Helen Deutsch drove us out to dinner at Max's house. Helen Deutsch at that time lived across the road from the entrance to Max's property, in a redone red barn. As we drove up, Mab was working the garden, in a little sunsuit, with a broad-brimmed straw hat, garden gloves, looking very pretty, with her deep violet eyes, apologizing for being found in these clothes. At the dinner were Helen Deutsch and the Andersons. There was a lot of talk about the theater, and after dinner Kurt played and I sang "Pirate Jenny" in German. Their daughter Hesper was then a very little girl, about four, with the look of a fairy princess, fragile, with long blonde hair. Max was writing *High Tor* at the time, and that night Mab read us a scene from *High Tor*, the scene with a sand shovel. Kurt felt it was such a pity we had not met Max earlier, because *High Tor* seemed to him an ideal subject for a musical play—and he always kept the

Opposite: Publicity photo taken for Le Ruban Bleu, 1938.

Lenya and Weill at Brook House, 1941. They bought the house in May 1941 using the profits from Lady in the Dark, *which enjoyed a long run and drew a then-record price for film rights from Paramount.*

idea that some day he would turn it into a musical. The friendship must have progressed rapidly, because this was not long before *Knickerbocker Holiday.*[45]

We rented a little house during the summer while Kurt was working with Maxwell Anderson on *Knickerbocker Holiday.* I used to walk up and down South Mountain Road and saw a house called "Brook House." I was fascinated by it and knocked on the door. It turned out to be owned by the actor Rollo Peters (he played Romeo to Eva Le Gallienne). After we talked about his career a bit, I asked him, "Have you ever thought about selling this house?" He said, "I would sell any of my other properties, but not this house. My heart is here." So I said, "Well, if you ever decide to sell it, will you call me first?" He said, "Yes, I can promise you." In 1941, when Kurt had his big success with *Lady in the Dark,* Rollo called up. "Are you still interested in the house." "Am I interested? Yes! Yes! Yes!" So we went out one afternoon and made the contract then and there. We paid $16,000 for it, a real steal. A beautiful house and 18 acres.[17]

I played for the first time here in a play that Maxwell Anderson wrote for Helen Hayes, *Candle in the Wind*. I played a little Austrian servant girl. Big deal. You could have woken me up at three o'clock in the morning when I was three years old and I could have played that part. I didn't have to rehearse. There was a very funny incident during the rehearsal for the show, which was directed by Alfred Lunt. Lynn Fontanne always sat in the audience to listen. There was a scene where I had to put a chair under the doorknob so the Nazis couldn't come in. Big protection that was, you know? One day I came to the rehearsal and Lunt said, "Darling, it's terrible but I have to tell you. We have to change from the left side with the doorknob and that chair, to the right side." I said, "That's okay." He said, "Well, let's rehearse it." I said, "Alfred, you don't have to rehearse it. All I have to do is cross the stage and put the chair on the other door. I can do it without rehearsal." Whereupon Alfred turned around to Lynn in the audience and said, "Lynn, isn't she a genius?" I was so embarrassed. I thought I'd die, you know?[17]

Lenya played an Austrian maid (Cissie), with Evelyn Varden (Maisie Tompkins), in Maxwell Anderson's Candle in the Wind. *The show opened 22 October 1941 at the Shubert Theater and played for 94 performances. Photo: Vandamm Collection, Billy Rose Theatre Collection, The New York Public Library for the Performing Arts, Astor, Lenox and Tilden Foundations*

The Japanese bombed Pearl Harbor on 7 December 1941, but that did not stop the cast of Candle in the Wind *from completing a five-month tour, from January-May 1942. Lenya's part was hardly satisfying, but the tour allowed her*

Cast of Candle in the Wind *on opening night. Seated far left: Helen Hayes; standing, left: Alfred Lunt; standing, right: Maxwell Anderson; seated fifth from left: Lenya. Photo: Vandamm Collection, Billy Rose Theatre Collection, The New York Public Library for the Performing Arts, Astor, Lenox and Tilden Foundations*

Lenya's citizenship papers, dated 5 May 1944. Weill had already received his citizenship in August 1943, his case having been expedited to allow him a greater role in the war effort. At Lenya's hearing, the judge asked only one question: the name of America's first president. Lenya's answer, "Abraham Lincoln," satisfied the judge. Lenya's friend, actress Dolores Sutton, reported that Lenya told her years later, "I'm lucky he asked me that one. If he'd asked me anything else about the presidents, I'd have answered wrong."

Lenya and Mab Anderson working the civil defense watchtower in Rockland County, New York.

Opposite: Publicity photo of Lenya, 1942. Photo: George Hoyningen-Huene/Frederick R. Koch Collection, The Harvard Theatre Collection, The Houghton Library

to experience middle America while passing through Pennsylvania, upstate New York, Ohio, Indiana, Missouri, Wisconsin, Michigan, Illinois, Kentucky, Florida, Tennessee, Georgia, Alabama, Mississippi, Texas, Arkansas, Oklahoma, Kansas, and Iowa.

Happy to be performing again, Lenya recorded six songs by Weill for Bost Records. Both Weill and Lenya participated in a number of programs designed to support the war effort, and Weill contributed music to We Will Never Die, a pageant intended to call attention to the plight of the Jews in Europe. Later in 1943, Weill's One Touch of Venus became an instant hit on Broadway, with Mary Martin in the starring role.

Weill made special musical arrangements for Lenya's debut recording in the U.S. of "Lost in the Stars," "Lover Man," "J'attends un navire," "Complainte de la Seine," "Soerabaja [sic] Johnny," and "Wie man sich bettet."

Lenya sang "Moritat vom Mackie Messer," "Surabaya-Johnny," "Seeräuberjenny," and "Und was bekam des Soldaten Weib?" (with Kurt Weill at the piano) at a concert given by exiled German artists to aid in the U.S. war effort. The program is autographed by cast members.

Cartoon by William V. Madison (1980's) depicts Brecht's visit to Brook House in May 1943. Brecht had hoped to interest Weill in collaborating on musical versions of The Good Soldier Schweyk and The Good Person of Szechwan.

We did a few recordings for the war effort—Voice of America, you know. I sang a song for the boys of America, "How Much Longer?" It was really an attack on Hitler, of course.[17]

Another little contribution to the war was manning an air raid tower in Rockland County. Usually we played canasta. Well, I tried to figure out where the planes were coming from. By the time I straightened out south, north, west, and south-west, etc., we could have easily lost the war![13]

Brecht came to visit Weill once at our country house in New City, New York with his Danish girlfriend, Ruth Berlau. I showed them to the guest room, a long, low-ceilinged room furnished in Early American style. In the time it took me to return with towels, Brecht had completely rearranged the room: took down the white organdy curtains, pushed the beds into a corner, set up a table and typewriter in the middle of the room, and tacked a Chinese linen scroll on the wall. In no time there were plates of cigar stubs everywhere. The smell of sweat, leather, and stogies stayed until he left.[45]

Weill wrote a part for Lenya in The Firebrand of Florence, *but it took some effort to persuade the producer and the other authors (Ira Gershwin and Edwin Justus Mayer) to use her as the Duchess playing opposite Melville Cooper. For her publicity shots Lenya tried an unconvincing make-over as a Hollywood starlet, but the artifice showed; she didn't come across the footlights as either sexy or funny, and many critics found her to be miscast in the role. Lenya's featured song, "Sing Me Not A Ballad," later became one of her most popular concert numbers. Reviews for the entire effort ran from decidedly mixed to negative, and the show closed a failure. Lenya never performed again in public during Weill's lifetime.*

The Firebrand of Florence: lovely music. You see, the part of the Duke was written for Walter Slezak, and with me as the Duchess, it would have been a marvelous combination. Then Walter couldn't do it for some reason. I think he had a cold—or a Hollywood commitment, or whatever. So Slezak was out and Melville Cooper was in. That left me absolutely out on a limb, because my style and Cooper's never jelled, you know? But this was not the only reason. The production by John Murray Anderson, which was light in the rehearsals, became bogged down by heavy, cement costumes—heavy and slow. Being set in Florence, it should have been light and floating. But it just moved like glue, you know? If that ever moves.[70]

Kurt always said, "*Firebrand* was my first smash flop." And it was. And from there on I said "Kurt, no. Listen to me. This is the last time you try to write for me in this country. Just forget about me. I'll do whatever you need for your comfort." And that's what I did for five years. I cleaned his room, very carefully around his scores so nothing should happen, you know? And I didn't miss performing, because I had it before, and had it in such a marvelous way, you know, which I never expected when I was in the little circus. So, I didn't regret it at all.

The Firebrand of Florence. *The operetta opened at the Alvin Theatre 22 March 1945 and was not a success, running only 43 performances. Top: Lenya (as Duchess) and Melville Cooper (as Duke); Middle: Lenya with Earl Wrightson (as Cellini); Left: Entrance of Duchess in Act I. Photos: Lucas-Pritchard/The John Bennewitz Collection, Museum of the City of New York*

Left to right: Alan Jay Lerner, Rita Weill (Kurt's sister-in-law), Lenya, and unidentified child on the grounds of Brook House, late 1940's.

In May, Weill and Lenya celebrated the end of the war in Europe. While Lenya played cards with her friends on South Mountain Road and continued relationships with various male admirers, Weill wrote and orchestrated a new show almost every season: Street Scene *with Elmer Rice and Langston Hughes* (1946); Love Life *with Alan Jay Lerner* (1948); Down in the Valley, *a school opera with Arnold Sundgaard* (1948); and Lost in the Stars *with Maxwell Anderson* (1949).

Lerner was well-bred and charming, and very much in love with his actress wife Marion Bell, who was gay and filled with wild fantasies. Alan looked like a college kid, alert, clever, with a head too big for his body. He had a well-built, small body, sensual mouth, and his hair grew so quickly that he always looked like a 19th-century poet. At that time Lerner visited a gay Hungarian psychoanalyst who liked to dance the czardas with me. Kurt liked Alan because he was very flexible, excited by ideas, and a wonderful listener. They usually worked over at Henry Varnum Poor's house.

Opposite: Publicity photo of Lenya, 1945.
Photo: Marcus Blechman

When we went to Indiana for the premiere of *Down in the Valley*, Alan and Marion were so relaxed you would never have guessed it was an opening. I, of course, was shaking for days.[45]

The successes Weill had in America were never as exciting as those in Berlin. They couldn't have been, because in Berlin it was the beginning. Here he was already established, and he could almost predict whether a show would be a success or not. The Broadway atmosphere was a quieter one, but happier. Brecht was also out of the picture.[72]

Early in the summer of 1948, my sister Mariedl wrote that mother had suddenly announced that she wanted to see Linnerl's house in America—not me, my house. They were ready to leave as soon as we arranged air passage from Vienna to New York. Kurt and I met them at LaGuardia. Mariedl and I ran into each other's arms, dissolved in tears, but mother greeted us with smiling composure. She was eighty and looked no more than sixty; her deep-set eyes dauntlessly clear, her hair still thick and iron-gray, her walk quick and purposeful. Mariedl was heavier, and her long gentle Austrian face marked by the hardships of recent years, but now she was aglow with happy excitement. I told them that we were driving right back to the country, so that they could lie down and rest. Mother laughed and said maybe Mariedl needed it, but she herself wasn't a bit tired. Her only request was that along the way we must stop at a church so they could offer thanks to God for their safe arrival.

St. Patrick's was the only Catholic church we could think of on short notice, so we went into Manhattan. Kurt waited in the car while I raced Mother and Mariedl into the cathedral. Then we drove west on 57th Street, mother staring intently out the window. Before we turned north on the West Side Highway, she had her first and most significant comment to make on America: "All American men walk with their hands in their pockets." A moment later she exclaimed, "Look, Mariedl, the Danube!" I told her that they had left the Danube on the other side of the ocean, that this was an American river, the Hudson. Mother kept staring out the window, then repeated with calm obstinacy, "The Danube, Mariedl, it's the Danube." Maria leaned over and whispered, "See how mean she can be?" It may have been meanness; it may have been hard Austrian logic—such a big and beautiful river, wherever it was, could only be the Danube.

When we got home, Mother inspected the house from top to bottom. She hopped up the stairs like a busy bird, flitted from room to room, never pausing with Mariedl to admire and exclaim. "How do you like it, mother?" I asked. "Fine for you, Linnerl, not for me," she said. And I think she was ready right then, mission accomplished, to fly back to Vienna.

That night, I asked mother if she remembered an old Tyrolean poem called "Frau Hütt," which had been one of my childhood favorites. She knew the whole poem, and rising from her chair, she gave us the whole blood-curdling story, about the starving beggar woman's curse turning proud Frau Hütt to stone, every gesture and inflection perfect. Later, we were reliving some of the endless grim dramas that had occurred in those two rooms where mother still lived, and remembering how the neighborhood respected my drunken, brutal father because he was a coachman. Mother was on her feet again with the story of the time she had suffered a miscarriage, the sad little remains had been placed in a shoebox, but the church would not grant burial. As she described the scene, her tiny figure stiffened, her eyes blazed, and she seemed to be confronting the priest then and there, "You cannot refuse the fruit of Herr Blamauer!" The shoebox was buried in consecrated ground—and hearing mother's voice ring out, observing the majesty of her stance, we guessed that the name of Blamauer had not turned the trick alone. Kurt was doubled up with laughter, as mother sat down again. At last, he said afterward, he understood the peculiar quality of my talent.

Early in the visit, as she put on her silver-rimmed glasses to knit, I noticed that the right lens was missing, but she refused to have it replaced. "Leave it as it is, I've seen enough of the world." We took her to see the sights, but she showed little interest. Radio City left her visibly bored. She let me buy her only one dress; she chose it herself, with a quick and unerring taste, a royal-blue knitted dress, expensive, simple. Anything Kurt and I told her about our life in America, Kurt's career, the people we knew, she listened to with interest, but with no questions of her own. It came to me that she was the most wonderfully adjusted woman I have ever known; modest in her wants, envying no one, arrived at the end of a long tough life with never a twinge of self-pity. She was delighted to have all her children gone and to be alone with her second husband.

Before they left, Mab Anderson gave a little farewell party for mother and Mariedl with our friends from South Mountain Road. Mariedl chatted away, hiding her emotion; but mother sat silently most of the evening, smiling down at three red roses Mab had cut for her in the garden, holding them stiffly but with a strong noble grace. And when it was time to leave for LaGuardia Airport, she hurried to the car without so much as a last glance around her. "Why do you cry now?" she asked Mariedl roughly.

Lenya's mother and sister visit in New York, 1948. Front, from left: Johanna Heinisch (Lenya's mother), Lenya, Maria Hubek (Lenya's sister). Back, from left: Mab Anderson, Rita Weill.

Lenya with her mother in the Brook House kitchen, New City, New York, 1948.

"We've had six wonderful weeks." At the airport, she shook hands with Kurt, spoke with grave formality, "Thank you, Herr Weill." I asked her if she would be glad to be home again, and she said, "*Aber ja!*" For a fleeting second our eyes met in the good-bye of a mother and daughter who would never see each other again. We embraced, and they were gone.

Mariedl's first letter said that I wouldn't have known mother that first week back in Vienna, bragging for hours about the plane ride, the New York skyscrapers, her Linnerl's house, her son-in-law's importance in America. All well within her husband's hearing, of course. And not a word about the Hudson.

Almost three years later my mother died peacefully in Rochus Hospital after a heart attack. Mariedl doesn't even know the people who have the old flat now. If I am ever in Vienna again, I will ask their permission to stand for a moment in the kitchen where I slept as a child, and another moment in my mother's bedroom, looking out at the gilded cupola of Steinhof. That is all I will need.[45]

Weill suffered a heart attack at Brook House on 17 March 1950. He began working on songs for his next project, Huck Finn, *while recuperating in the hospital.*

Kurt is improving steadily and my only worry now is that the better he feels, the more restless he will get to do things too soon. He has to remain at the hospital another four weeks, which I think is just nothing considering the seriousness of his illness.[76]

Lenya knew Weill only too well, and her fears were well-founded; Weill died four days later, on 3 April 1950, at the age of 50. Friends rallied around Lenya while Weill lay in state in the front room of Brook House. Two days later the simple graveside service consisted only of Maxwell Anderson's brief eulogy, which included the lyric from Lost in the Stars *that Lenya had chosen for Weill's gravestone:*

A bird of passage out of night
Flies in at a lighted door,
Flies through and on in its darkened flight
And then is seen no more.
This is the life of men on earth:
Out of darkness we come at birth
Into a lamp-lit room, and then
Go forward into dark again.[5]

Kurt Weill dies suddenly on 3 April 1950 of a heart attack. New York Times obituary, 4 April 1950.

KURT WEILL DEAD; COMPOSER, WAS 50

Wrote Music for 'One Touch of Venus,' 'Lady in the Dark' and Other Broadway Hits

ALSO TURNED OUT OPERAS

'Der Protagonist' and 'Tsar Has Himself Photographed' His Best-Known Works

Kurt Weill, the composer, died at 7 oclock last night in the Flower-Fifth Avenue Hospital, after an illness of two weeks. He was 50 years old.

Mr. Weill, whose melodies like "September Song" and "Speak Low" won the plaudits of Broadway, and whose more serious musical achievements were hailed in

KURT WEILL 1947

In 1926, collaborating with Georg Kaiser, he wrote the opera "Der Protagonist," which was produced by the Dresden State Opera. After composing two other operas, "Royal Palace," with Ivan Goll, and "The Tsar Has Himself Photographed," again with Herr

---

KURT WEILL IS BURIED

Maxwell Anderson Speaks at Rites for Noted Composer

Special to THE NEW YORK TIMES.

NEW CITY, N. Y., April 5—Kurt Weill, composer, was buried this afternoon in Mount Repose Cemetery at near-by Haverstraw after a brief ceremony by his friends at his home here on South Mountain Road.

There was no religious service. Maxwell Anderson spoke. He is a next-door neighbor and had been a collaborator with Mr. Weill in several Broadway shows. Mr. Anderson told of Mr. Weill's career and their close association.

Leo Sohn, a brother-in-law, also spoke. Mr. Weill's parents and brother are in Palestine and Mrs. Sohn, the former Ruth Weill, was the only close relative here.

Among those at the burial were Mrs. Maxwell Anderson, Mr. and Mrs. Rouben Mamoulian, Mr. and Mrs. Max Dreyfus, Robert Sherwood, Mr. and Mrs. Elmer Rice, Mrs. Walter Huston, Mark Blitzstein, Charles MacArthur, Arthur Schwartz, Mr. and Mrs. Milton Caniff and Marc Connelly.

New York Times funeral notice for Weill, 6 April 1950.

Kurt Weill — Musiker des epischen Theaters

Von Theodor W. Adorno

Die Figur des Komponisten, der in Amerika starb, wird vom Begriff des Komponisten kaum recht getroffen. Seine Begabung wie seine Wirkung beruhte weit weniger auf der musikalischen Leistung als solcher, auf Gebilden, die nach Substanz und Faktur für sich allein

Zusammenarbeit von Dichter und Musiker ist bis heute unerreicht geblieben. An den Stücken und Songs hat Weill aktiv mitgeholfen; und manche der berühmt gewordenen Melodien gehen auf Brecht zurück. Die schlagendsten Ergebnisse waren „Mahagonny" — besonders

Kurt was a very difficult man to know. When he was lying there in his coffin for two days in our house in New City, I stood in front of him and said, "You know, Kurt, it's only in the last week that I understand you." I had this feeling of never really having known him. Although I *did* know him, I did not.[72]

This is just to thank you [music critic Olin Downes] for your wonderful article in last Sunday's *Times* [10 April 1950]. Kurt would have loved nothing better than to be called "people's composer," because that is what he was and wanted to be.[24]

It has been five weeks now since Kurt passed away, and I have not been able to take even one step forward. The only thing that keeps me in this world is his music and the only desire I still retain—everything I have learned through him in these twenty-five years—is to fight for this music, to keep it alive, to do everything within my power for it. There are only a few who know about his importance, especially here, where only a part of his work is known. And I believe that it will have to be the task of my life to make this music known. Everything is still very hazy and I don't know where to begin. But the only thought that emerges over and over out of my confused inner self is about his music: don't trust anyone with it; nobody should dig around in his works. This is the only thing that still keeps me alive. And again and again I have to think of the last line in *Der Silbersee*:

He who wants to forge ahead
Will be carried by the Silver Lake.[33]

I had given up hope that I would ever be able to give the right answer to those innumerable letters I get from his friends asking me, "Why did you let him work so hard, why didn't you stop him from writing one show after the other." And the only answer there is, you [Olin Downes] gave when you said, "he was born to do exactly what he did, and to work steadily and successfully toward a modern art of the musical theater." And nobody ever before has stated this so clearly and with so much understanding and knowledge of his work and what he was aiming at. You know as well as I do that it was his life to write music and his very existence to search continuously for new forms in the musical theater. I will never forget the horror he created at the music festival in Baden-Baden in 1927, when he suddenly stopped writing atonal music and wrote the first short version of *Mahagonny*. I still can see his colleagues rushing up to him after the performance and almost shouting, "Weill, do you know what you're doing? You are writing in G major!" And Kurt smiled and said very calmly, "I know what's wrong with it. It's not a new invention."

It wasn't easy for Kurt to start all over again, but I never saw him falter or look backwards for one moment. He was only interested to achieve in this country what he had started in Europe. Just before he was taken ill, he said to me, "There are two more things I want to do most. That's *Huck Finn* and *Moby Dick* as an opera. And then I promise you, I will take a little rest."[24]

I will be in San Francisco for the opening of *Lost in the Stars* on August 7th. We are going by train. I thought first I could take the car and drive, but I am too tired to undertake such a long

Mab Anderson, Lenya, and Maxwell Anderson at Lewisohn Stadium, New York, for a Kurt Weill memorial concert, 10 July 1950, at which Anderson read a short eulogy. Photo: Institut für Theater- Film- und Fernsehwissenschaft, Universität zu Köln

trip. I don't know what happens from one day to the other. And after the concert, which after a two-day postponement finally went on and was a big success, I really completely collapsed. I just have to wait and see what every day brings. It's sometimes so hard for me and everything looks hopeless and senseless to keep on living, and it's not even that I don't want to try. I had such a wonderful life with Kurt, that I don't see any reason of going on and try to do—What?[1]

I had a strange dream the other day about Kurt. He was lying in sort of a bed and his head had slipped down from his pillows. And I kept piling up his pillows to make him feel comfortable and whenever I turned, there he had slipped away again. I woke up in tears and unhappy for days, and happy still that I had at least seen him alive.[21]

Legends: On Weill

Portrait of Kurt Weill by Karsh, 1946.

She is a miserable housewife, but a very good actress.

She can't read music, but when she sings, people listen as if it were Caruso. (For that matter, I pity any composer whose wife can read music.)

She doesn't meddle in my work (that is one of her foremost attributes). But she would be very upset if I took no interest in hers.

She always has a couple of male friends, which she explains by saying that she doesn't get along with women. (But perhaps she doesn't get along with women precisely because she always has a couple of male friends.)

She married me because she enjoyed horror, and she claims that this desire has now been fulfilled sufficiently.

My wife's name is Lotte Lenya.[74]   —KURT WEILL, 1929

Weill was a tiny man, five feet four, incredibly shy, with a curious childlike smile, and cool, ironic eyes.

His brother Hans looked like his mother's side of the family, but Kurt, Ruth, and Nathan looked more like the father: high cheekbones, brown eyes, wavy dark brown hair, small boned, slender wrists and ankles, a delicacy of features that made them seem rather fragile, even though they were very healthy. High blood pressure was inherited from the father's family.

116

A complex relationship is captured in this famous photo of Lenya and Weill, Berlin, 1929.
Photo: Ullstein

Kurt Weill with sheepdog Wooly, a gift from Moss Hart,
at Brook House, mid-1940's.

Kurt's ears were remarkable, small, close to the head, beautifully shaped, round like shells, no lobes, and sensitive to the touch—he especially hated when barbers touched them.

Very delicate slender hands, fingers wider at the base and narrowing at the tips, strong defined lines in his palms. Five feet, three-and-one-half inches tall, size nine shoes, wide shoulders and deep chest (probably developed in part by swimming), narrow hips, strong good chin, a large, pleasantly sensual mouth, like Charles Boyer. Small, straight nose, strongly defined eyebrows, perfect teeth, face dominated by forehead, which rose high and straight from the brows.

Spoke with a soft voice, with a slight mockery that often made people think he was arrogant and sarcastic. Always knew what he wanted to say and how to say it.

When he was angry his voice became almost inaudible, cold and direct, knife-like. Open to criticism on a completely professional level.

He could be funny and humorous, ironic and satirical, but not bitchy.

He slept with open hands, thumbs slightly drawn into the palms, hands level with his shoulders—from childhood until death.

Always meticulous and neat, like the whole family, great

personal sense of possession of his clothes, wanted nothing of his own touched by others, could never bear anything wrinkled, stained, or spotted.

Loved monotone ties, socks, sweaters. Came to love American country clothes, leather jackets.

Loved walking, swimming.

Never liked violence in any form, but he liked watching Joe Louis because of the stalking way he moved.

While walking, he used to suddenly lift up his pants with his forearms. When absorbed in thought, he would walk back and forth with his right index finger on the side of his nose.[45]

Some people thought Kurt was arrogant. But he wasn't arrogant at all; he was just terribly shy, and that shyness kept people away from him, like a wall he built around himself. Nobody really knew Kurt Weill. I wonder sometimes whether I knew him. I was married to him twenty-four years and we lived together two years without being married, so it was twenty-six years together. When he died, I looked at him, and I wasn't sure I really knew him.[3]

All the Weill children brought friends home after school and weekends. Their home was always a center of activity because it was in the same building as the Jewish community center. All the Weill children acted in the plays that were produced at the center, and Kurt chose music when it was needed and played the piano.

The four Weill children, ca. 1910. From left: Ruth, Nathan, Kurt, Hans. Photo: P. Clasen

A page from the catalog of the Nazi exhibition, "Entartete Musik" ("Degenerate Music"), held in Düsseldorf, 1938. Contemporary reports indicate that the display devoted to music from Die Dreigroschenoper *had to be shut down by the Nazis because it was too popular. The musical quotation, from "Die Ballade vom angenehmen Leben," is meant to portray Weill as a sympathizer with the idle rich.*

that little body and those fragile hands, all with a passion that was fascinating. For me, this was always a great, great thrill.

Weill never reacted strongly to attacks against his music in the Nazi newspapers. He just read them and said nothing, holding it all in. I was much more emotional about it. But I wasn't Jewish, either. There must be some kind of immunity developed, a protection, after those thousand years of persecution. He never showed emotion about the big things, very self-controlled. When he had his doubts, they were buried. He only got visibly mad about little things, like when his pencils hadn't been properly sharpened.[72]

There is only one Weill. There is no American Weill, there is no German Weill. There's only Weill. It's the most stupid thing when the Germans say, "Of course, our Weill was much better. He sold out to Broadway." You have heard that many times. They don't know that our whole theater takes place on Broadway. That's the only place we have. There's music, drama, name it. It takes place on Broadway. So he sold out to Broadway. What does that mean?[59]

For me, *The Eternal Road* is still very close to this whole European background. I can't separate the Kurt Weill from 1924 from the Kurt Weill from 1950, the day he died, because there's a very clear development in his music. A lot of people think Weill became softer in this country, but I don't think so. The curve is very clear to me.[52]

The subjects Weill had on Broadway were different subjects from the *Threepenny Opera*. The problems were different problems here. So, that's why the stupid ones think he changed. He didn't change. He found very good literature. Maxwell Anderson was a good one. Ogden Nash. All those very highly successful musicals. And *Lost in the Stars*? My god, it's almost as aggressive as *Threepenny Opera*, dealing with the blacks in Johannesburg. I'll tell you about one incident, with *Knickerbocker Holiday*. Now, *Knickerbocker Holiday* was a great departure from the usual American musicals, as far as the libretto was concerned. Larry Hart was sitting in front of us at the opening. At one point he turned around to Kurt and said, "Kurt, I think we'll have to change our librettists from now on." So, he knew that something new was happening. I think Kurt Weill was extremely lucky in this country. It has something to do with his talent, of course it has. But that he made it. If you think of it, he had only fifteen years, from 1935 until 1950. Look what he did with a completely new medium. And what influence he had in those fifteen years.[70]

Maxwell Anderson, Lenya, and Weill in Brook House, 1949, during the creation of Weill's last musical, Lost in the Stars *(based on Alan Paton's novel* Cry, the Beloved Country*). Anderson was Weill's closest friend in the U.S., and according to Lenya, the closest to him of all his collaborators. "As a purely working relationship, I would put Max with Brecht, as far as Kurt was concerned; and of course Kurt loved Max as a person."*

"Pirate Jenny" is a song of revenge. It's the song of the eternal underdog. There she dreams of the day when she can repay all those rats who have treated her so badly. "Trouble Man" is a torch song by a woman in love who, no matter what—it's much closer to "Surabaya Johnny," see?[8]

The problem is this: German critics will accept anything from America, as long as it has an American composer. (I know Fritz Loewe is Viennese, but he was never a German composer of Kurt's stature.) From Kurt they expect something else, no matter how good his American musicals were, they still would not accept it. You can read in every German newspaper that he got cheap, Broadwayish, and all that crap. They even said it about *Lost in the Stars*.[67]

Kurt couldn't stand Adorno. You see, I would almost call Kurt a peasant—he was a very simple man, not complicated at all. He didn't want to get involved with all those highfalutin' things. He understood them, but he didn't *want* to understand them. He wanted to live a simpler life, he didn't want this kind of life.

Kurt Weill at work, 1943. "He was the most meticulous man you ever met in his method of working, and very conscientious about working every day. He always lived for his music." Photo: Vandamm Collection, Billy Rose Theatre Collection, The New York Public Library for the Performing Arts, Astor, Lenox and Tilden Foundations

Opposite: Lenya's favorite photo of Weill and her together.

Erika Neher, wife of Caspar, with Weill, early 1930's.

Sure, Weill got depressed because of being misunderstood, but no critic could ever make him insecure. He was absolutely secure in what he wanted to do. Just sometimes he would like to read something more pleasant, than, for instance, the time his violin concerto was played in Dessau. The stupid critic wrote, "There was an expectant mother in the first row. We hope that her milk won't get sour from hearing this music."[72]

I'll tell you what it was with Kurt: he didn't have so many affairs. But he had affairs that were rather serious, because Kurt was very emotional and honest in his love. He was very much in love with the wife of Caspar Neher, Erika. That was a lovely affair. She loved him, but nothing disturbed—that was a wall I didn't touch. Of course I was in Vienna with my Flying Dutchman [Pasetti] at the time. He never talked to me about it. Erika had other affairs too, like with another friend of Caspar's, Johannes Küpper. She was like a little sexy pony, blonde, sturdy, and witty. I wonder if Cas ever *knew*.

Kurt could really laugh; he could never finish a joke because he was laughing so much—tears streaming down his face, you know? Once we went to the old Met to hear an opera by Rossini, *Barbier* I think. When we came out, two real dowagers were walking behind us, talking. One said to the other, "Did you know that Rossini was lying in bed when he composed the first overture, and the window was open, and a gust of wind blew his manuscript right out the window. Rather than getting up to get it, he just wrote another one!" And the other said, "I'm glaaaad." And just the way she said it, "I'm glaaaad." So stupid. I'll never forget Kurt, leaning against the wall and laughing himself silly.

Another time at *Suor Angelica*, we were sitting in the gallery and he was so bored. He leaned over and whispered to me, "All those nuns *und kein Schwanz in der Nähe* [and not a dick in sight]! I couldn't listen to the music for the next five minutes. We had lots of fun together. Really. That was a happy time.[72]

So much nonsense has been said about Weill and myself, and if I would get upset about everything I could easily develop a nervous breakdown. It ain't worth it.[49]

The Saga of Pirate Jenny 1951-1960

Painting by Arbit Blatas of Lenya playing Jenny, inspired by the production of The Threepenny Opera *at the Theater de Lys, New York, 1954.*

When Lenya stepped to the front of the stage in the second act to sing "Pirate Jenny," the miniature confines of the theater stretched and were replaced by a broad and sweeping arena of genuine sentiment. For that's what art can do, and that's what the artist does.[38]
— JAY HARRISON, *New York Herald Tribune*

Devastated by Weill's death, Lenya for weeks refused to sleep alone in Brook House. One old friend who eased Lenya's loneliness was George Davis, a fiction editor for Vanity Fair *and* Harper's Bazaar. *Davis began his career as a writer and published his only novel,* The Opening of a Door, *while living in Paris in 1931. Upon returning to America, he exerted substantial influence on popular literary culture, "discovering" such writers as Truman Capote and Carson McCullers. During the 1940s he presided over a house-cum-artist's commune at 7 Middagh Street in Brooklyn that served as a temporary home for a circle of influential friends, including Gypsy Rose Lee, Benjamin Britten, Peter Pears, and W.H. Auden.*

After Kurt died, I really sank to the bottom of the ocean. George Davis, who had been our friend since 1936 when he had us photographed for *Harper's Bazaar*, called me and asked, "Lenya, can I help you in any way?" And so, we started

Lenya's second husband, George Davis, remade her into a tireless promoter of Weill's music. New York, 1952.

to get together sometimes. I think he married me out of friendship, just so I wouldn't be alone. He is the one who really started my second career. I fought him bitterly, and hated him for doing it.[17]

Opposite: Publicity photo, 1951.
Photo: Louise Dahl-Wolfe/Staley-Wise Gallery, New York

We gave a concert at Town Hall of Weill's music, and I sang. And that evening, before the concert, I remember my voice just disappeared. I said, "My god, what am I going to do?" Then the curtain went up and I had to go out. And I saw that

Poster for Lenya's second Kurt Weill Concert, 23 February 1952. Lenya gave her first Town Hall concert in 1951. One of the concert's organizers, Ernst Josef Aufricht, had produced the original production of Die Dreigroschenoper *in Berlin, 1928.*

Opening night program of Maxwell Anderson's play Barefoot in Athens *at the Martin Beck Theatre, 31 October 1951. The play about the life of Socrates had a disappointing run of 30 performances. Lenya played Xantippe, Socrates's shrewish wife. In spite of positive reviews for Lenya during out-of-town tryouts, the producers replaced her with an actress who didn't have an accent. They then invited Lenya back for the Broadway opening.*

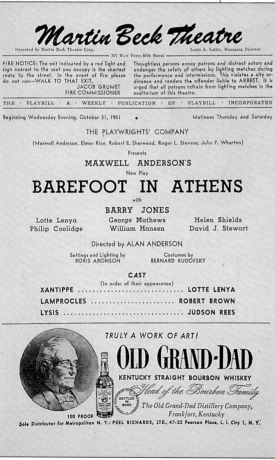

full packed house, you know? I said, "Oh, come on, Lenya, he would have been happy to see that, so do something." And the voice was there, it came back. I didn't do anything. Just the thought of how much he would have loved to see that packed house come to hear his music, and that did it. My voice was never clearer and I became a performer again that night. The concert was so successful that we had to repeat it three times.[28, 70]

I'm having a great many problems because of dear "Bidi" [Brecht]. He signs contracts on my behalf which he has no rights to whatsoever, and I have to fight like hell over here to put things in order again. He probably still clings to his old philosophy: "There is nothing for man to depend upon" (about which he really is not entirely wrong).[50]

Lenny Bernstein was very interested in doing a concert version of *Threepenny Opera*, and we did it at Brandeis in 1952—Marc Blitzstein as narrator, and Lenny conducting. It was a big success. What a marvelous sight, looking out the window during the rehearsal and seeing the students sitting around listening, some even singing the "Moritat" already. I don't think I will ever hear the music played as beautifully as when Lenny did it. It was so magical and effortless.

And the next day four or five big American producers came to me and said, "We want to do it." I said, "Well, that's wonderful. How do you want to do it?" One said, "Well, I want to set it in San Francisco." I said, "Why in San Francisco? If Brecht didn't think of San Francisco, why do you?" "Well, I just feel that way."

I said, "Well, thank you very much." The other one came and said, "Well, I'd love to do it, but first of all we have to get rid of that corny orchestration." I said "Well, thank you very much. No." He said, "Well, if you're that difficult you can wait until doomsday." I said, "Then I'll wait."

Well, I didn't have to wait until doomsday. Eventually two young producers came, Carmen Capalbo and Stanley Chase, completely unknown, and they said, "Miss Lenya, we would love to do *Threepenny Opera*. We have no background, nothing, but we just love the work, and we want to do it." I said, "Well, would you do it the way it's written?" "Yes, exactly, we won't change a thing." I said, "Take it. You get to do it." It opened in 1954 and ran three months short of seven years.

No one knew *The Threepenny Opera* would be such a big success, and we had to close after three months because another show was booked to come into the theater during the summer. Brooks Atkinson was really responsible for bringing it back. He would always end his theater reviews with, "Bring back *The Threepenny Opera*. We never had it so good." We opened again in September, after the theater was free. The rest is history.

Leonard Bernstein revived The Threepenny Opera *in a concert performance of Blitzstein's adaptation, Brandeis University, July 1952. Lenya sang the part of Jenny. Photo: Zachery Freyman*

A meeting of the Threepenny Opera *brain trust, ca. 1954. From left: Marc Blitzstein, Stanley Chase, Lenya, Carmen Capalbo.*

Theater de Lys, *a 299-seat house on Christopher Street in
Greenwich Village, was home to* The Threepenny Opera
*for seven years. Photo: Friedman-Abeles
Below: Poster for* The Threepenny Opera *at the Theater
de Lys, drawn by David Stone Martin.*

Opposite: Publicity photo of Lenya and Scott Merrill in
The Threepenny Opera. *Photo: Louise Dahl-Wolfe/
Staley-Wise Gallery, New York*

By now *Threepenny* is a big success. I am very happy about
it, most happy about Kurt's wonderful notices for his music. I am
pushed around from one TV show to the other, all for publicity,
but it is worth it. At the moment I am utterly exhausted, but
nobody seems to care and so I go on.[21]

The only major change we made in *Threepenny* was
that Polly sings the "Bilbao Song" in the stable scene instead of
the "Pirate Ballad," and Jenny sings the "Pirate Ballad" in the
brothel scene with a few introductory lines added for the songs.
That worked beautifully, and me singing the song in that spot
added considerably to the success of the production. The rest was
pretty much the same.[39]

Marc Blitzstein's adaptation of *The Threepenny Opera* is a
masterpiece, because his changes are hardly noticeable. Everyone
thinks the translation is muted, but I think it's just a matter
of language. The German language has a harder sound than
English, and you can't get away from that. Even Auden and
Kallman's translation of *The Seven Deadly Sins*, which is as close
as anyone can come to Brecht, sounds softer than the German.

Brecht is never vulgar. Never, ever. In the "Tango Ballade"
the advice he gives there to those two people is, for me, almost a

lesson in morals. He just tells you not to disturb a pregnancy, and that's all he does. If you have a dirty mind, you can say it's dirty. For me it's pure.

It would be a very poor sign if Weill's works could only survive through my presence. When I left *The Threepenny Opera*, finally, after two years, they were all heartbroken and horrified. They said, "Miss Lenya, look—we'll have to close the show." I said, "You will not. Don't be silly. This is a marvelous work, and it would be very poor sign for Brecht and Weill if its success depended on the minor role. If Jenny ever becomes a major role, then there's something goddamn wrong with the whole production."[8]

In the process of inheriting Weill's artistic legacy, Lenya also assumed by default the management of his business dealings. Weill had always dealt directly with his publishers and managed most of his own affairs, using agents and lawyers only for major contracts. Forced emigration had left Weill's musical rights scattered

Above and opposite: Lenya getting ready to play Jenny in The Threepenny Opera, *1954. Opposite photo: Gena Jackson*

Scott Merrill (Macheath) and Lenya (Jenny) in The Threepenny Opera, *Theater de Lys, 1954. Photo: Neil Fujita*

among three publishers on two continents and divided between "serious" music publishers (Universal Edition) and popular music publishers (Chappell & Co.). Assisted by various advisors over the years, Lenya would be embroiled for the rest of her life in contractual disputes and disagreements with publishers who, for the most part, wanted to exploit Weill's music without investing in printing, promotion, distribution, and protection of musical integrity. Throughout the next two decades she would also carry on an infamous "widows' war" with Brecht's wife, Helene Weigel, in an attempt to keep the well-oiled East German Brecht machine from making changes to Weill's music. Upon her death Lenya left file cabinets full of letters like the two that follow, many of them written for her by George Davis or David Drew.

Below: Assorted beggars and prostitutes in a scene from The Threepenny Opera, Theater de Lys, 1954. Lenya is at the far right. Photo: Neil Fujita

Before I could answer you [Alfred Schlee, Universal Edition] about the royalty allocations as far as the print sales are concerned, I wanted to wait for Mr. Blitzstein's answer. My agent

Right: The brothel scene, Lenya is second from left.

SAGA OF PIRATE JENNY 1951–1960   137

(who also happens to be Mr. Blitzstein's, which somewhat complicates matters) let me know that Mr. Blitzstein wants 5% for his adaptation. I understand your problem very well, 18% is quite high. Your proposal to bring this down to 15% is quite understandable. Only I don't see why I should have to make this sacrifice alone. It is entirely Brecht's problem to reach an understanding with his adaptor. I am willing to come down to 10%. Dear Mr. Schlee, as you very well know, Brecht always took advantage of Weill's good nature, and it makes me sick to think that this sort of thing is supposed to continue in the same manner. As far as the *Dreigroschenoper* is concerned, I had to agree to everything, since evidently nothing can be changed in the original contract. Nobody over here would have thought of reviving the *Dreigroschenoper* only because of Brecht. It was Weill's popularity and my indefatigable endeavors that have made it so successful. The recordings have received marvelous reviews and the fact that MGM now is doing a *Mahagonny* Suite is the result of the successful *Dreigroschenoper* production. I am now insisting on my rights out of simple justice. And the fact that I'm coming down from 13% to 10% is not due to my love for Mr. Brecht. I want to accommodate you as much as possible. The fact that Brecht never answers letters is an old and proven trick of his. But I have found that when he is faced with an ultimatum, he can answer very well. He tried the same trick in the present *Dreigroschenoper* production, when he never answered questions until I let him know that if he didn't answer by a certain date, the whole production would go to pieces. The answer was here within a few days. Perhaps he is not interested in a publication of the English version, and perhaps he figures that there will always be the Bentley adaptation (the publication of which I would never consent to) and whom he probably would compensate by writing him a nice letter. Please do let him know that Blitzstein asks for 5% (just between us: Blitzstein is much more interested that his adaptation will be published and promoted in the right way, and he might be agreeable to much less—2%—it's worth a try). As soon as you have Blitzstein's agreement, set Brecht a time limit and see how he reacts. As to sales of the piano-vocal score: none of us will be able to earn Rockefeller fortunes. But this time, it is for me a question of principle. I don't understand one thing. Why do you have to have Brecht's agreement if, for instance, someone wants to do *Dreigroschenoper* in Mexico? I know that the theatrical distribution rights have not been cleared as yet, but

One of a series of lithographs by Arbit Blatas depicting scenes from The Threepenny Opera *(based on the Theater de Lys production); this one shows the brothel scene.*

Below: Word of the success of The Threepenny Opera *in New York spread as far as East Germany, where the magazine* Theater der Zeit *ran a feature article in the September 1956 issue, one month after Brecht's death.*

what could he have against it? I have the old Felix Bloch Erben [German theatrical publisher and original publisher of *Die Dreigroschenoper*] contract here, and as soon as I have some time I'll get in touch with my lawyer and see whether the rights can't be cleared. Is it not possible for Universal Edition to clear this up? All his life Brecht has figured that people were afraid of him, and that's how he has made his best business deals. But after all, there still exists something called the law. And it must be possible to find out whether the theatrical rights went back to U.E. after the dissolution of Bloch Erben. I would be a lot happier if that was the case.

It was most kind of you [Alfred Kalmus, Universal Edition] to send me a copy of the letter to Brecht—how, I wonder, will he react to an Earl and a Viscount wishing to sponsor his beggars and whores in English theater? Quite amicably, I should say! Meanwhile, I would like to put down some of my own reactions to the production proposed by the English Stage Society.

First, the English version to be used. I assume that by the pre-war version they mean the Eric Bentley-Desmond Vesey version (the version used in the first American production was, by common consent, pathetically inadequate.) The Bentley-Vesey version has been published here and performed a few times by college and amateur groups. Mr. Bentley had hopes that Kurt would give it his blessing. Needless to say, Kurt refused. Their version seemed to Kurt stilted, flavorless, the lyrics unsingable, the score quite distorted. Last winter, several unauthorized performances of this work were given in Chicago, to a very bad press. Nevertheless, Mr. Bentley is bitter about the Blitzstein version, attacking it cautiously in print, and viciously in private.

As to the Blitzstein version, it was made principally for American performance, and its use of American slang is of course deliberate. Its great success with theater audiences and critics is now being repeated with the large record public and record reviewers. It is, above all, wonderfully *singable*, probably because Marc himself is a composer, and theatrically most effective, because Marc has had long experience in the theater. Because of this, and because all previous versions so completely lacked these qualities, I worry about a new version. Is there no possibility that Marc's version could be used in England? I realize that all the Americanisms of necessity would be cut, and I admit that I cannot judge whether they are vital to his version or merely a kind of colorful addition. Could a man like Wolf Mankowitz do such a job, or would he insist on a completely original version? If so, it would be possible to ask him to do first his own versions of "Moritat," "Seeräuberjenny," and perhaps "Wovon lebt der Mensch"? It may be that Mankowitz, like Marc Blitzstein, has his own unique qualities that would make him perfect for an English production. His name is unfamiliar to me; my husband says that he knows the name, but nothing of his work. Has he written anything that could be sent to me?

By the way, I have discussed none of this with Marc Blitzstein. He might object strongly to having his version touched in any way. I must tell you in confidence that Marc, like Mr. Bentley, wished to have his version made the one authorized English-language version, and I would not agree to this, despite the admiration I have for his work, and my feeling that no other existing version gives a hint of Brecht's poetry and power. I doubt that he has taken his disappointment well, but this present discussion about the English Stage Society's production would not have

The original off-Broadway cast recording of The Threepenny Opera *was recorded and released in 1954 by MGM Records.*

Poster for Martin Vale's play The Two Mrs. Carrolls, *staged in July 1954 at the Lakeside Summer Theatre in Lake Hopatcong, New Jersey. Lenya played Mrs. Carroll; Scott Merrill also appeared as Denis Pennington.*

been possible if I had made such a step! Meanwhile, all this might affect Universal-Edition's printing of the Blitzstein version . . . or not? What do you think?[69]

George Davis negotiated with MGM Records to make the premiere recording of Kurt Weill's Violin Concerto and the cast recording of the American Threepenny Opera, *followed by Lenya's famous and often-reissued recordings made in Germany for Philips and Columbia. She often had the music transposed or arranged to suit her aging and lower voice, a fact she tried to hide from the press. Lenya and Davis made numerous trips across the Atlantic between 1955 and 1958 to make recordings or to attend premieres of important productions of Weill's stage works.*

Above: Studying the score in preparation for the premiere recording on MGM Records of Weill's Violin Concerto. From left: violinist Anahid Ajemian, conductor Izler Solomon, Lenya, and producer Ed Cole, March 1955.

Right: George Davis and Lenya arrive in Hamburg for the first of many European recording sessions that Davis arranged with Columbia and Philips Records, 1955. Photo: Klaus Kallmorgen

Surveying Berlin's ruins during her first postwar visit, 1955.

I went back to Berlin for the first time in 1955 to make my records for Columbia. And that's when I saw this beloved city of mine completely destroyed. And I just wanted to go straight back home again. There I see that city I really loved, where I met Kurt Weill, and we were happy there and made our career there. So, I stayed because I had to make those records. After three days, when I walked through that destroyed city, nothing touched me at all. It was like walking through Pompeii. I had become so removed from it because it had no resemblance any more to what it was.[16]

A Berlin railyard, 1955.

By now we are used to the rubble, which they clear up religiously and indefatigably. What a determination to get on top again. One could admire it, if one would not be afraid that somewhere there lurks another Hitler. You can't find a single Nazi in Germany! Nobody was one. It was all a dream.[21]

I just sent you [Elisabeth Hauptmann] a wire about the German texts for a record I made in Hamburg for Columbia. I persuaded them to print Brecht's lyrics in German on the record cover. They are so beautiful, and I want them to be on the cover, along with a literary translation in English which George and I did on the boat. Tell Brecht that I did, besides "Seeräuber," "Surabaya," "Barbara," "Moritat," etc., also "Die Ballade vom ertrunkenen Mädchen," with two men's voices humming, one guitar, and me singing. It turned out beautiful (nothing for the Hit Parade, but I love it and so it was sung). I need also Brecht's agreement in principle with a production of *Die sieben Todsünden*, which Frankfurt wants to do in a big house together with a ballet by Stravinsky and a premiere of a ballet by Boris Blacher. Please ask Brecht whether there are still old agreements or contracts with Edward James and Boris Kochno that we might be bound to. The only material in my possession is the full score, from which the orchestra parts would have to be extracted. I think it is a wonderful opportunity to revive this work, and it might lead to further performances. I am waiting for Brecht's suggestions.[39]

Singing at a reception at the Atlantic Hotel in Hamburg, 1955.
Photo: Klaus Kallmorgen

Come on, Brecht invented his theories much later—this epic theater, and all that. When I did the first recording for Columbia, *Lotte Lenya Sings Berlin Theater Songs,* and I went over to Berlin—I went over to the East Zone—to talk to Brecht about the album. He said, "Lenya, I really hardly remember some of those songs." I was all alone with him. He was sitting in a very high, gothic chair, with his cap on, you know, with the leather jacket. No piano, nothing. "Well, could you sing one?" I said, "Yes. Would you like to hear 'Surabaya Johnny'?" He said, "That would be lovely. Could you do it?" I said, "Sure." So I started, and right in the middle, I don't know what happened, but I stopped. "Brecht, I want to ask you something. Now, with your epic theater. . .maybe you want me to sing this song different—less emotional—than the way I

Philips Records made Lenya's first postwar recording in Germany, 1955. The collection of Weill's German theater songs, Lotte Lenya singt Kurt Weill, *has been re-released many times. Reproduced courtesy PolyGram Records.*

sing it." Whereupon he got up from his chair, touched my cheeks—he did that—and he said, "Lenya, darling, whatever you do is epic enough for me." That is a true story. This is what he said. I should have had a witness; but there was nobody there.

And another strange thing happened there, too. I sang the "Ballade vom ertrunkenen Mädchen" from *Berliner Requiem*, which was written about Rosa Luxemburg, you know? And so I sang that. I knew Brecht so well—I knew he had something on his mind. The meeting was over, and I was walking towards the door, and he had the door knob already in his hand. He said, "Lenya, darling, can I ask you something?" I said, "Sure." "Would you—could you possibly come and sing that 'Ballade vom ertrunkenen Mädchen' for my archive? Could you do that?" I said "Brecht, I would hate to lose my American passport. But, if you promise me that you will really only use it for your archive and not publish it ever." Because it would have been unfair to be engaged by Columbia and go ahead and sing it for him first, you know? He said, "No, I promise you, I will never use it. Only for my students, to show them how that song should be sung." That was on a Thursday, and the next Saturday I went over to the Schiffbauerdamm Theater and they were backstage packing for their first engagement to go to Paris with the Berliner Ensemble. So the asbestos curtain was down, but still there was hammering going on. And he took me into a little box where he had everything prepared for that song. Of course there was so much noise—one couldn't hear—too much interference. So I saw him going behind the asbestos curtain. He shouted, "Quiet back there! I'm doing something which will last much longer than what you are doing there." And I said, "Brecht, I think you have to get used to the idea that you're behind the iron curtain." So he laughed loud. He said "HA-HA-HA!" And then he turned around, looking to see whether anyone heard that.[59]

You think Brecht liked to be poor? No! He wanted to be rich, and he is. Sure, he was a Communist, and lived like one in a beautiful house in East Berlin. He had everything you could possibly get. If that is being a Communist, I'll take it.[52]

The president of Philips is crazy about my record. Every time they play it for people, they get the same reaction. As a result the biggest broadcasting company will devote a full hour to

Lotte Lenya sings Kurt Weill, *with a newly designed cover for the British release by Philips Records featuring a painting of Mackie Messer by Emmerich Weninger. Reproduced courtesy PolyGram Records.*

Below: Saul Bolasni's painting of Lenya appeared on the U.S. release by Columbia, under the title Lotte Lenya Sings Berlin Theatre Songs by Kurt Weill. *Reproduced courtesy Sony Records.*

it. This makes me very happy because when Columbia sent me there, they didn't know what they were getting (neither did I at the time).[21]

"Surabaya Johnny" is a most difficult song to sing. Also the most simple, but you have to catch the right mood and meaning of the lyrics. I think it's one of Brecht's greatest poems, and musically it's so beautiful.[17]

In summer 1955, Lenya and Davis returned to the U.S. and took an apartment in Manhattan at 994 Second Avenue so that they could attend to business more easily. The Threepenny Opera *reopened in September at the Theater de Lys.*

I am very excited about moving to the apartment in the city. I like the idea of spending the winter in town and working there with the piano on hand. It's no good out in the country, and in town we will have many people who can play and we can plan for new records and get Kurt's music really going. Isn't it fun how everything seems to fall into place since we made that trip to Europe? I am so happy for George. He seems to have found himself now that we have an apartment in town where he can have people to communicate with (which he needs more than anybody I have ever known). Surely we will have our ups and downs, but who hasn't. But at last we know now how to cope (is that the word?) with it and not get so frantic anymore.

I am home, but I should be at the theater. I caught a nasty cold, driving home late at night dog-tired and all the rest of the usual responsibilities which go with *Threepenny Opera*. But it will be very good. We found wonderful new people and it is worth all the effort one makes. And dear George remains helpful in his unique way, watching over the record cover (he knows so well how it should look and what should be told on the back of the album). And then angel Ed Cole, the producer, comes in with his great talent and experience, and his enthusiasm for Madame Lenya has to be kept down considerably. And so between the two and a great art director at Columbia, Mr. Neil Fujita, who loves the album and takes great pride in doing a special job, at least it will look wonderful.

It was quite a strain, this whole adventure at the Theater de Lys. But *The Threepenny Opera* turned out beautifully, much better than last year. We got wonderful notices and so everybody is happy. Four performances over the weekend knocks the hell out of me. (I can't take it less seriously, otherwise it won't be good.) So today was supposed to be my day of rest and what did I do? I got up at ten, started washing my dirty clothes, ironed them as I took them off the line, looked at the wonderful fall leaves for a while, and wished I could stay in the country just a few more days.

Today we got the reviews from Berlin, where *Silbersee*, Kurt's last show before he had to leave Germany and which was the first show banned by Hitler, was given at the Berlin Festival. I had a lot to do with it last summer, when the publisher had already given it to a little experimental group, and I was racing around Berlin trying to convince them it was the wrong place. I finally got my way with them and was able to place it in the Festival. It is such a tremendous success, and the publisher wrote me a letter to apologize and sent the reviews. I am very happy about it, but tired too. What a fight that was. But the result is what counts, and so I can't feel bad about it. Kurt would have

Opposite: Lenya in her dressing room at the Theater de Lys. Photo: Gena Jackson

giggled too if he would have seen me, running from one brasshead to the other to make them see it my way. What next??

Last week I did something very funny. Does Turk Murphy mean anything to you? Well, he has a band, a Dixie band, and he plays the trombone. He was making records for Columbia and they asked me to come over after the show and listen to it. So I did, and then they asked me if I would sing, just for fun, with his band—the Moritat from *Threepenny*. Well, it turned out

*Turk Murphy and Lotte Lenya recording "Moritat."
The record was not released commercially in the U.S. because
the producers feared competition with Louis Armstrong's.*

*Right: Louis Armstrong and Lotte Lenya recording
"Moritat" for Columbia Records in 1956.*

*Lenya and Louis Armstrong with the band
during rehearsals for the recording of
"Mack the Knife."*

to be so good and funny that Columbia is bringing it out. Me
singing with the band. I had more fun doing it and they all loved
it. And George was sitting there and you should have seen his
face! Beaming is not the right word for it. It's strange how much
confidence he gives me. I would never have dared things like
that. And here I go. Sail right into it without thinking twice.
Well, that's enough now about that "great artist". . .[21]

Shortly before Louis Armstrong made his recording of
"Mack the Knife," I made one with Turk Murphy. I sang it in
German, and then he came in with his jazz band. It was a very
good record. But Louis made his the next day, and it was better.
So Goddard Lieberson said to me, "We'll have to shelve that
Turk man for a later time and bring out Louis's recording
instead." I will never forget the recording session. Armstrong
came in with his whole entourage. They started playing what
sounded like a jam session—you couldn't hear one note of "Mack
the Knife" in the midst of all that noise. Finally, someone said,
"Okay, Louie let's go." And they all started into "Mack the
Knife" and played it like they had heard it all their lives. I looked
at George astonished. But George said, "Now, Louie, let's take

In Dusseldorf with members of the cast of the German premiere of Street Scene *(Weill, Elmer Rice, Langston Hughes, 1947), November 1955. Photo: Elfi Hess*

one more, just for security, in case something happens to this one." In the middle, when he came to the names—Jenny Diver, Lucy Brown—I saw George stop him for a second and whisper something in his ear. Louis did it again, and this time he sang "Jenny Diver, Lucy Brown, dah, da, dah, Lotte Lenya." Now that was million-dollar publicity. And then later Bobby Darin did the same thing. I've always been lucky in my life, I really was.[17]

Weill would have loved Armstrong's recording. Of course, he knew all of Armstrong's earlier recordings. Once I brought home a very modern jazz arrangement of "September Song." He listened very hard, and finally said, "What is it?" Well, soon a faint snippet of the melody came in and he said, "Oh, yes." I asked, "How do you like it?" He answered with a line from *The Threepenny Opera*, "Well, it's possible this way, but it's also possible the other way." But Armstrong he would have adored, and also Bobby Darin. See, because they didn't change the melody. The melody was intact.[52]

One evening, long before "Mack the Knife" became so famous, Kurt and I had been invited to dinner at Billy Rose's in New York. We had not been in the country very long and didn't have much money. At one point in the evening Billy says, "Kurt, you know there is one song which I would like to buy from you, and I'll pay you all the money you want." Kurt, suspicious, stood back and said, "What song is it?" Billy replied, "I want to buy the 'Moritat.'" Kurt remained silent for a few moments and then said, "Billy, I'll sell you the whole *Threepenny Opera* if you want to buy it, but I won't sell you that song."[68]

The Moritat has been recorded now by 17 different companies. You hear it coming out of bars, juke boxes, taxis, wherever you go. Kurt would have loved that. A taxi driver whistling his tunes would have pleased him more than winning the Pulitzer Prize.

Opposite: Supervising the orchestra, conducted by Wilhelm Brückner-Rüggeberg, during sessions for Aufstieg und Fall der Stadt Mahagonny, *Hamburg, 1956.*

The state department will pay for my trip to Germany in November [1955] for the opening of *Street Scene.* George got that for me. Now he can come with me and help me to say the right thing to the press and the people who represent American culture over there. What fun it will be to hear *Street Scene* again. Kurt would be so proud. And that George running around and working on so many things at the same time that I get dizzy listening.[21]

I returned to Hamburg in 1956 to do another recording. I'll never forget the newspaper the day I arrived. On the same page: "Lotte Lenya Arrives in Hamburg." "Bertolt Brecht died last night." I still shiver when I think about it. It was such a shock.[17]

Top: Sheet music of "Mack the Knife" issued by Harms in 1956.

Bottom: Jacket of Die sieben Todsünden *for Philips, 1956—the first recording of one of Weill's most popular works. Conductor Wilhelm Brückner-Rüggeberg made a transposed arrangement suitable to Lenya's 58-year-old voice. Reproduced courtesy PolyGram Records.*

Yesterday I finished *The Seven Deadly Sins* recording and everybody thinks it's beautiful. I was, as usual, deeply depressed and could not see anything good in what I did, and I needed a night's sleep to make me realize that it really is lovely. It's such a beautiful work, and the four singers representing the family are excellent, and Miss Lenya does a very moving and sometimes bitter job of getting her sister Anna to understand about the cruelty of this world.

George is so comforting in a crisis like the after-effects from a week of recording. He is able to detach himself and float on what he is hearing on the record. Afterwards he is able to analyze it in a few words like, "impeccable taste, harsh, and infinitely moving." It helps to make me believe that what I did is good. And you know how severe a critic he can be and *must* be when it comes to things one wishes to last for a long time.[21]

I wanted the *Mahagonny* recording to be authentic— Weill wanted it to be performed by singers. Jimmy Mahoney has to sing, you know? Weill really wrote it with the melodies in it, as sustaining melodies, which he wanted to have sung, you know? The "*Nur die Nacht darf nicht aufhör'n, nur die Nacht darf nicht sein,*" that's an aria which has to be sung. You cannot speak it. It's like a Verdi aria, you know? So, that's why I took singers. Wonderful singers. That tenor Heinz Sauerbaum is fantastic.

I don't sing the songs now any differently than when I sang them in Berlin. Maybe a little bit more mature. You learn, naturally, you learn. You use all the wisdom you have accumulated as a human being. It's a maturer Jenny, it's a maturer "Surabaya Johnny" than it was in 1929. But the style, the motion, the meaning; it's exactly the same.[8]

Another premiere recording: Aufstieg und Fall der Stadt Mahagonny, *made for Philips in November, 1956. Tenor Heinz Sauerbaum sang the role of Jimmy and Brückner-Rüggeberg conducted. Reproduced courtesy Sony Records.*

Of course I should have called the Intendant of the Vienna State Opera. But you know, that would have put me once more right into the midst of things, and after four months of dealing with an opera house and opera singers in Hamburg—wonderful as it was—I just wanted to have some peace and quiet. You'll [Caspar Neher] understand that better than anyone else. Or do you? One can't forever be doing business. And so instead, I sat down in the kitchen where I "have eaten two heifers, and after that still another one" [from *Mahagonny*]. And as result of this gluttony, I have to run around in my skiing pants, since my behind refuses to be squeezed into anything else. But for *Die Bürgschaft* I'll be streamlined again.[50]

It's fun to be back with Victor Carl [Guarneri, close friend of Davis and Lenya] running in and out of the apartment, screaming and cursing about all the things he has to do for me (loving every minute of it) and with that whole gang there on Second Avenue, which makes my being stuck at the apartment cheerful and bearable. Only when Friday comes do I show my strength and determination to spend the weekend in the "ghost-house."[21]

Your Erika, who apparently has the unpleasant task of finding the letters you [Caspar Neher's] are too lazy to mail, has finally sent me your letter in which you complain bitterly about injustice to humanity because they don't want to pay you to use four *Mahagonny* drawings. Just to avoid the possibility of your dying from starvation, I went to Columbia with my shoes torn to a frazzle. As a result they will pay you 1,500 Marks, which—between you and me—I find far too much. For all of this, I expect to be invited to a wonderful Austrian dinner in Casa

Neher when I come to Berlin in October. We're going to stay here all summer. I would have loved to go to the ocean, but unfortunately George doesn't like the water. For him a vacation means sitting all day in some library reading. That's George.[50]

Rumor has it that I will be awarded the *Freiheitsglocke* [Freedom Bell, from the city of West Berlin]. I can't imagine what that is, but we shall see. On the 2nd I have to attend a big press conference (I dread those things, but it has to be done) and then I hope I can work in peace and get all the things done I have in mind. The people at the record company are really tremendously helpful to me, and I find working there very exciting. No rush, no union man behind me, and the orchestra is usually very exuberant. So it's real fun working in

Above: Recording the "Havana Song" from Aufstieg und Fall der Stadt Mahagonny, *with accordion. Photo: Scheel.*

Right: Recording session, Hamburg, 1956. Photo: Harcken.

Above: Exhausted, during the final session.

Below: Listening to the playbacks with George Davis.
Photos: Philips Records

A television appearance in Stuttgart, on Süddeutscher Rundfunk, 7 October 1956. The program, entitled Lotte Lenya, *featured Weill songs and an interview by Josef Müller-Marein. Photo: Wolfgang und Liselotte Fischer*

Right: Actor Burgess Meredith (left), a long-time friend from New City, and Lenya, at the recording session for Johnny Johnson *(Weill and Paul Green, 1936). Photo: MGM Records.*

Berlin. I don't know how I would feel about living there again. That thought never entered my mind. So why even ask.[40]

Later on, in the States, I got an award at the German Embassy. They gave me a big pin for carrying German culture to the United States. I wouldn't be caught dead wearing it, of course. The luncheon was very good and I asked the hostess, "Would you tell me what's in the sauerkraut that makes it so delicious?" She said, "Miss Lenya, of course I'll tell you, but please don't tell anyone else. Most of these American women wouldn't want to know what goes into sauerkraut."[17]

George and I had to take a plane from Hamburg to Berlin, only 55 minutes but brother were they rough. Benjamin Britten, who is an old friend of George's, was in the same plane coming from London. They hardly had a chance to say hello to each other for fear of vomiting in each other's face. It was that bad. We were met at the airport by Margot Aufricht, our old friend, and

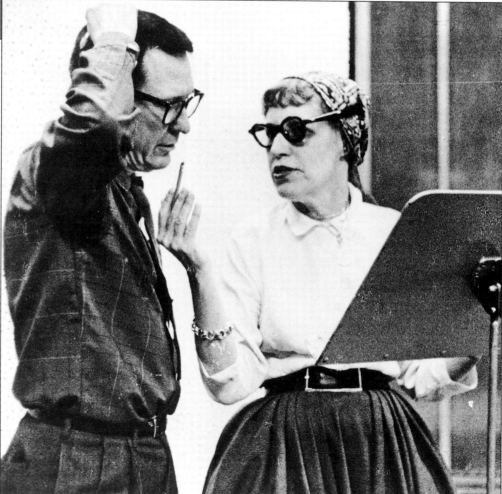

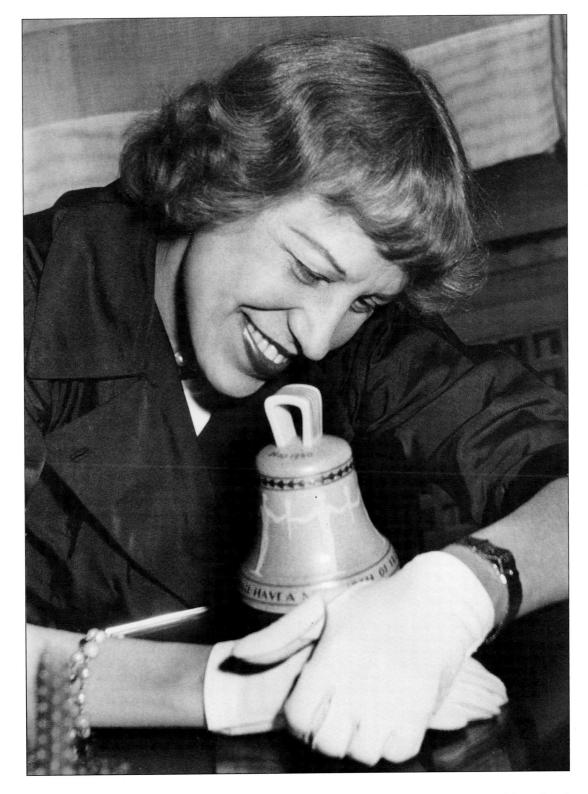

Above: Awarded the Freedom Bell, the highest cultural award given by the city of West Berlin, 11 November 1957. Photo: Ilse Buhns

Following pages: Record store display window at 54th Street and Lexington Avenue, New York, ca. 1957.

taken to our apartment. It looks exactly like Sally Bowles' apartment, and one could almost hear the landlady asking for "Mister Ischywoo." But no landlady here. The apartment belongs to a Rumanian, and it looks it. They cleaned for days to get the grease off the walls, but we love it now.

September Songs and other American Theater
Songs of Kurt Weill, *Columbia Records, August 1957.
Reproduced courtesy Sony Records.*

I saw three rehearsals of *Die Bürgschaft*, Kurt's most important opera. I'm not happy with the cuts they made, but the production and the cast and choruses (and they play an extremely important part) could not have been better. After we had a few battles about the changed ending and meaning, the premiere took place and was a tremendous success by critics and audience. You see, all the young people in Germany today know Kurt only from the *Threepenny Opera*, and nothing more. Now here they learn about a new work, and it was so important that it be a success.

Now my battle with the Hamburg Opera House starts. They don't have the right choreographer for the *Sins*; the premiere has been announced for February 18th with me singing the lead. I felt like an ant when I was trying out on that huge stage to see whether my voice could be heard. And it could—damn it. So I must find a good choreographer like Roland Petit or some foreigner. Otherwise it will not be a success.

Thank God I don't have to worry about the Hamburg production of *7 Sins*. The Brecht heirs are so difficult at the moment and want such high royalties, that I stopped all productions until

*Above: At the opening of the first post-war
production of Kurt Weill's opera,* Die Bürgschaft,
Berlin, 6 October 1957. Photo: Ilse Buhns

*Right: Wilhelm Brückner-Rüggeberg and Lenya
(center) are flanked by two singers from the Berlin
revival of* Die Bürgschaft. *Photo: Harcken*

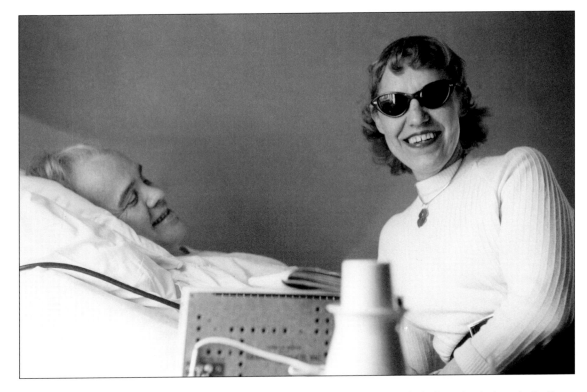

Lenya visiting George Davis during a hospital stay in Berlin.
Davis died in the hospital of a heart attack, 25 November 1957.

Soon after Davis's death, Lenya had to record Die
Dreigroschenoper *in Berlin, January 1958. Photo: Paul
Moor/Philips Records*

they come to their senses. You know, I always had my doubts
about that big opera house in Hamburg and me getting lost on
that stage. No Walküre am I. It's on records, and that's good
enough for the time being.

The English writer, David Drew, who is thinking of writing
a biography about Kurt is a dream of a guy. Young, witty, and
extremely clever. I think we would have fun with him in the
house for a few months. He was with me during the rehearsals,
George not feeling too well, and a blessing it was to have him
with me so that I could rebel (musically—me not reading a note
as you well know—he helped out there with his musicologist's
brain), and we had fun besides, just raising hell.[21]

George died in a hospital a stone's throw from the Russian
zone. The doctor there said to him, "Well, Mr. Davis, even if you
have to leave this world, you won't be missing much."
Whereupon George put his hands behind his head and said, "Oh,
doctor, I don't agree with you at all. I think it's a lovely world
and I love my life. I wouldn't change it, not for a million dollars.
I don't think it's a bad world. We'll change for the better." He

died that night. You see, there was no bitterness in George. He looked at disasters philosophically, and this gave me great, great, strength.[17]

Philips/Columbia recording of Die Dreigroschenoper, *1958. Brückner-Rüggeberg once again conducted, and the cast included such stars as Willy Trenk-Trebitsch, Trude Hesterberg, and Wolfgang Neuss. The cover drawing is by Ben Shahn. Reproduced courtesy Polygram Records.*

How I wish you [Mary Daniel] could be with me to hold my aching head, to tell me that George knew that I loved him dearly in spite of our quarrels. Why does one always remember the bad things first, and why do I always feel guilty?

I have started working with my actors on the *Threepenny* recording. I must work very hard in order to do a good job. And I am grateful that I can work and have not too much time to think. The nights are drowned out by sleeping pills that the doctor gave me. But I still have those terrible nightmares, where I am in the hospital, trying desperately to work the oxygen mask, and can't, and poor George looking at me with big eyes. One should think that to go through something like that once would be enough. It's lonesome without him and to work alone without his guiding hand is not easy, but still I must try. This is what he would want me to do most. Margarethe Kaiser is with me, and, bless her heart, tries to hold my head up. I cannot write more today, my back hurts, my eyes are blurry, and it's living hell right now. Let's see what that bragging Austrian can do with her so-often mentioned courage. Does not look too good to me right now.[21]

It is so hard to believe that George is gone and I am not able to write about it yet. But I have finished the important part of my job here, the recording of the *Threepenny Opera* with a German cast. It's a beautiful recording and I feel I have done my best to make George and Kurt proud. I have canceled the remaining two records, which only concern me, and I can wait with them until I have caught up my strength. I am very tired and burnt out from too many heartaches and too many tears in these last eight years. But also so many happy times I have had in my life, that I am not complaining about my fate, it's just that I need a little more time to readjust myself once again. It was a happy and useful life I had with George and I do miss him so very much. Six years is such a short time. But this I felt when Kurt died and I had him for twenty-four years. It's always too soon, it seems. And how lucky I am to be able to say that.

Opposite: With George Davis, ca. 1956.

*Lenya takes her concert program to Lewisohn
Stadium, New York, July 1958.*

Right at the moment I am jittery about the K. Weill concert at Lewisohn Stadium. It's such a frightening place. Soooo big![60] At the first rehearsal I felt like the last of the Christians being thrown to the tigers. But then at night, when the spotlight hits you, the vastness of the stadium disappears. Then it's only you and the microphone.[17]

I was singing all day long with that croaky voice from far too many cigarettes. But I will stop smoking as soon as I get into town and start working on *Seven Deadly Sins* which the City Center is doing around Christmas. Balanchine is doing the choreography. Allegra Kent, his prima ballerina, is doing the part of Anna 2, and I am Anna 1. Isn't that exciting? Auden has done a beautiful translation. So life begins to look more cheerful now. Well, that's all the news. Martini time has come, and I am thirsty.[21]

I had given up smoking for three months before the opening of *The Seven Deadly Sins* at the New York City Ballet, which was very hard for me, being a chain-smoker. I gave it up and sang clear as a bell. When the reviews came in—and they were beautiful—one of them said, "Here she is again, with that inimitable, husky, marvellous voice of hers." When I read that I went into the drugstore, bought a pack of cigarettes, and practically ate them. I was so mad.[52]

Above: Lenya as Anna I at the New York City Ballet.

George Balanchine (left) and Lenya (right), preparing for the American premiere of **The Seven Deadly Sins** *at the New York City Ballet, 1958. The ballet was in repertory for the 1958-59 season, featuring Lenya as Anna I and Allegra Kent as Anna II. Photo: New York City Ballet*

Balanchine's production of The Seven Deadly Sins, *New York City Ballet, 1958-59. Lenya (Anna I) snaps Allegra Kent's (Anna II) picture. Photo: New York City Ballet*

Sunday afternoon I went to a lovely concert at Town Hall with Auden and his friend Chester Kallman: Stravinsky's new work *Threni*, Schoenberg, Alban Berg. Stravinsky was there and he will come to hear the *7 Sins* on Wednesday. I don't think it will be to his taste. But I think he remembers it from Paris. He was there at that time. Afterwards is a little party at Auden's house for him. I hope he will come.[21]

My television interview was a bad one. So flippant and rather stupid. It was only topped a week later by Ed Fitzgerald, who had me on and insisted that *One Touch of Venus* had a Chinese background, and I was introduced as the great European operatic star Lotte Lehmann! I lashed out at him; I've just had enough of emerging as a full idiot with those interviewers. This last one, I won.

The Carnegie Hall concert was a tremendous success, sold out and the audience could not have been more enthusiastic. The manager called me up the other day to ask if I would be willing to repeat it on March 30th. There was not a moment's hesitation in my voice when I said no. Before the concert someone wrote me a note telling me that I don't have to prove myself anymore, and I should not take it too seriously. Well, that's one way of looking at it, but with that attitude I would cheat my audience, which loves to cry and laugh with me.[21]

Lenya's three Carnegie Hall concerts (1959, 1960, and 1965) drew wide acclaim. The 1965 concert was preserved on a pirated LP.

Now here I will give you the facts as I remember them: Felix Gerstman (now deceased), the producer of my Carnegie Hall concert in 1965, had a tape made of the concert—as he had done with all his concert presentations. He gave me a copy of this tape, of which I subsequently made a few copies for my friends. Such a friend was Mr. Vivian Liff in London, an ardent record collector. I gave him a copy as a Christmas present. I do not recall having given permission for publication, and surely no contract for commercial exploitation was offered to me.

In reference to the paragraph you question in Mr. Ross's letter: Mr. Ross states that the "tape we used for making Rococo 4008 was made by Mme. Lenya, and supplied to us by herself." I never gave a tape to anyone except the aforementioned Mr. Vivian Liff. Now Mr. Ross "should like us to add that previous permission was obtained through our mutual personal friend Mr. Vivian Liff, of Tunbridge Wells, London, England, that both Mme. Lenya and Mr. David Drew agreed to the publication." No such proposition was considered or discussed.

Mr. Ross claims further that "they" got in touch with me during my stay in London recently and I "again was pleased that the disc was issued" and I am supposed to have asked that some copies be sent to me!!! (The only copy I have is the one I BOUGHT for six dollars and seventy-five cents!!!)

I can only quote Mr. Ross again: "There must be a mistake somewhere!"

I have nothing against this "floating" record, except that I want to get my usual artist's royalties. I am also curious about what "evidence" is supposedly in their possession. Don't you think it advisable to ask them to produce whatever they claim to have?

"Carnegie Hall." Painting by Russell Detwiler in honor of Lenya's 1965 concert.

Left: Rehearsal for Carnegie Hall concert, 7 February 1960. From left: Maurice Edwards, Polyna Stoska, Didy van Eyck, Ludwig Donath, Lenya, and conductor Maurice Levine. Photo: Don Hunstein

Following page: Richard Ely designed a poster for one of Lenya's Carnegie Hall concerts. About the portrait, Lenya wrote, "I love it very much. It's strong and arrogant."[27]

Of course, you will know whether there is "actually no law against recording and publishing such a recital" in Canada. But still . . . they are also selling it in the USA. Nu???[44]

Next Monday I start working with the director on the Kafka stories. I tried out one myself on my recorder and it sounds pretty good. Julie Sloane read "The Hunger Artist" for me, and it was interesting for me to hear what she did with it. It would never go on a record.

Mr. Hammarskjold called after his return from the near East to show us the U.N. Champagne was served and he showed us around personally, which was quite an impressive sight. He is gone to visit Latin America. In the meanwhile, I have found out that there is no Mrs. Hammarskjold. Not a female, anyway. But I like him enormously and hope that I will see him again.[21]

Left: The Stories of Kafka *read (in English) by Lenya. The album was recorded in the summer of 1959 and released late in 1962.*

Below: The single 45-rpm release of Bobby Darin's rendition of "Mack the Knife," one of the best-known popular versions of the song, earned two Grammy awards in 1959. WCBS radio banned the song from the airwaves because disc jockeys had developed a rather morbid habit of playing the song immediately following the latest news report of youth stabbings in an already charged summer of gang violence in New York. Reproduced courtesy Atlantic Recording Corp.

Invitation to German Poetry read by Lenya, recorded August 1958 and released late in 1960. Reproduced courtesy Dover Publications.

I am happy that you [Kurt Pinthus] liked the record of German poetry. All the marvelous things you said about it made me listen to it again and enjoy it. One always is so critical about oneself and needs a little support. And coming from you, it gives me great courage.[56]

Right: Last recording for Philips/Columbia: Weill and Brecht's Happy End, *in which Lenya sang all the solo parts (with choral backing), recorded July 1960, again with conductor Wilhelm Brückner-Rüggeberg. Reproduced courtesy PolyGram Records.*

I did another revival of *The Seven Deadly Sins*, in Frankfurt with the marvelous dancer Karen von Aroldingen. We did it for many months at the opera house. She had one dream: to come to America and dance for Balanchine. So I arranged for them to meet in Frankfurt, and Balanchine took her, but only for the corps. So that shows how much she wanted it. In Germany, she was a big star. Well, after spending five years in the corps, she became a prima ballerina again, of course.[17]

Right: With Karen von Aroldingen (Anna II) in the German stage premiere of Die sieben Todsünden, *produced as a repertory piece in Frankfurt at the Städtische Bühnen, beginning 6 April 1960. The production was choreographed by Tatjana Gsovsky and designed by Hein Heckroth. Photo: Jack Hochscheid*

Below: At the Musica Viva concert in Munich, 6 May 1960. The all-Weill program featured Mahagonny Songspiel, *selected German songs, and* Die sieben Todsünden. *Photo: Felicitas*

So What?
1961-1981

As the Contessa in The Roman Spring of Mrs. Stone. *"You see, I have never quite been able to get out of the whorehouse!" Photo: Warner Bros.*

I was told that Lenya was one difficult lady, so beware! But she was the antithesis of difficult. . . . There was not a hypocritic bone in Lenya's body. She was also very straightforward. If you ever convoluted the reply to a question, you were in deep trouble.[58]

—HAROLD PRINCE, stage director

If Lenya spent the 1950s in the shadow of Weill and guided by the hand of George Davis, she reclaimed her own identity in the 1960s and, in many respects, reached the peak of her fame. Once again she took to the stage as an actress in works unrelated to Weill and eagerly accepted most of the limited film offers that came her way. Feeling the effect of age and cigarettes on her voice, she began to sing Weill's music less often, but she continued to guard his legacy and promote authentic performances.

In 1960 José Quintero called me and asked if I wanted to play the Contessa in *The Roman Spring of Mrs. Stone*. I was so surprised I didn't think he really meant it. I thought he would change his mind. But he didn't.[55]

I've been in London since 29 November and am doing my first movie in thirty years. It is so easy that one could teach it to a jackass in just a few days.[50]

Above: The Roman Spring of Mrs. Stone, *1961. Lenya,
as the procuress Contessa Magda Terribili-Gonzalez, meets
with Vivien Leigh as Mrs. Stone, and Warren Beatty as
the gigolo Paolo. Photo: Corbis-Bettmann*

*Lenya's Oscar nomination for Best Supporting Actress for her
performance in* The Roman Spring of Mrs. Stone, *1961. Rita
Moreno won the prize for her performance in* West Side Story.

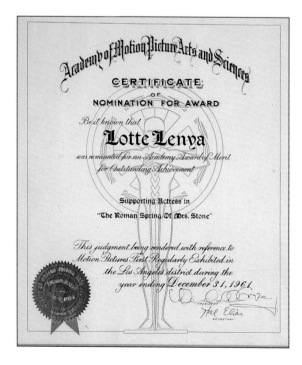

The original conception of the part of the Contessa, who
procures boys for older women, was that of an elegant, fussy
person, and I wondered why they didn't get someone like
Martha Hunt for the part. I didn't see the part that way. I told
José I saw her as a Middle European woman who was once rich
but no longer. So she started her service to make money. To her
it was a business and she was cold and businesslike about it. He
let me do it that way.

I think Warren Beatty acts strangely because he has a
complex about his sister. I got along with him because I didn't
know he was Shirley MacLaine's brother. It is better to be
ignorant sometimes.

At home I have a whole box of awards. Everybody says,
"Why don't you put them up?" I say, "I have enough hanging up
already." I really don't believe in those things, you know? It's
nice when you get one, but it doesn't shake me.[70]

*Opposite: A photograph by artist and patron Carl Van Vechten, New York, February 1962.
Photo reproduced courtesy Joseph Solomon, Executor of the Estate of Carl Van Vechten*

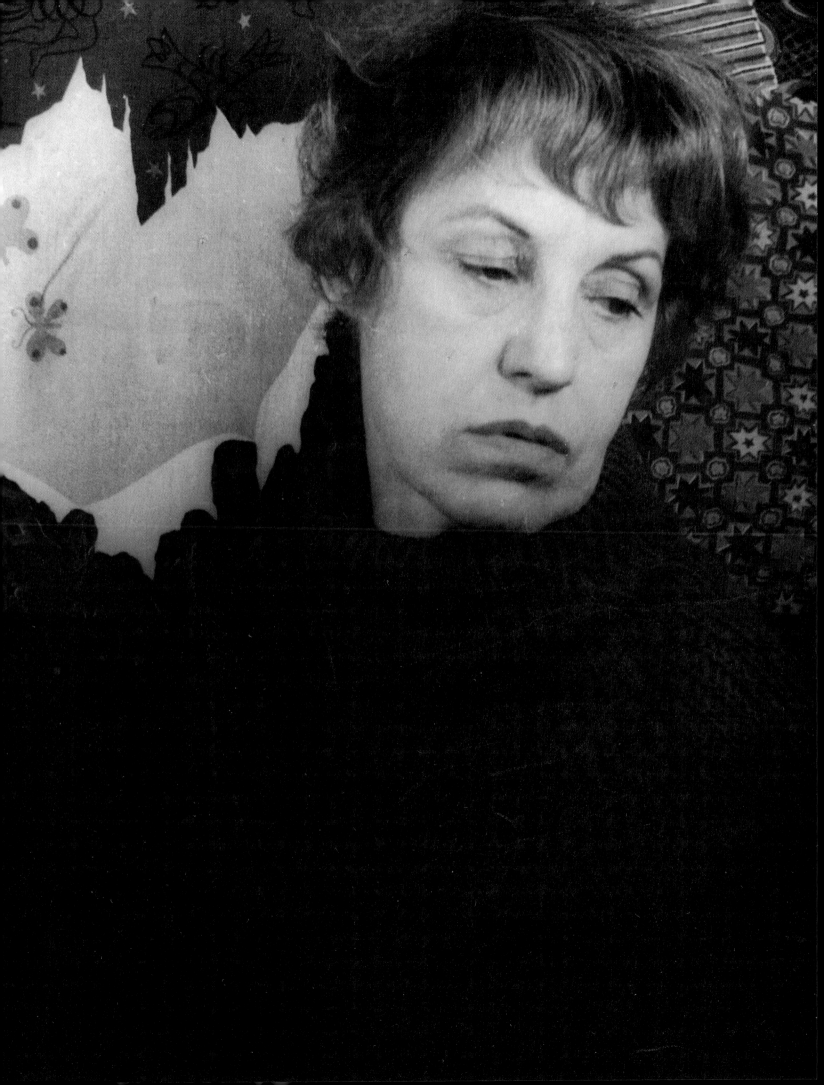

Rehearsing **Brecht on Brecht,** *a revue of Brecht's poems and songs compiled and translated by George Tabori, in London, September 1962. Photo: Sandra Lousada*

George Tabori, who is a very good translator of Brecht, one of the best, came up with the idea for *Brecht on Brecht*. And Gene Frankel directed, who had no idea of Brecht's poetry, which was my mother's milk. I came to the cast a few days after the rest had begun rehearsing. I saw those actors reciting those poems with so much— you know—with them swinging their heads and their legs and God knows what else. And then I came with the first poem I had to read, "To Be Friendly." I stood there; I said it, quietly. Lee Strasberg was sitting in the theater. When I came back he said, "I learned something."

The show is a big success and I am (once more) in the MIDDLE! The toast of the town and you know how big London is. The matinees are always a little rough, and it's hard work all around. I am doing so much more in the show than I did in New York. But the audience is nuts about me, and I think that is as it should be. I don't know whether the show will move to the West End, but we are staying six weeks at the Royal Court. You would like the billing I have: pictures and notices of mine all over the place and my name in lights above the title.[14]

While Lenya was playing in Brecht on Brecht *at the Theater de Lys in New York, before it moved to London, Vera Stravinsky introduced her to Russell Detwiler, an artist 27 years her junior. "He's an alcoholic," Lenya told a friend, "but I can handle him." Detwiler followed Lenya to London, where they married. Detwiler had studied painting at the Academy of Fine Arts in Philadelphia and the Art Students League in New York. Both Vera Stravinsky and*

soprano Jennie Tourel owned a number of his dark, impressionistic paintings, and they helped to have his work shown in a few New York galleries. Lenya, whenever she wasn't dealing with his drinking binges, also promoted his work.

I haven't rushed into this like a silly girl. When you are really in love, age just becomes something written in your passport. They can say what they like. We're in love and we don't care. Besides, I got tired of him asking me four times a day to marry him.[6]

Rosa Klebb in *From Russia with Love*: my most famous role. I was working at the Royal Court playing in *Brecht on Brecht* when the call came, "Miss Lenya, we have a part for you. We wonder whether you're interested in it." I said, "What is it?" The

Top: Lenya enjoyed her top billing at the Royal Court Theatre production of Brecht on Brecht.

Below: Original cast recording of Brecht on Brecht, *released by Columbia, 1963. Reproduced courtesy Sony Records*

With her third husband, the American painter Russell Detwiler, shortly after their wedding in London, which took place during the run of Brecht on Brecht, *2 November 1962. Lenya was 64 and Detwiler 37. Photo: Keystone Press Agency*

Opposite: With Detwiler in their New York apartment, posing under his portrait of Lenya.

producer, a Mr. Saltzman, said, "It's an Ian Fleming story." I said, "I'm very sorry about my ignorance, but I don't know who Ian Fleming is." So, he said, "Well, we'll send you a book over in the afternoon. Could you read it and we can talk to you tomorrow?" I said, "Oh, sure, I'll read it." On the first page was a description of Rosa Klebb: she weighs 240 pounds, her bosom is very catholic down to her knee. And that was the description. Saltzman invited me to meet with him, so I went to his office, looking very slim then. I said, "Mr. Saltzman, have you seen what it says about her?" He said, "Don't pay any attention to that. That's not important. Are you interested in the part?" "Very much." "All right, we'll get in touch with you." I didn't hear anything from him by the time I went back to America, so I figured nothing would come of it. Lo and behold, a week later I got in touch with my agent and an offer had come in, paying very good money. And that's how it was. That's how I got the part. When I came to London to make the movie, the wardrobe mistress, accounting for the 240 pounds, had already made a pattern to pad me, to make me fat. I tried it on and said, "My god. I couldn't walk a step in this thing. It's like Golem, you know? Let me just wear a uniform." They said, "Oh, my god, no. The director. No, no, no. You *must* wear it." I said, "There's no *must*. I'll walk like I weigh 240. The director won't even notice." And that's exactly what happened. I walked on for the first take with a mannish hair cut, because she was a lesbian, and wearing a uniform. No padding, nothing. Terence Young took one look at me and said, "Doesn't she look fabulous?"[70]

I adore making pictures, especially shooting all the scenes out of order. I have a terrific ability to concentrate, so it's no problem for me. Once during the filming of *From Russia with Love*, the director, Terence Young, said to me, "Lenya, darling, at this point, please look straight into the camera." I said, "Where is it?" I was surrounded by six cameras but didn't see any of them. That's how deeply I get into it.

Sean Connery was an absolute dream of a guy to work with. When that last fight came on—you know, with the chair—Terence said to him, "Well, Sean, this time you really have to fight," because usually the other things were done with stuntmen. After that scene I looked like I had been beaten up by a sadist. Black and blue all over, but it worked. But everyone remembers the shoe. I always get stopped on the street by someone saying, "Look! There's the lady with the knife in her shoe!"[17]

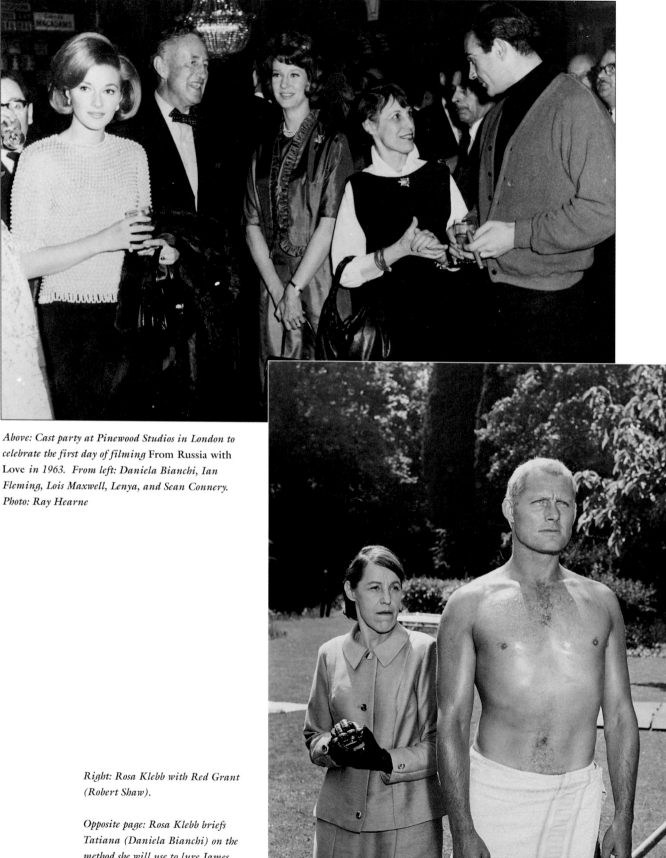

Above: Cast party at Pinewood Studios in London to celebrate the first day of filming From Russia with Love *in 1963. From left: Daniela Bianchi, Ian Fleming, Lois Maxwell, Lenya, and Sean Connery. Photo: Ray Hearne*

Right: Rosa Klebb with Red Grant (Robert Shaw).

Opposite page: Rosa Klebb briefs Tatiana (Daniela Bianchi) on the method she will use to lure James Bond to his death.

Photos: United Artists

Above: Lenya in her best-known film appearance as
Rosa Klebb, From Russia with Love, *1963.*

Right: In a climactic scene, Lenya as Rosa Klebb
threatens James Bond with a knife hidden in her shoe.

Below: Attacked by Klebb, James Bond (Sean Connery)
has no choice but to defend himself and the Western
world. Photos: United Artists

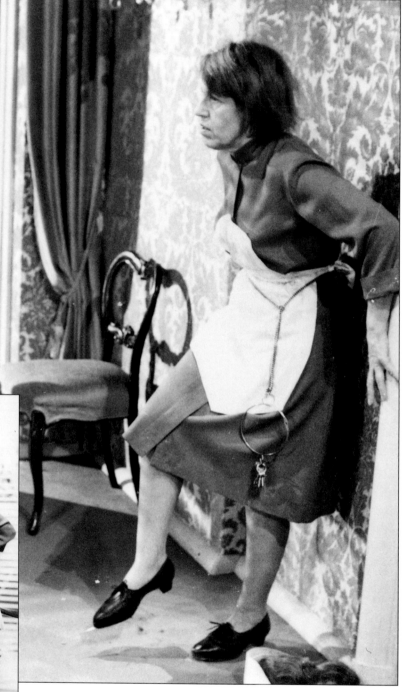

[Letter to a German theater]

Thank you for your letter of October 22. My apologies for replying in English, but I have to dictate this as I am at present on tour. For the same reason, I must reply rather briefly. I am already acquainted with the so-called "Holliger-Fassung" and with Herr Holliger's views on the *Mahagonny* Songspiel. And I have already made it quite clear, through Universal-Edition, that I am entirely opposed to any attempt to interfere with Weill's wishes concerning the opera and the Songspiel. And I am wholeheartedly against any attempt to amalgamate the opera and the Songspiel. I must quote from a letter Weill wrote in 1932 to an organization that wished to make a "Songspiel" version of the opera:

> *What I want to avoid most of all is that the piece will be cut down to nothing except songs or song-like sections, and I would principally prefer that a single song is omitted here and there rather than leaving out all of the musically demanding sections.*

That, for me, is final. But I would like to add one thing. There has been a fundamental misunderstanding of what the Songspiel is. There is only one version, and that is the version Weill wrote in 1927 for Baden-Baden, in which I appeared. (There is no "Paris version": what was performed in Paris was the best selection from the opera and the Songspiel that could be managed with the resources available, and it was intended for that occasion and that place only—a single concert performance.) The 1927 Songspiel is *quite distinct* from the opera, and that is what no one understands. There are no *characters* in the Songspiel. No lumberjacks, no escaping criminals, no prostitutes. The four men appear in tails and the girls (two) are described as "Soubrettes." There is no "drama." It is simply a little "scenic cantata" based on the "Mahagonny Songs" from Brecht's *Hauspostille*, with orchestral interludes between each of the vocal numbers. It is, I admit, difficult to produce, but if it is produced with understanding, it cannot fail, because the musical form is perfect. It even seems to succeed when it is *not* produced with understanding—again, for musical reasons. But the moment you start introducing new bits here and there, the moment you introduce an element of "drama" where none existed, you confuse the whole issue.

At an opening of a Detwiler exhibition.

I assure you, dear Dr. Barfuss, that Weill's authentic Songspiel has more in common with Stravinsky's *A Soldier's Tale*—a work that Weill loved—than does the formless pot-pourri of this "Holliger-Fassung." If you and Herr Holliger do not think the authentic Songspiel is worth performing, then you are perfectly entitled to your opinion (though I disagree with it, and can cite a number of recent performances in my support). You must find some other work to go with the Stravinsky. But please do not ask me to give my consent to something which I know is wholly contrary to the composer's intentions and indeed to artistic principle.[78]

[Letter to agent Bertha Case]

Tomorrow my Russi arrives with his "fiancée" Anna Krebs, who took care of him. Madame Weigel from the East Zone wishes a third division of royalties earned from the London production of *Happy End*, even though a new contract was made with Bloch Erben in 1958 which says nothing of the kind. I wrote to B.E. that it is not enough for Mme. Weigel to "wish" and that I insist on the terms of my contract. It's going to be fun . . . To "dear" S.o.B. B. [Brecht's son, Stefan] I wrote that I was not a bit surprised that Auden refused to do a new translation "alone" as S.B. so "tact-fully" suggested. Darling, we just have to think of another way to make money. What about a coffee shop with something going on in the back? We'll dig up something when I get back.[15]

Right: Helene Weigel, Bertolt Brecht's wife, stars in the Berliner Ensemble production of Mutter Courage, *East Berlin, 1949.*

Opposite: Lenya rivals Weigel's Mutter Courage in a production at the Ruhrfestspiele in Recklinghausen, 12 June–25 July 1965, directed by Harry Buckwitz. The German critics compared her performance negatively to Weigel's. Photo: Rosemarie Pierer

Weigel was a toughie. Weigel was Jewish—a Yenta. With all my dislikes of her, I liked her because she was so tough and had such a *jiddisches Köpfchen* [clever little Jewish head]. I wish I had an inch of that.[72]

Paul Dessau is a different type of composer than Weill. He succumbs to Brecht completely, you know? I've heard Weigel sing the *Mutter Courage* song, and it didn't make any impression at all. It went by unnoticed.[8]

For me, *Mother Courage* was a real challenge. The character is on stage in twelve out of thirteen scenes, and the scope of the role is terrific. I love the end, when she's all alone, having lost her children, she picks up the wagon and goes on. It was one of the most meaningful roles to me personally.[17]

I'm still a little tired from all the work I did in Germany, but it was fun up to the very last day. I finished *Mother Courage* on the 25th of July, went to Cologne on the 27th, and sang on the 30th and 31st at the festival in a sports arena (seating 7,000)—five songs in a Brecht evening. I wish you could have heard the applause. If you think Carnegie Hall was great (and it was), you should have heard what went on there. I could not leave the stage. Thank God I only had music to five songs, which I had to repeat. Otherwise I would still be singing there.

Above: Mother Courage (Lenya) comforts her daughter Kattrin (Ida Krottendorf).

Right: Hannsernst Jäger[?] as Der Koch with Mutter Courage, Recklinghausen, 1965. Photos: Rosemarie Pierer

Opposite page: Russell Nype and Lenya in a scene from "Lotte Lenya: The Broadway Years of Kurt Weill," a CBS television special broadcast in October 1964 in the "Stage 2" series. Photo: J. Peter Happel

Recreating "The Saga of Jenny" in "The World of Kurt Weill," filmed in May 1966 and broadcast on WGBH-TV in February 1967.

I am preparing an hour-long TV show for WGBH in Boston, which I will do between 9 and 20 May. All Kurt Weill songs and a narration, which I also will do. It's lots of work and I need all the little time I have right now to prepare it. For me it is always like starting from scratch. I forget the lyrics from one time to the next. It's unbelievable but it is the truth. I never forget the music, but the lyrics fly right out of my head.[48]

I knew *I am a Camera* and Christopher Isherwood very well from Berlin. So, Hal Prince called my agent and said, "We have a part for Miss Lenya. Could we get in touch with her?" Kander and Ebb played me a few songs from *Cabaret*, but not the ones they wrote especially for me. I liked them very much. Prince said, "Well, can we make a contract for a year?" I said, "Mr. Prince, I don't want to sign that because, you see, if I like the show, then I stay forever. If I want to get out of the contract,

I can get out of it, you know that. So, just believe me. I love it, and I will do it."[70]

I loved doing every minute of *Cabaret*. Sometimes I'd get so annoyed with that young girl that played Sally Bowles. After three or four weeks she kept complaining, "I'm so bored." And I told her, "Then get the hell out of the theater. You have no right to be here."[17]

Russ has been moved out of the psychiatric ward and transferred to the regular surgical one, which of course is much better for his morale. He will be at the hospital for many months to come, which will give him a good chance to recover also from his drinking problems. And it will give me a chance to recover from last year's nightmare of living in constant fear of what I will find when I get home from work.[48]

I got an invitation to luncheon at the White House during the Johnson administration, held in honor of the Minister of

Top: Martin Sheen (Kilroy) with Lenya as the Gypsy in a scene from a television film of Tennessee Williams's one-act play Ten Blocks on the Camino Real, *broadcast on WHYY-TV (New York) in October 1966.*

Bottom: Ten Blocks on the Camino Real. *Photo: Ted Mitchell*

Hal Prince directing Lenya in Cabaret. *In the show she sang "So What?", "It Couldn't Please Me More," "Married," and "What Would You Do?"*

Right: Dancing with sailors during the Act I finale of Cabaret.

Opposite: Lenya (foreground) with the original cast of Cabaret, *1966.*

Iceland. I was amazed that no one even searched me before going in. Johnson entered with all the fanfare, but he was really very amusing, with a twinkle in his eye that I thought he never had. We all sat down and Johnson made a very funny speech. Then the Minister of Iceland started, "Our history goes on for nine hundred years." Everyone thought, "Oh no, we have to listen to nine hundred years of history." Well, he got up to about three hundred, and I'm convinced that Lady Bird just kicked him under the table, because he just stopped abruptly.

I don't remember the first course, but the main course was lamb chops—the tiniest ones you ever saw! I mean, mini, mini! The butler was very nice, though. He said, "Take

[Letter to publisher Univeral Edition]

Today is Weill's birthday and I wish more than ever that he was still alive to explain to you my reasons why *Mahagonny* would not be suitable for the Schauspielhaus in Zurich. Mr. Voelker has not mentioned in his letter how much the orchestra would have to be reduced in order to facilitate a performance in his theater. Weill's score calls for 34 or more musicians, and the absolute minimum would be 26. I know the Zurich Schauspielhaus very well since I spent a good part of my young years there, and it is a mystery to me how he could accommodate 26 musicians. I am afraid that Mr. Voelker intends to convert *Mahagonny* into the *Dreigroschenoper* by magic. The Volksoper in Vienna is quite another matter—they do have an orchestra pit. Also, I believe that they can afford an orchestra. If Theodor Adorno now maintains that actors are better for *Mahagonny* than singers, it seems to me that Adorno lives somewhat in the past and hasn't noticed that there is now a new generation of singers able to perform *Mahagonny*, histrionically as well as vocally. This is no longer a problem. I repeat here (as I have already said in my telegram) what the very same Adorno said after the Berlin performance of *Mahagonny*—cast mostly with actors: Harald Paulsen, Trude Hesterberg, and me. In his criticism he wrote, "But the real *Mahagonny* belongs in an opera house." Why this "oracle" has now changed his mind does not interest me in the least.[69]

Lenya feared poverty as much as loneliness, always consulting her accountant before making an expensive purchase. Some called her thrifty, others had more negative terms for her constant concern about money. In September 1968, one month before her 70th birthday, she accepted an advance of $250,000 from a publisher of "popular" music, The Richmond Organization, for the transfer of the American rights in Weill's music, even though her assets at the time equaled many times that figure. Weill business never ceased, but friends say she tired of working, even passing on an opportunity to play Coco Chanel in a musical by Alan Jay Lerner.

I am agreeable to have Mr. Luciano Berio record and arrange "Surabaya Johnny" and "Ballade von der sexuellen Hörigkeit" as he sees fit. However, I am *NOT* agreeable to any performance of "Ballade vom ertrunkenen Mädchen" in any form other than Weill's original scoring. Should Mr. Berio decide

Opposite: Lenya (Emma Valadier) sets up a rendezvous in The Appointment. *Photo: M-G-M*

Lenya on camera during shooting for the television program Lotte Lenya singt Kurt Weill, *filmed by UFA for German television in 1967. The half-hour documentary program featured an introduction, narration, and singing by Lenya, and was later dubbed into English.*

to record the song exactly as written and scored by Weill, I would have no objection to his doing so. But under no circumstances will I allow any arrangement of this composition.[57]

Lenya and Stefan Brecht tried to prevent a theater version of Mahagonny *from opening off-Broadway at the Anderson Theatre because of distortions to the text and music. Produced by Carmen Capalbo (who mounted* The Threepenny Opera *at the Theater de Lys), the show featured Barbara Harris, Estelle Parsons, and Mort Shuman in the principal roles.*

I've been involved in a production of *Mahagonny* here, and not in a way I like to be involved. I saw the first preview February 20th and was about to commit suicide. It was a complete disaster. We went into arbitration (endless meetings) and I was able to restore the music, which did help somewhat. At least all the reviews were extremely favorable as far as the music was concerned (which showed me what deaf ears the critics have). The notes were there, but played with a sledgehammer. It finally opened April 28 and closed after 6 performances. I was greatly relieved when it closed. The arbitration still goes on, fighting for subsidiary rights.[41]

Your review of the ill-fated *Mahagonny* production at the Anderson Theatre prompted me to write you [Clive Barnes] this note. I had to let you know how very deeply I appreciate the fact that you were able to evaluate the importance of the work, and the beauty and significance of the score, through the vast distortions of this production.

It is entirely true—and not just a rumor—that Stefan Brecht and I fought body and soul to prevent the "show" from opening. But—alas—we did not succeed. The work would indeed be dead for the United States for some time to come, were it not for your knowledgeable review, which will keep interest in the work alive. Please accept my heartfelt thanks and gratitude.[7]

In late October 1969, at age 44, Russell Detwiler died from a fall at Brook House caused by an alcohol- and narcotics-induced seizure. Lenya buried him in a plot near Weill's in Mount Repose Cemetery, not far from Brook House. Later Lenya told a friend, "Of all my husbands I loved Russi the most. Because he needed me the most."

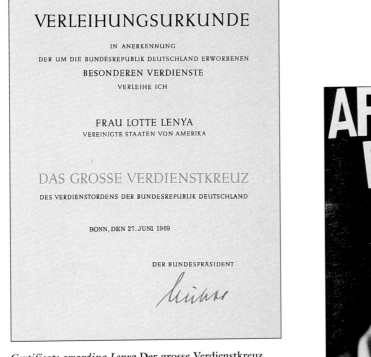

Certificate awarding Lenya **Der grosse Verdienstkreuz** *(the Great Service Cross) in recognition of "her merits in the German and American theater and for furthering cultural relations between Germany and America." The award was granted by the West German government 27 June 1969 and presented on 9 September.*

A feature interview in After Dark, *an American entertainment magazine, July 1969. The cover shows Lenya in Lion Feuchtwanger's* Petroleuminseln, *Berlin, 1928.*

Richard Avedon took the cover photo for The Lotte Lenya Album *released by Columbia in 1970. The two-LP set contains reissues of two recordings made in the 1950's:* Lotte Lenya singt Kurt Weill *(German songs, 1955) and* September Songs and other American Theatre Songs of Kurt Weill *(1957). Photo: Sony Records*

With Russell Detwiler at Brook House in New City, NY,
August 1966. Photo: Ted Mitchell

No, you don't have to pray for me. I don't believe in that escape either—I'd rather face whatever my fate has lined up for me. I admit, the other way is easier, and I have seen it work, but why try to escape pain and despair for someone I loved so dearly? Does he not deserve that grief I feel? I think it is a healthier and more honest way of facing life. I look out the window and see the seasons change and know, since we are part of nature, that I too will change and will find a purpose again for existence.[30]

People ask me what it's like to be married and widowed three times. Look at me and tell me what it does. You cannot explain what it does to you. I am sure many other women have gone through the same thing. Many young women with children right now, with the war in Vietnam, are going through the same thing. You just take it. There are many beautiful things still in life, which you can enjoy and should enjoy. I am sure each one of my three husbands, whom I loved very dearly, would not want me to sit there in my mourning clothes and never get out of it. I think they would like what I'm doing now—that I keep working, that I keep alive. Sometimes it's difficult to be alone, and especially for me because I'm a person who loves to share, whether it's bad or good, but I like to share my life with someone. And if that person is taken away from you, it takes time to adjust to the loneliness. I'm learning that again for the third time.[52]

Last week I had a one-hour interview with Ed Newman for colored TV. I think it went awfully well, and I made a few charming remarks about old man Brecht. I also said the reason for the exceptionally marvelous Berlin audience was because 95% of them were Jewish. The Goyim will love me for that. I don't give a sh—.[67]

I wish I had more time to study guitar, an instrument I like very much. It goes with my voice. The reissued Berlin Theatre Songs and American ones (2 records in one album) are out, with a new photograph by R. Avedon. I was surprised to see myself in windows again.[30]

Photo: Ted Mitchell

On 10 June 1971, shortly before leaving for The Netherlands to participate in a performance of Weill's Der Silbersee, Lenya abruptly married Richard Siemanowski, a documentary film-maker and nephew of composer Karol Szymanowski. Siemanowski hoped to produce a television documentary about Lenya, but it was never completed. Lenya kept the marriage largely a secret; she never mentioned it in correspondence to even her closest friends. The two never lived together. Lenya's succession of marriages after Weill's death, to three homosexual men, two of them alcoholics, ended with her divorce from Siemanowski on 11 June 1973.

I heard from London that a very exciting original orchestration of the Israeli national anthem by Weill has been found. I am leaving for Holland on the 16th of June. They're giving Der Silbersee and Royal Palace at the Holland Festival, with me doing the narrations.[62]

Lenya's "secret," fourth husband, Richard Siemanowski.

The rehearsals for *Mother Courage* are going very well indeed, and Herbert Machiz does a terrific job. I am still struggling with the enormity of the dialog. It's a tapeworm and just to handle all the props is a job in itself. The students are wonderful and needless to say, I am getting along with them beautifully. They gave me a surprise birthday party on stage and it could not have been sweeter. Its really lovely out here and the daily drive along the ocean to the university is a sheer delight. God, I wish I would have had the opportunity to learn under such ideal circumstances. It's just staggering the luxury of instruments, rehearsal halls, and God knows what. No wonder most of them delay their graduation. I would too.[67]

Shortly after marrying Siemanowski, Lenya went to Amsterdam to take part in a concert performance of Der Silbersee *(Weill and Georg Kaiser, 1933). Shown here rehearsing with Mary Lindsey (Fennimore), Lenya served as narrator. Photo: Maria Austria*

THE UNIVERSITY OF CALIFORNIA, IRVINE   SCHOOL OF FINE ARTS   PRESENTS

LOTTE LENYA
in
Bertolt Brecht's

MOTHER COURAGE

**Directed by
Herbert Machiz**

November 17-20, 23, 24, 26, 27   8:30 P.M.
Village Theatre   Gen. Admission $4.50
UCI Students $2.00   Tickets Available at the
Fine Arts Box Office   714/833-6617

At age seventy-three Lenya tackles Mother Courage, *in English, at the University of California at Irvine, November 1971, directed by Herbert Machiz.*

I worked with Brecht for three days on *Mother Courage* and he told me, "Lenya, you're much gentler. Your Mother Courage does not have to be a hyena of the battlefield." Overplaying the part—to play it like a Greek heroine—is, I think, just wrong. You have to keep the part in the frame in which it was written.

When I read the reviews of the Irvine production, I was amazed how little the critics bothered with the character of Mother Courage. Who was she? What does she deal in? She's a market tender who follows the camp and deals in socks, a little bit of brandy, whatever she can pick up. She's not a member of the Krupp family. She is fighting for survival, right? She's only making a living through the war; that doesn't mean she's *responsible* for it. (She's not a war criminal; this is a religious war, and

*Opposite: Lenya on Laguna Beach, 1971.
Photo: Ted Mitchell*

Following pages: Blocking with director Herbert Machiz; Lenya as Mother Courage, *Irvine, 1971.*

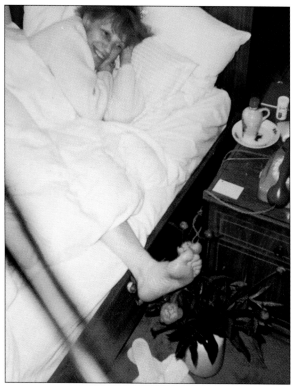

Relaxing at home during the 1970's.

New City neighbor and confidant, Martus Granirer, captures Lenya in the 1970s.

Mother Courage didn't start it.) She doesn't get rich from the war; she remains poor to the very end. Mother Courage is just trying to make a living for herself and her children, and she's trying to protect her children. Her first entrance she says, "You're not going to make war with my children." Then in the third scene, when Eilif asks how the others are, she says, "Thank God, Swiss Cheese has become paymaster, and I've kept him out of the fighting." So she protects her children all the way through. *That's* her function. The only time she falters is when she haggles about paying $200 for Swiss Cheese. She says she can't pay it; she has to have something left in her hand, because if she has nothing, any bastard could throw her in the gutter. Even then, though, she tries to rescue him: "Run," she says, "and tell them I'll pay the $200." But it's too late, and Swiss Cheese gets killed.

All those things have not been mentioned in the reviews. I think the function of a critic is to review not only the performer, but also to go into the play. This play says so much about corruption, religion, you name it. If the critics would only *listen*, it would practically write their reviews for them. I think they don't understand the play, so they skip over it as fast as they can—"just another Brecht"—and praise or attack the performer. That's the easiest way out. The critics' responsibility must be to educate the audience, and they haven't done it.

A critic must be very intelligent to praise for the right reasons. Also, a critic must be very intelligent not to tear down for the wrong reasons. In this case, they've torn down for the wrong reasons. Have you ever heard of an actress who was "tired" on opening night? I would like to find that actress. Or did I "play down" on account of the students? I didn't have to do that; these students were excellent. On the contrary, I played *up* to them, gave them all I had. I gave them everything I understood about the character of Mother Courage, and this I *discussed* with Brecht![79]

Somehow it feels good to be home again, though I had a wonderful time out there. I am most happy when I am on stage. But that's no news to me, I only forget it once in a while.[67]

In the middle of March I go to Tallahassee for the *Threepenny Opera* in which I play Jenny—I hope for the last time! After that, I am not doing a thing and will take care of my house and myself for a change.[48]

Indeed Lenya's Jenny at the University of Florida was the last role she played in a theater. She spent her last decade enjoying her reputation by giving television interviews, accepting limited guest appearances, taking a cameo role in a film, and collecting awards.

I am not doing anything, and I sometimes wonder whether I will ever do anything worthwhile again. Got an offer for a Polanski film [*What?*, starring Sydne Rome and Marcello Mastroianni] but it was just too foolish a part. No lines at all—just appearing in a nurse's uniform. I don't know what he had in mind offering me a part like that, which could easily be played by any nurse out of a hospital.

When Russi's paintings arrived from the exhibition in Tallahassee about two weeks ago and the driver did not find me in, he parked his truck on 123rd St. and 3rd Ave., the worst crime district in the city. When he returned after dinner, the truck had been broken into and two of my most beloved paintings—The *7 Deadly Sins* and *Surabaya Johnny*—were missing. Ever since I have spent a lot of time at the police and the FBI trying to get them back. I also put out a reward of $1,000 for their return. Since they were evidently stolen by some drug addicts, the police are very doubtful about their return.

October 30th was three years since Russi's death, and I still miss him very much. It's lonesome without him, difficult as he was sometimes. I visited his parents a few months ago. I looked at his father's hands, which are so very much like Russi's. I wonder how much damage he did to Russi. He surely did not understand that complicated creature.[48]

It's awful to live alone. I am thinking of selling the house eventually. It lost its function. I am not quite ready yet, there is still a thread, no matter how slender, that keeps me here. When Kurt died I was convinced that I would never smile again. I was wrong. And that I must remember in these days of depression, when I feel like running away but not knowing where to go. So, here I'll stay until the time when I can leave and take all the memories with me without pain. I don't know what got me into that mood. It's a lovely, sunny day. Forget this gloomy letter. I have not written too many of those.[4]

Top: **Surabaya Johnny** *by Russell Detwiler at the LeMoyne Art Foundation, Tallahassee, Florida, 16 April-7 May 1972. The exhibit, entitled "Detwiler Paints: The Music of Kurt Weill / The World of Lotte Lenya," was held in conjunction with Lenya's last stage appearance, at the age of 73, as Jenny in* The Threepenny Opera. *Bottom:* **The Seven Deadly Sins.** *Photos: Joe Kairis*

Weill scholar, business associate, and friend David Drew in the late 1950's, shortly after they met. Photo: Neil Fujita

With Lys Symonette in 1975, who worked with Weill from 1945 until his death and became Lenya's accompanist and musical adviser. Photo: Berkey

In 1973 Lenya engaged David Drew to be the "European Manager of the Kurt Weill Estate." Drew encouraged her to demystify the recorded story of her life.

David made me write the first episode of my life. He told me to just write five lines and then he would tell me whether to go on. Well, I got so mad at myself for stalling for so many years that I just sat down and wrote two pages. He was very happy with the result, so now I'm trying to write two pages every week to send to him. I think the more I write, the easier it will get. Maybe not, because maybe it gets more difficult when you discover the danger of trying to make up stories. But I am already fully aware of that, so "schtick" to the truth Kid—it's bad enough.[13]

I canceled the Dick Cavett show for the time being. My accompanist, Lys Symonette, is on vacation and without her, I am lost. I also did want to sing a new song, "Nannas Lied," and for that I need her help. So maybe I will do the show in September, or later. Right now he is a little mad at me. But I want to do a good job and not jacking along like one of the Gabor sisters.[13, 48]

Last week through x-rays they found what is going on beyond the 38th parallel—it's called a "hiatus hernia." Harmless as they say, incurable as they say, something one has to learn to live with, which means, no liquor, no spicy foods, no cold drinks, no raw vegetables or salads. With one word, as dull a diet as possible. Well, if that is all they want, they shall have it. I gave up smoking overnight, and surely can adjust my life to that diet. Its harmless enough.

I did a small part in a TV play for Play-Time 90 CBS, written by Steven Rossen. It was fun doing it, but it was canceled after a few tries.[4, 13]

How do you like Novotny's suggestion to let another singer [in a Lenya portrait] sing a song. F,,, them. The script was so bad anyway. Siemanowski's was almost a classic compared to theirs. I am glad I got out of that. They will hate me in my home town, but who cares?[67]

Today is the first day I try to stop smoking. I was up to almost two packs a day and the result is a devastating one. Headaches, dizziness and listlessness, beside trembling like Parkinson's disease. It's 3 P.M. and I have not tried to sneak one in. But the day is not over yet. Anyway, it's worth trying. . . . Well darling, I just broke down and had my first cigarette, which isn't too bad.[47]

[Letter to Universal Edition]

If I answer your letter of 9 December only today it is because of the following reason: I was so shocked by the content of your letter that I needed a bit of time to recover from it. Ever since Weill passed away in 1950, I have been working uninterruptedly in one form or another to promote his music. When I returned in 1951 for the first time since the war, I didn't find a trace of Weill displayed in any of the music stores, whereas almost every well-known or unknown composer was represented. It seemed as if Weill had never existed at all. Only through my recordings as they came along throughout the years: *Mahagonny, Dreigroschenoper, Happy End, The Seven Deadly Sins* and through the many concerts I have given in Carnegie Hall and various universities has the "Weill Renaissance" been given a start.

And now, as far as the movie deal is concerned, you claim, "on the other hand, there is, of course, this cursed temptation of money." In the course of these years I have spent a small fortune to promote Weill's music, and I will continue to do so. So please don't talk to me about "temptation of money." If it was up to me, this movie needs never to be made, and I wouldn't shed a tear if the entire project comes to naught. By the way: I have not *recently* acquired an attorney, thus inducing you to engage one for yourself. I have had my attorney for years, and he is by no means a recent "acquisition."[69]

Above: Portrait of Lenya by Richard Ely.
Below: Bertha Case (left) and Lenya. Case, an artist's agent,
represented the interests of Bertolt Brecht's estate in the U.S.
for many years and also represented Lenya. She was Lenya's
close friend and frequent card table partner.

I just came back from Philadelphia, where the Curtis Institute for Music gave an all-Weill evening with great success. Hearing those young people sing his music made me very happy.[4]

As soon as I have caught up with my accumulated mail I will see you [Bertha Case] and then you can clobber me in Canasti (as our one-time friend Jimmy called it). Anna Krebs, my friend from Hamburg, is arriving Saturday for three weeks. She will clean my house, which she loves to do, being German. While I was away I read Logan's autobiography (excellent) and Mary Hemingway's, which will come out in September. She sure can write. Kenji the cat had an operation while I was away but is fine now. He did not "talk" to me for two days. Mad as hell because I was away. The fat one Teeko just rolled on his back to show me what he has not got anymore.[15]

I got a movie job. Cameo part, a masseuse with an accent. I will have the pleasure of digging into Burt Reynolds. Could be worse. Only a day and a half shooting and good money.

I was in Miami for one day of shooting "Semi Tough" with Burt Reynolds, who is a dream to work with. It was 95 degrees in the studio and I kept drinking water from a fountain all day long. I studied Rolfing technique a little bit to prepare for the part. Burt looked like a huge tree trunk lying on the massage table. I dug into him and said, "Burt, I'm so afraid I'm hurting you." He said, "No, not at all. I rather enjoy it." The next day I came down with a fierce dysentery and had to stay in bed for 3 days. They cut my hair (what hair?) for the picture and I look like an old Frankie Adams out of "Member of the Wedding." It might do my hair good in the end to have it so radically cut. Those are the things one does for the "Arts."[17, 47]

Bertha Case, my agent, will be here for three days. She is fun, loves to play cards, and drinks a lot.[47]

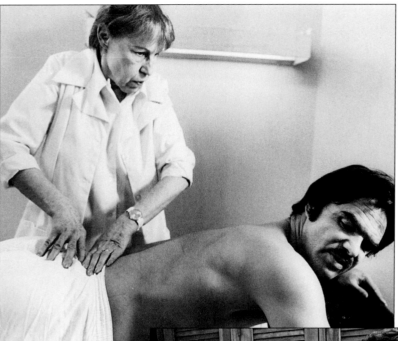

[Letter to Universal Edition]
First let me say that I am very pleased that you want to include the English text in a printed *Drei-groschenoper.* Now when you ask me whether I feel that the new Manheim-Willett transla-tion is the best one, I must say that presently I prefer the one by Marc Blitzstein. I find it infinitely more singable and com-patible to the musical values. If you would ask Stefan Brecht, however, he would probably prefer the new Manheim-Willett version. There will be a new cast album of the present NY performances coming out next season. Why don't you wait until I send it to you so you can judge yourself by comparing it to the recording of the Blitzstein version.[69]

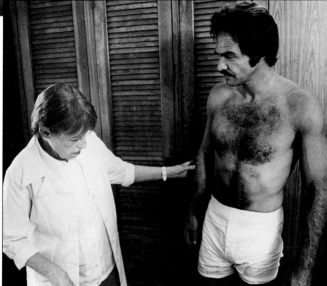

Top: Lenya, as Dr. Clara Pelf, working on Burt Reynolds in a scene from the film Semi-Tough, *1977. Bottom: Examining the patient. Photos: United Artists*

I am preparing—and what a job it is!—an exhibition for the Lincoln Center Library: Kurt Weill & Lotte Lenya. Collecting all the music, photos, scores, etc., will keep me busy all summer long. The *Threepenny Opera* is playing at Lincoln Center and a great success. I have not seen it yet, but friends tell me it is very good. Walter Kerr wrote beautiful things about it in the Sunday *Times.* Needless to say, that made me very happy.[48]

The exhibition will be the 5th of November, and I will be glad when it's over. You can't imagine how much work is involved, and I am sick and tired looking at my pictures and reading whatever has been written about me. And there is quite a lot.[47]

There is a little bit more in the exhibition on my career than on Kurt Weill's, but this is because Kurt Weill died in 1950 and I'm still here. He left his whole estate to me, and I don't feel like

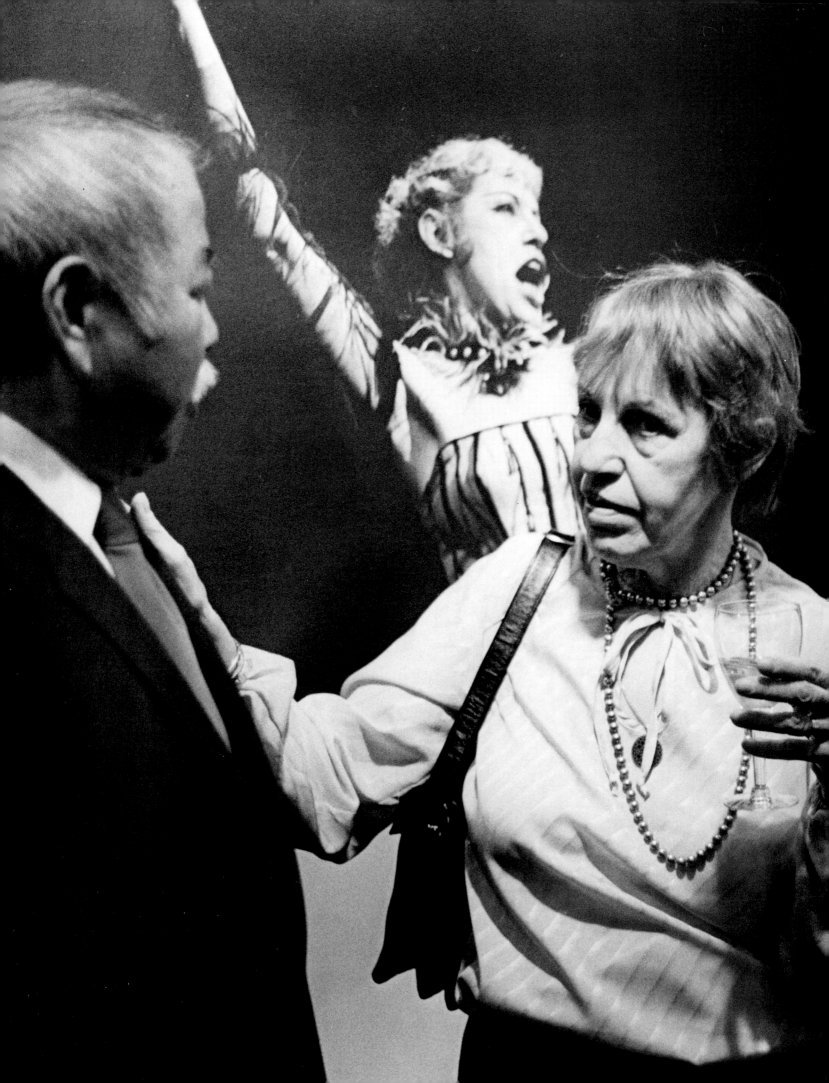

sitting back and collecting royalties the way so many widows do. That is why we are having the exhibition of stage sets, photographs, manuscripts, and drawings. Besides my work on stage, the major part of my life is Kurt Weill. I'm not so important.[18]

[Letter to Universal Edition]
Thank you for your letter of 26 April in which you inform me of your decision to leave the adaptation of *Die Bürgschaft* in the hands of Gottfried von Einem and his wife. I doubt very much whether any *Bürgschaft* sketches can be found in Neher's estate. I consider this work to perhaps be the most important one among all of Weill's works, and the very thought of having it "adapted" disturbs me greatly. It is a very somber work and has been conceived as such. In all of the operatic repertoire it is certainly not the only one with a tragic ending. Making cuts is a rather well known procedure and perhaps it should be left to the director to—as they say— "tighten" it. "Adaptation" is something else altogether. I would be most grateful if you could let me know what exactly Mr. von Einem has in mind by "re-modeling" the work.[69]

I am still recovering from that rather severe operation. Margo Harris is a great help to me. She nursed her late husband for five years and knows how to treat me when I get impatient.[48]

My aim now is to bring back the music from Weill's classical period, which is not known in this country. Everyone knows Weill from all those song programs like "a gala evening with Miss so and so," as if he had done nothing but write theater songs. But he was a full-fledged composer who wrote operas, oratorios, symphonies, and no one knows anything about it. The Greenwich Symphony just did a concert at Avery Fisher Hall with the *Symphony no. 1, Little Threepenny Music, The New Orpheus,* and *Quodlibet.* Now, that's a first.[17]

The 80 years lie comfortably on my shoulders. It's such a pleasure not to have to count anymore. As a matter of fact, I never lied about my age. I think it is a blessing to have reached that age and not need crutches. I am invited to a cocktail party for Vera Stravinsky's 90th birthday. She is as lively as a bird on the wings (lyrics by Hammerstein) I was told. It's snowing the first

Hirschfeld's caricature of Weill and Lenya printed in the New York Times *report on the* Weill-Lenya *exhibition, 12 November 1976. © Al Hirschfeld. Art reproduced by special arrangement with Hirschfeld's exclusive representative, The Margo Feiden Galleries Ltd. New York*

Opposite: The New York Public Library mounted the first exhibition devoted to documenting Weill's and Lenya's careers, 1976. To honor the occasion, Lenya donated Weill's manuscript score of Die sieben Todsünden *to the library. Lenya is pictured here with photographer and designer Neil Fujita. Photo: Lee Snider*

Made up "glamourous," ca. 1976.

Advertisement for two half-hour interviews given by Lenya to Schuyler Chapin for public television, December 1978-January 1979 (the interviews were aired early in 1979). The segments were entitled "Lenya: The Berlin Years" and "Lenya: Paris—New York." Photo: C. Brownie Harris

Opposite: Being interviewed by Schuyler Chapin, 1978.

snow, and I wish I could stay in the house hibernating until the first crocuses. I *am* tired from last year—two major operations and now an injured hand. I've had it. Otherwise, I'm OK. My hand is tired now from typing with one finger, so I say goodbye.[49]

It's a great blessing to celebrate your eightieth birthday. I'm interested in counting the years, not in dying. I was never worried by age. Not at fifty, not at seventy. I enjoy living. I can think of only a few American actresses who readily admit their age. Actually, three: Ruth Gordon, Marlene Dietrich, and Lotte Lenya.[17]

I feel fine looking forward to *Mahagonny* at the Met and next year's production of *Silbersee* which has Hal Prince doing it. It is in good hands. The Met rehearsals start October 16th, the opening on November 16th. They have a good cast and a good stage designer, Jocelyn Herbert, who was the girlfriend of George

LENYA
THE BERLIN YEARS

Lenya congratulating the Greenwich Philharmonic after a concert at Lincoln Center honoring her eightieth birthday. The all-Weill program consisted of the Symphony no. 1 *(1921),* Kleine Dreigroschenmusik *(for wind band, 1928),* Der neue Orpheus *(a cantata for soprano, violin, and orchestra, text by Ivan Goll, 1925), and* Quodlibet *(suite for orchestra, 1923). Lenya had broken her wrist a few weeks earlier and concealed her sling by wearing a bright red bathrobe to the concert. Photo: Gretchen Tatge*

Lenya (left) being feted at a dinner after the first performance of The Rise and Fall of the City of Mahagonny *at the Metropolitan Opera, New York.*

Devine, a good friend of mine from the days I played at the Royal Court Theater in London. I will be at the rehearsals of *Mahagonny* everyday. Good Luck Miss L....![49]

None of the young singers can sing Kurt Weill. None of them. There's only one, and that's Teresa Stratas. She's born with it, you know? She loved the music, and she can do no wrong. So, when she sang Jenny in *Mahagonny* at the Met, I met her after. I said "Teresa, here is my crown. I give it to you now. You are the one, so you carry on." And now she sings Weill like he wrote it for her.[70]

I am happy about the big success of *Mahagonny* which has put Kurt where he belongs. Away from just a writer of songs. The most important composer of the 20th century. That was my xmas present—a happy one.

I finally got to listen to the recording of *Die Bürgschaft* [Sender Freies Berlin, conducted by Janos Kulka]. What in heaven's sake had the conductor in mind cutting two bars here, four bars there, etc. Terrible tempos. I'm afraid to say what I really think about it. So many cuts for no reason (maybe for length?). The singers—well, they depend on the conductor. I can't say I like any of them. Thomas Stewart was the best, but still not good enough.[49]

Soprano Teresa Stratas at her famous Whitney Museum recital, 4 January 1980.

Lenya died on 27 November 1981 of ovarian cancer. She had undergone two operations for the disease, and its progression was probably accelerated by senseless cosmetic breast surgery nine months before her death. In spite of her weakened condition, she continued to watch over Weill's legacy and share her realistic philosophies on life.

I never gave permission nor will I ever give authorization to Barbara Schall-Brecht or anyone else to alter instrumentation or make any musical changes in *Threepenny* performances in East Berlin.[69]

I would go on stage again, of course I would! But movies would be even better. I would like to play in a movie again. It's somehow easier. I'd enjoy that very much.[26]

Bootlicking was never one of my talents and I'm not going to start now.[21]

Oh well, one cannot do right by everybody. Kick back once in awhile. It's a healthy and well-liked reaction. Better than to duck. I learned that the hard way. I better stop now before I spread around too much Readers Digest wisdom.[21]

Opera News *devoted the 1 December 1979 issue to the Metropolitan Opera premiere of* Rise and Fall of the City of Mahagonny. *The photo of Weill is by Lotte Jacabi, Berlin, 1929.* © Opera News 1998

If you let anger get a hold of you, you will usually lose out in the end. This I learned the "hard way" but now I know how to preserve my strength. I've wanted to spit sometimes too (the black widow), and I smiled instead.[42]

Pete brought me a heavenly vase full with autumn leaves today. They look so beautiful. How much closer to God can one get? And a beautiful blue heron flew over the brook. Nature can make me cry faster than anything.[21]

Applause is a fading thing. So is fame. So, don't rely too much on it. Whether you have instant recognition or get it a little later, what difference does it make?[70]

Lenya on the grounds of Brook House, May 1981. Photos: Ted Mitchell

Legends: On Life and Art

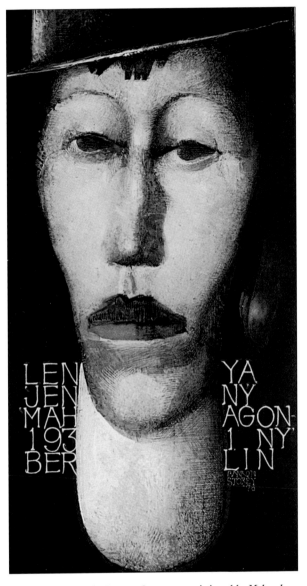

Portrait of Lenya by Barron Storey, commissioned by Mohawk Paper, 1976. The work commemorates Lenya's characterization of Jenny in Mahagonny, *Berlin, 1931.*

Lenya's passing is indeed very sad, but remember that she accomplished her mission to place Kurt Weill on the top list of composers and without her zest and zeal he could have been forgotten. How fortunate we all are for her belief, which in turn is our belief in her.[35]

—LILLIAN GISH, actress

The kind of songs that Trude Hesterberg and Rosa Valetti were singing in the cabarets had absolutely nothing to do with Kurt Weill. I mean, take Dietrich's "*Ich bin von Kopf bis Fuss auf Liebe eingestellt*" ["Falling in love again, never wanted to."] That has nothing to do with Brecht and Weill. That's a typical cabaret song. The standards were completely different in cabaret, you know?[8]

Anita Berber was a very beautiful girl, and a dancer. And she danced primarily in night clubs. And in the nude. So, if you think we are so far ahead now with the nudity, no, we had it all in Berlin forty years ago. And, of course, at that time drugs were different kinds of drugs. I think she took cocaine, and morphine, and died at the age of twenty-eight, which was very sad. But

Reclining in the South of France, late 1920's.

Below: Fritzi Massary in costume, ca. 1925. Photo: Bildarchiv Preussischer Kulturbesitz

many, many lesser known people died the same way at that time. People now make such a big deal about her famous "Dance of Lust" but it would be like going into a kindergarten now. I loved her too much to call her dirty. She was just exotic and strange, and that's what made her so special, you know?[16]

Heinz Tietjen once said, since Massary—Fritzi Massary—he hasn't heard anyone with diction like mine. She was an operetta singer in Berlin, the greatest who ever lived. Marvelous. Wonderful. Elegant. My god, I couldn't have been more flattered. It was one of the greatest compliments I've ever gotten, to be compared with her.[8]

You know the fabulous Twenties. Everyone was a *femme fatale* and everybody slept with everybody. Nobody took it very seriously. But what era wouldn't be decadent if you lose a war? It was as decadent then as it is here. Don't you think disco is decadent? I don't think that Berlin decadence is romanticized—it was real—but do you think they all were spending the night in nightclubs? People always forget that in Berlin there were some people who really got up in the morning and went to work! I think *The Blue Angel* and *The Threepenny Opera* were very close, true to life. It was a time from 1926 to '33. How could it ever come back? You will have your own time, because look at it today.[71, 72]

Walter Huston? Well, you see, it's a personality. That crackly voice of his, that's the personality, and that has a great deal to do with how people sing the songs. For instance, I have heard "September Song" sung beautifully by two people very different from each other. One by Eddie Albert, who sang it heartbreakingly beautiful. And Jimmy Durante.

Oh, I could barely hold back my tears when he sang it, it was so lovely. But there you are. You couldn't find two more different people.

You can't really compare Mary Martin to Dietrich. Mary was fabulous in *Venus*. Dietrich didn't want to do it, maybe because of the sustained tune in "Speak Low." Mary Martin has a very trained voice, which is different than Dietrich.[8]

I sure love the Billie Holiday record. She is my favorite singer. My heart starts aching when I hear her sing. Tonight I am going to see the movie with Diana Ross in the B.H. story. She got marvelous reviews. I am still doubtful that I will like her. Nobody can sing like Holiday. . . . Yes, I saw *The Lady Sings the Blues*. Diana Ross is a very gifted singer, but of course it's impossible to reproduce a Billie Holiday. She did the best she could. The whole picture was done to make money, and that's what they are going to get. That too shall pass.[48]

Barbra Streisand can do no wrong. She excited me very much, but Judy Garland just breaks my heart. Barbra Streisand is so wonderful, but I don't understand some of her movies. That *Up in the Sandbox*, or whatever it was called—I wanted to walk out. I just saw *On a Clear Day*. Streisand is just incredibly marvelous. I dislike the movie and the score I found completely uninspired. One bad song after the other. And my dreamboy Yves Montand, I found not so good. Language does hamper him.[18]

Signing autographs after a concert, Lewisohn Stadium, New York, July 1958. Photo: Bernard Seeman

Did you hear that boring concert by Pavarotti from Montreal?[67]

Opera singers have to be both good singers and actors. Callas and Schwarzkopf are brilliant examples. Look how Schwarzkopf develops the role of the Marschallin in *Rosenkavalier*. Whereas Lotte Lehmann was resigned from the start, Schwarzkopf is happily in love at the beginning and only becomes resigned—and tragic—at the end. This is great acting.

Like a friend of mine said, "I love that voice of Lenya, it's one octave below laryngitis." Which is not true, there are much deeper voices. Lauren Bacall. Her voice is down in the cellar. So is Katharine Hepburn's voice. [Imitating Hepburn] "My god, ee-oo."[8]

Swimming in the Mediterranean,
South of France, 1928.

South of France, 1928.

Below: London, 1934. Photo: Gerty Simon

Skiing in the Alps, late 1920s or early 1930s.

Kurt talked a great deal about Busoni's humor, about all the little dirty jokes he used to tell them in between teaching. Busoni was also very superstitious. He had a woman there, a little hunchback named Rita Boetticher. Busoni thought it was good luck to touch her. Kurt thought she was a horror, but she was there all the time watching over Busoni, in spite of his wife Gerda. Rita belonged to the house.[72]

Well, yes, Carl Orff is very much influenced by Kurt Weill, but everybody knows that, including himself. I saw a very, very good opera of his, *Die Kluge*, done by the Komische Oper in East Berlin with Felsenstein. Very much influenced by Kurt Weill. The whole beginning was just taken out of *Die Bürgschaft*.[8]

Among modern composers my favorite is Britten. I love everything of his, and I have every record of his music available. I love Stravinsky, of course, and Bartók and Hindemith, but these are of the older generation. Of younger composers, apart from Britten, I think I find Henze the most interesting.[63]

Lenya celebrates in her New York apartment after her last Carnegie Hall concert, 8 January 1965. Photo: Ted Mitchell

I think surely Leonard Bernstein knows every note of Kurt Weill. I'm sure he does. Oh, he knows more than the *Threepenny Opera*. And he is the one who took up after Weill's death. I think Leonard Bernstein is the closest to Kurt Weill. His *West Side Story*—which I think is lovely and beautiful—his *Candide*, which I think is a marvelous score. So, you see, those are the things Kurt Weill would have done, too, if he would have lived, you know?[8]

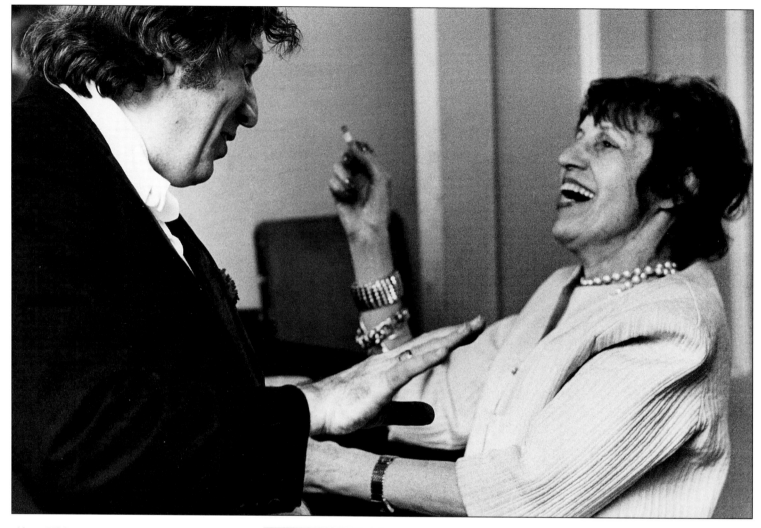

Above: With composer Gunther Schuller at the Holland Festival, June 1971. Schuller had reorchestrated Weill's early opera, Royal Palace *(1927) after the original score and parts were lost. Photo: Fletcher Drake*

Right: With Alan Jay Lerner (left) at a banquet, ca. 1978.

Once Weill picked up a book from Brecht's nightstand. The dust jacket said *Das Kapital* but inside was an Edgar Wallace thriller.

Brecht once went with Aufricht to von Mendelssohn's home, a huge house filled with treasures, El Grecos, Rembrandts, Renoirs, fabulous furniture, rugs, etc. Brecht sat down and looked around. When Aufricht asked him what he thought, he said, "If they'd clear out all this shit, it would make a nice house."[45]

To say that Brecht was a good director is an understatement. He was incredible. That was his second genius. And what always amazed me was the incredible patience he had with actors. Never yelling, just showing. So, you couldn't fail, you know?[70]

One cannot explain Brecht easily or shove him in a corner by saying his work was just an expression of his communism. I don't think he took his political life too seriously. What he did take seriously were the human aspects of life. In the last verse of one of his ballads he writes, "We who wished to plant the seeds of kindness, Could not ourselves be kind. But you to be born in a time, When man to man is a helper at last, Think of us in the past, With understanding." He knew that not all good could survive and there were times when we had to be evil. But he believed in what lay ahead. This is where the misunderstanding of Brecht arises.[32]

I think that an opera like *Street Scene* could have very well been written by Brecht. It attacks poverty, and it shows the melting pot of those poor people in that tenement house. It could have been written by Brecht. And also, when he went back to East Germany, he still had the same things to attack which he had attacked before. But in this country there was less to attack.[8]

Anna sent me the book by Klaus Mann, *Mephisto*. For a *roman à clef* it's easy to guess whom he means. It's well written, but I don't think it would go well here. One has to have lived in Berlin to know the secrets. Why it was forbidden in 1968 is beyond me. Don't the Germans like to be reminded of their glorious times?[49]

Have you read *Lolita*? It's beautifully written and a tender story. Not at all dirty as so many people (with a dirty mind) say.[21]

Lenya was fascinated by Greta Garbo and kept two pictures of her in New York apartment.

If you have talent for an art, it shows early in life. My late husband Russell Detwiler was an artist and wanted me to try to paint. But if I'd had the talent, it would have showed early. It didn't.[9]

I was invited to the Hornicks for New Year's. They are great collectors of modern paintings, and the neighborhood gets upset with their ultra modern sculptures on the lawn. I find them rather beautiful, but I have been around—as they say—that's why I like them.

A funny story. I saw in Philadelphia the unveiling of a marvelous, powerful sculpture by Jacques Lipschitz, and the band (consisting of firemen) played with an Irish tenor singing at the top of his Irish lungs "Get me to the church on time." I saw Mrs. Lipschitz bowing her head . . .[4]

They should shoot television! Except for educational television. I never got a television job, and I don't care. They should remove it from the earth. Gunsmoke! Smoky Guns! Gun Does What? How many tricks does a gun do? It never ends. This generation will be a generation of nitwits![25]

The young actors of today are very dedicated. What spoils them is if they are grabbed by Hollywood and become stars. Then the modesty of the profession goes out the window.[36]

I think the young actresses of today are marvelous, especially the movie actresses. Everyone always goes back to Bette Davis or to Joan Crawford. Sure, they were very good, surely excellent, but there are so many good young ones too. Like Jill Clayburgh, who is a dream of an actress. She's fascinating in *Unmarried Woman.* Many young ones are just as fabulous as the old ones were. There's no such thing as a "golden age of talent." The United States right now is full of talent. Kurt was always floored at the range of talent he found when he held auditions. He'd say, "It's staggering." In a way, New York City today is like Berlin of the twenties, but without Hitler.[17]

It's too hot to go into town, but I did make myself go see *Hamlet* with Richard Burton. Quite an experience. He is a completely unorthodox Hamlet, humorous and tragic, with a peasant-like elegance. So very, very different from all the Hamlets I have ever seen. When we left the theater, there were thousands

*With soprano Birgit
Nilsson and actress
Liv Ullmann, 1980.*

of people standing in line, with mounted police around them, just to see Miss Taylor and him riding by in their closed limousine. Needless to say, we did not wait for this event, as much as we love them.[48]

I don't want to have actors over to my house. Actors' stories are so boring, but I love Katharine Hepburn, Tammy Grimes and Ruth Gordon. Just lately I have been invited out many times myself. I went to that terrible party NBC had at Sardi's. I go out when Fred Ebb is doing something, and the other night I went to see Chita Rivera. Now I am looking forward to a little peace, and to raking my leaves in the country.[18]

I adore Bea Arthur's *Maude*, because for two years I shared the same little dressing room with her when we did the *Threepenny Opera*. I think she's a marvelous comedienne.[36]

I go to the theater very often. I love musicals. I saw *Chorus Line* and I saw *Chicago* three

With soprano Astrid Varnay, 1975.

From left: famous boxer Max Schmeling, Lothar Olias,
singer Greta Keller, and Lenya, in Hamburg, mid-1950's.
Photo: H. Meyer-Pfundt

times. I adore it. I haven't seen the new *Porgy* but I sat next to Gershwin when it opened, and he was heartbroken because it was a failure. I saw *The Wiz*, but no matter how I tried I couldn't forget Judy Garland.[18]

I don't want to see *Oh, Calcutta!* [a play performed largely in the nude]. I wouldn't be able to concentrate on what the actors are saying. I am not a prude, but what do the actors hang on to? The Folies Bergères does it better and does it deliberately.

The Boys in the Band clears the air. Homosexuality has existed for thousands of years and did not disappear just because we closed our eyes. I believe in "live and let live." If people are born that way, it's fine with me. The very fact that we can now talk about homosexuality in plays and on the screen is a great step forward. There are enough people marrying and having children as it is.[31]

Speaking of dancing, I went to see *On Your Toes*. I didn't care too much for the show, but I was utterly enchanted by

With Kenji Fujita, Lenya's godson and son of Neil Fujita,
artist and friend of Lenya who designed several album jackets
for her. Photo: Neil Fujita

Zorina in her ballet, "Slaughter on 10th Ave." First, she looked
ravishingly beautiful in a very Berlin 20s way, and danced better
than I had ever seen her before.[12]

Sweeney Todd! Something I never thought I'd see—Max
Reinhardt meets Bert Brecht![71]

I didn't think I could have children because of two abor-
tions I had in Zurich when I was young—fifteen or sixteen. Later,
in Vienna, a doctor told me I could have the passages unblocked
and have a child. I was with Pasetti at the time, and he wanted us
to have a child together. So, I went to Kurt, "Pasetti wants a
child." He looked at me and said, "But that would hurt me very
much." Later, at the age of 42, I brought up the topic with Kurt
again. "Do you want a child or not, because soon the gate will be
closed, and I'd really love to have one." He said, "Darling, I'm

Brook House, New City, New York, mid-60's:

Opposite page: Outside in autumn.
Top, left: Raking leaves.
Top, right: Gardening in April.
Left: Relaxing incognito on the porch.

Playing with Wooly, the Weills' sheepdog, in New City, mid-1940's.

scared to death that something would happen to you. I must tell you something. I don't have any vanity that my name should live on through my son. I hope my name lives on through my music." That was his vanity.[72]

Here at the hotel is a little girl six years old, an Armenian child, speaks Arabic, Turkish, English, and a little French. The parents leave her alone all day and she and I have become good friends. I wish she were an orphan. That's the kind of child I would like to have. She has the most beautiful dark eyes, dark hair, and as fragile as a lotus flower. But what a temperament. Cheats like a Turk and is quick as a lizard. What a dreamchild![21]

When I was a child I asked my mother if I was pretty. "No," she told me truthfully, then wisely added, "But men will always love you." Love, of course is the greatest beauty secret of them all. There is one democracy we all live under: time. We all grow older, and we must learn to accept what time does to us. I have always been a character actress so I never needed to worry about the lines in my face—they are better for me—but maybe in ten years I might want to have them removed. I see nothing wrong when a woman does so. But I often wonder what good it does when the hands and elbows are so revealing, anyway. I believe it's better not to worry about such things, to be yourself and not take life too seriously. My early years as a circus performer and dancer have been invaluable. I don't exercise anymore, but I love to take long walks in the country with my two dogs. I don't wear make-up, except lipstick and eyeshadow unless I'm going out. I think the skin should have a chance to breathe and besides I like shiny faces. I adore false eyelashes. They are the greatest invention since the zipper and Scotch tape. On stage I wear two pairs. I have never thought much about glamor because I have never "sold" glamor. I'm more interested in what people are. Maybe I'm a sucker for being so optimistic about life, but it keeps me happy.[19]

Recording session. Photo: Sony Records

Remember, I'm not a German, I'm Viennese. There's an old saying: "In Berlin the situation is serious but not hopeless. In Vienna the situation is hopeless but not serious."[20]

Reagan scares the shit out of everybody, so one chooses the lesser evil Carter. At least he knows what a *Geistes Kind* he is [what kind of person he is].

My Christmas was boring as I find all mass holidays. That explosion of sudden kindness makes me sick. As soon as the Christmas tree loses its needles, people are as bitchy as they were before.[49]

Every September my royalties go up![17]

The greater they are, the simpler they are. Einstein impressed me most of anyone I have ever met. He knew how to keep quiet. When he had nothing to say, he didn't talk.[9]

I cannot cook, and have no intention of learning. I can boil eggs. I have not quite recovered from my two major operations, and have to take it easy. So no disco dancing at 54 Club.[4]

Gretel Kaiser was in heaven. It was just one more experience for her to see what it means to be an American. The friendliness of the people, their warmth to take one in immediately, means a lot to her. I hope she won't forget it when she goes back to Germany.[21]

There is nothing wrong with being romantic, as long as one knows it oneself. It's much easier to cope with life if one knows a little bit about oneself.[4]

I don't play bridge, I play poker. I'm a great poker player.[8]

It's not always wise to trust women.[49]

Woman's liberation bores me to death. It's so nice to be dependent on a man. I can't think of anything nicer. Besides, I was born free and remain that way.[23]

To be loved by everybody—I would wonder about that kind of love.

When someone studies you to the point of hating you, it may be disconcerting, but it's also a fantastic compliment.[34]

I really don't know what the mystery is. The youngsters look at me as if I'm a living legend—or a ghost![54]

It's nice being called a legend. Why should I mind being called that? I think it's very flattering, don't you, to be a legend and still be alive and kicking. If you become a legend you must have made your point somewhere. Perhaps I did something which, if you want to get hifalutin, is recognized as art.[23]

Opposite: A classic portrait from the 1940's.

CHRONOLOGY

This chronology lists Lenya's major performances, records key events in her life, and presents a skeletal picture of her movements and relationships. Only the most significant of her hundreds of appearances on radio and television are included. Lenya recalls a number of performances—especially from her time in Zurich and early years in Berlin—for which there is no corroborating record; such performances are not included in this listing. Accounts of her early life are largely based on her own recollections, which, in many cases, are vague or contradictory. Under these circumstances, dates have been assigned as exactly as possible, at least to within a year. Doubtful dates are noted with a question mark.

October 18, 1898: Karoline Wilhelmine Charlotte Blamauer born at Linzerstrasse 87 in the Penzing district of Vienna to Franz Paul Blamauer and Johanna Teuschl Blamauer. She was the third child born to the Blamauers; the first, also named Karoline, had died; the second, Franz, was born in 1897. Her brother Maximilian was born in 1900; her sister Maria in 1906.

1902 or 1903: The family moves to Ameisgasse 38 in the same district. Karoline sings and dances in a neighborhood circus with a tambourine and learns how to walk a tightrope.

1905: Begins Volksschule (elementary school), then moves to a different school after one year. After the third year she moves to a school for gifted children in Hietzing, a more prosperous area than Penzing.

1910: Begins Bürgerschule (middle school).

1913: Graduates from Bürgerschule, and spends the summer working in the Ita hat factory in Vienna, in what is supposed to be the beginning of a four-year apprenticeship.

Summer 1913: Travels to Zurich, arrives on 18 September 1913, and moves in with her aunt on Zeunerstrasse 7. She begins taking ballet lessons with Steffi Herzeg, the ballet mistress at the Stadttheater, and earns money as a maid for a theatrical photographer Alexander Ehrenzweig. Within a few months, she moves into the Ehrenzweig home at Kreuzstrasse 10.

6 May 1914: Returns to Vienna for the summer, where she learns that her parents have separated. World War I begins on 3 August 1914. Unable to travel without a contract from the Zurich Stadttheater, she writes a frantic letter to the Intendant, Alfred Reucker, who provides it.

31 August 1914: Returns to Zurich by train, moving back into the Ehrenzweig home. She continues ballet lessons and acting training at the theater.

Autumn 1914: Formally hired as an apprentice in the Zurich Stadttheater ballet company, at a salary of 60 francs per month. Late in 1914 or early in 1915, she begins taking private acting lessons with young director Richard Révy. Later Révy will use her in some of the productions he directs.

1914-1915 season: Appears in small roles in the following works: Zurich Pfauen Theater: Kehm and Frehsee's *Als ich noch im Flügelkleide* (Jettchen Uenzen), Hermann's *Jettchen Gebert* (Rosalie Jacoby; her first performance under Révy's direction), Suppé's *Fatinitza* (Gregor).

Spring 1915?: Moves in with the Edelmanns; her best friend is their daughter Greta, also a ballet student.

1915-1916 season: Appears in small roles in the following works: Pfauen Theater: *Als ich noch im Flügelkleide* (Jettchen Uenzen), Anzengruber's *Der G'wissenswurm* (Annemirl). Stadttheater: Will's *Dornröschen*, Vorspiel only (Immergrün), *Als ich noch im Flügelkleide* (Jettchen Uenzen), Lehár's *Die lustige Witwe* (Margot), R. Strauss's *Der Rosenkavalier* (hairdresser's assistant).

Autumn 1916?: Becomes a full-fledged member of the *corps de ballet*, at a salary of 160 francs per month. Her salary increases every year thereafter.

17 October 1916: Moves to Kilchberg, Switzerland.

1916-1917 season: Appears in small roles in the following works: Pfauen Theater: Blumenthal and Kadelburg's *Im weissen Rössl* (Mirzl), Friedmann-Friedrich's *Logierbesuch* (Rosie). Stadttheater: Weinberger's *Drei arme Teufel* (erstes Mädchen), Fall's *Der Waltenbummler* (erste Freundin), Blumenthal and Kadelburg's *Im weissen Rössl* (Mirzl).

26 February 1917: Moves back to Zurich.

9 March 1917: Appears in a Tanzabend (Dance Evening) at the Pfauen Theater, dancing to J. Strauss's "Leichtes Blut," Gounod's "Bacchanale," Lanner's "'D'Schönbrunner' Walzer," an ensemble number, and several "National-Tänze."

1917-1918 season: Appears in small roles in the following works: Pfauen Theater: Shaw's *Cäsar und Cleopatra* (Iras), Wedekind's *Franziska* (Karaminka; directed by Wedekind), Blümner's (adapted from Aristophanes) *Krieg und Frieden* (Megarer's daughter), Bahr's *Das Konzert* (Selma Maier), Wedekind's *Der Kammersänger* (ein Listjunge). Stadttheater: Lehár's *Der Sterngucker* (Mizzi), *Der Rosenkavalier*, conducted by Richard Strauss (hairdresser's assistant), Stolz's *Lang, lang ist's her* (Lauserl), Offenbach's *Blaubart* (third page).

11 September 1917: Appears in a Tanzabend at the Pfauen Theater, dancing to Roswitsch's "Russischer Nationaltanz" and J. Strauss's "Kaiserwalzer."

Spring 1918: With Greta Edelmann, becomes embroiled in a contract dispute with the Stadttheater. Despite the qualms of some members of the theater management, their contracts are renewed for the 1918-1919 season.

2 July 1918: Performs in a Tanzabend at the Pfauen Theater, dancing to Brahms's *Dance in F-sharp minor* and a Strauss waltz.

Summer 1918: Visits her family in Vienna. She finds that her mother has taken up with Ernst Heinisch, who now lives with the family on Ameisgasse.

Summer 1918: Ingeborg Ruvina becomes *Ballettmeisterin* at the Stadttheater. She emphasizes the Dalcroze method, which Karoline prefers to more traditional ballet instruction. However, a personality conflict soon manifests itself, and becomes worse over the next three years.

1918-1919 season: Appears in small roles in the following works: Pfauen Theater: Fulda's *Die verlorene Tochter* (Margot Straub), *Jettchen Gebert* (Rosalie Jacoby), *Im weissen Rössl* (Resi), Kornfeld's *Die Verführung* (Dancer), Auernheimer's *Die grosse Leidenschaft* (Emilie), *Cäsar und Cleopatra* (Iras), Faesi's *Die Fassade* (Lady), Schnitzler's *Das weite Land* (a Frenchwoman). Stadttheater: Lehár's *Wo die Lerche singt* (Juleza), J. Strauss's *Der Zigeunerbaron* (Sepl), Hermann's *Der gestiefelte Kater* (rescued child), Fall's *Die Rose von Stambul* (Fatme), *Cäsar und Cleopatra* (Iras).

4 September 1918: Dances in the second act of J. Strauss's *Die Fledermaus* in the Stadttheater. She dances with three others, including her teacher and her friend Greta Edelmann, to "An der schönen blauen Donau."

1919: Moves to Pension Griese at Dufourstrasse 177. She has previously been living with a Swiss sculptor named Mario Petrucci, and apparently moves to avoid scandal. At some point during 1919, Karoline becomes pregnant and has an abortion in Geneva.

22 January 1919: Opens as Lisiska in Frank Wedekind's *Tod und Teufel* in the Pfauen Theater, directed by Wedekind.

8 May 1919: Opens as Minna in Kurt Götz's *Nachtbeleuchtung* at the Pfauen Theater, directed by Richard Révy.

1919-1920 season: Appears in small roles in the following works: Pfauen Theater: Frank and Geyer's *Ein reizender Mensch* (Monika), Strindberg's *Kamaraden* (Therese), Rivoire and Besnard's *Mein Freund Teddy* (Francine), Gordon and Götz's *Die Rutschbahn* (young lady), Anzengruber's *Der Meineidbauer* (Crescenz), Kaiser's *Von Morgens bis Mitternachts* (first daughter), Tolstoy's *Der lebende Leichnam* (Sascha), Enderlin's *Die Fräulein von Saint-Cyr* (Marie von Havrincourt), *Die verlorene Tochter* (Margot Straub), *Tod und Teufel* (Lisiska). Stadttheater: Offenbach's *Die schöne Helena* (Leaena), Schubert's *Hannerl* (Frau Dussek), Lehár's *Eva* (Schischi), Ascher's *Der Künstlerpreis* (Mila), *Der Meineidbauer* (Crescenz), Eysler's *Ein Tag im Paradies* (Baroness Traxler), Millöcker's *Der Bettelstudent* (von Richthofen), *Mein Freund Teddy* (Francine).

October 1919: Mario Petrucci goes to Vienna and arranges for her sister Maria to visit Switzerland. She spends two months in Zurich with Karoline, then spends two months at a rest home in the Alps, returning to Vienna in January 1920.

3 February 1920: Appears in a Tanzabend at the Pfauen Theater, dancing in the following works: "Miniaturen," "Grillen," "Der Tag," "Danse," and two ensemble numbers.

13 March 1920: Dances in the third act of Nedbal's *Polenblut* at the Stadttheater, performing "Krakoviac" with fellow ballerinas Greta Edelmann and Nina Zutter.

23 March 1920: With Greta Edelmann and Nina Zutter, files a complaint against Frau Ruvina, accusing her of chronic lateness to rehearsals, discourtesy, and favoritism. A month later, after several meetings, Frau Ruvina is mildly reprimanded by the theater, but Karoline undergoes a series of hearings and police investigations culminating in an order of deportation issued by the Zurich police on 26 June 1920. According to the order, the grounds for deportation are failure to pay full taxes and an immoral lifestyle, which includes living in "concubinage" with Mario Petrucci. The order is appealed, and the Stadttheater's Employees' Council, which includes Richard Révy, springs to her defense. The appeal continues for several months and causes a great deal of conflict within the ballet company and between the theater and the city government.

23 April 1920: Appears in a dance recital program following Bizet's *Djamileh* at the Stadttheater. She dances in Dalcroze's "Der Tag" and two ensemble numbers.

1920-1921 season: Appears in small roles in the following works: Pfauen Theater: G. Hauptmann's *Rose Bernd* (Marthel; listed in the program as "Lotte Blamauer" for the first time), *Als ich noch im Flügelkleide* (Wilhelmine Müller), Wedekind's *Lulu* (Hugenberg), Tagore's *Das Postamt* (Ludha), O. Straus's *Der letzte Walzer* (Petruschka), Büchner's *Wozzek* (Käthe), Shakespeare's *König Heinrich IV* (Franz), Shakespeare's *König Heinrich V* (Boy). Stadttheater: *Fatinitza* (Dimitri and Zuleika), Jessel's *Schwarzwaldmädel* (Lorle), *Rose Bernd* (Marthel), *Der letzte Walzer* (Petruschka).

June 1921: Stays in Flims, Switzerland (about 50 miles southeast of Zurich). Around this time, Richard Révy resigns from the Stadttheater and prepares to move to Berlin. He encourages her to try her luck there as well.

Summer 1921?: Karoline Blamauer adopts the stage name Lotte Lenja (changed to Lenya shortly after she moves to the U.S.) on the advice of Richard Révy. "Lotte" comes from one of her given names, Charlotte. The origin of "Lenja" is not so clear, but it is probably invented by Révy, based on the character Jelena in Chekhov's play *Uncle Vanya*. Her nickname for Révy is "Vanya."

3 October 1921: Leaves Zurich for Berlin with Greta Edelmann. It is unclear if she is expelled from Switzerland, or leaves of her own free will. She moves into a boarding house on the Lützowstrasse.

1922: Lives by selling jewelry, a gift from a wealthy lover in Zurich, and looks for work in the theater. Auditions for *Zaubernacht*, Kurt Weill's first stage score, and he plays "The Blue Danube" for the audition. They do not see each other again for almost two years.

4 May 1923: Swiss order of deportation against Lenya is formally lifted.

September 1923: Gets a job with a troupe that tours the Berlin suburbs performing Shakespeare, with a producer-director named Otto Kirchner. She plays Maria in *Twelfth Night*, at a salary of three million Marks per performance, which later in the year inflates to more than one billion Marks.

Autumn 1923: Révy brings Georg Kaiser, one of Germany's leading Expressionist playwrights, to a performance of *Twelfth Night*. Révy introduces the two after the performance, and Kaiser takes a liking to Lenya. After her engagement ends, he invites her to his country house at Grünheide, an eastern suburb of Berlin on Lake Peetz, for the weekend. Shortly thereafter, the Kaisers invite her to live with them, working as a nanny and housekeeper. She accepts the offer and moves to Grünheide.

1924: Performs in Franz Grillparzer's play, *Weh' dem, der lügt*, in Berlin [role and theater unknown].

May-June 1924: Meets Kurt Weill when he is invited to Grünheide to continue a collaboration with Georg Kaiser. According to Lenya's later recollections, she met him at the train station at Kaiser's request and rowed him across the lake to the Kaisers' home. During the crossing, Weill recalled her audition for *Zaubernacht* nearly two years before. They begin their relationship shortly thereafter.

May 1925: Kaiser offers Weill the use of his small Berlin apartment at Luisenplatz 3. Lenya moves from Grünheide, and Weill and Lenya begin living together, although Lenya frequently stays at Grünheide and continues to do so for the next two or three years.

28 January 1926: Lenya and Weill are married in a civil ceremony in the Charlottenburg section of Berlin. Lenya later recalled that they got married to eliminate local gossip.

May-June 1926: Plays the role of Feemy Evans in George Bernard Shaw's *The Shewing-Up of Blanco Posnet* at the Wallnertheater in Berlin, directed by Emil Lind.

June-July 1926: Weill and Lenya take a delayed honeymoon in Zurich, northern Italy, and Cannes.

Autumn 1926: Plays the role of Kukuli in an unknown stage work (possibly Ferdinand Kauer's *Der Wundervogel*) in Berlin.

Winter 1926-27: Lenya plays Juliet in Shakespeare's *Romeo and Juliet* at the Wallnertheater in Berlin, directed by Emil Lind.

17 July 1927: For the first time, Lenya performs in a work by Kurt Weill, *Mahagonny*, singing the role of Jessie, directed by Walther Brügmann. The *"Songspiel,"* with texts by Bertolt Brecht, was staged at the Deutsche Kammermusik in Baden-Baden, along with short operas by Ernst Toch, Paul Hindemith, and Darius Milhaud. Lenya, who had not been well known before, and had not been known at all as a singer, attracts notice.

May 1928: Weill and Brecht, with Lenya and others, travel to the French Riviera to complete work on their new show, tentatively entitled *Die Ludenoper*, based on John Gay's *Beggar's Opera*.

31 August 1928: The premiere of Weill and Brecht's *Die Dreigroschenoper* at the Theater am Schiffbauerdamm in Berlin, with Lenya in the role of Jenny. Lenya's success leads to an active career for the next three years, including additional stints in *Die Dreigroschenoper* as Jenny and Lucy.

October 1928: Lenya and Weill move to a new apartment at Bayernallee 14, Charlottenburg.

28 November 1928: Opens as Charmian Peruchacha in Lion Feuchtwanger's play *Die Petroleuminseln* at the Berliner Staatstheater, directed by Jürgen Fehling.

20 December 1928: Lenya's father, Franz Blamauer, dies in Vienna at the age of 63.

4 January 1929: Opens as Ismene in Sophocles's *Oedipus auf Kolonos* at the Berliner Staatstheater, directed by Leopold Jessner.

30 March 1929: Opens as Alma in Marieluise Fleisser's play *Pioniere in Ingolstadt* at the Theater am Schiffbauerdamm, directed by Jacob Geis.

31 August 1929: Opens as Lucille in Georg Büchner's play *Dantons Tod* at the Volksbühne, directed by Karl Heinze Martin.

14 October 1929: Opens as Ilse in Frank Wedekind's play *Frühlings Erwachen* at the Volksbühne, directed by Karl Heinze Martin.

31 December 1929: Plays the role of Fern Barry, "a dancer," in Ferdinand Reyher's play *Harte Bandagen* at the Berliner Staatstheater, directed by Leopold Jessner.

24 February 1930: Records two songs from the Weill-Brecht opera *Aufstieg und Fall der Stadt Mahagonny*: "Alabama-Song" and "Denn wie man sich bettet" with "The Three Admirals," conducted by Theo Mackeben, on Ultraphon 371.

9 March 1930: Attends premiere of Weill-Brecht opera *Aufstieg und Fall der Stadt Mahagonny* in Leipzig. The performance is disrupted by Nazi demonstrators.

31 March 1930: Plays the role of Sally, "a thin mulatto," in Michael Gold's "Negerstück" *Das Lied von Hoboken* at the Volksbühne, directed by Heinz Dietrich Kenter.

Autumn 1930?: Records two songs by Weill and Brecht from the play *Happy End*: "Surabaya-Johnny" and "Bilbao-Song," for Orchestrola (2311), conducted by Theo Mackeben, musical director for the stage performance.

Autumn? 1930: Records two songs from the Weill-Brecht opera *Aufstieg und Fall der Stadt Mahagonny*: "Alabama-Song" and "Denn wie man sich bettet" with ensemble and orchestra for Homocord (H3671).

19 September-15 November 1930: Filming of the German version of Georg Wilhelm Pabst's *Die Dreigroschenoper*. Lenya, as Jenny, sings "Seeräuberjenny," making it one of her signature songs (the song was sung by Polly in the stage version). The film is released 19 February 1931.

7 October 1930: Opens as Frau Götz in Paul Kornfeld's play *Jud Süss* at the Theater am Schiffbauerdamm, directed by Leopold Jessner.

December 1930: Appears as Tanja in Valentin Katayev's play *Die Quadratur des Kreises* at the Theater am Schiffbauerdamm, directed by Francesco von Mendelssohn.

7 December 1930: Records "Aus der Drei-Groschen-Oper" (Selections from *Die Dreigroschenoper*) with Kurt Gerron, Erich Ponto, Willy Trenk-Trebitsch, Erika Helmke, and the Lewis Ruth Band conducted by Theo Mackeben for Ultraphon (A752-A755). She sings "Seeräuberjenny," "Barbara-Song," "Zuhälter-ballade," "Eifersuchtsduett," and "Moritat und Schlusschoral," taking several songs from Polly's role. She also sings the part of Mrs. Peachum in the "Erstes Dreigroschenfinale," taking the notes down one octave.

June 1931: Erwin Piscator offers Lenya a role in a film based on Anna Seghers's novel, *Der Aufstand der Fischer von Santa Barbara*, to be filmed in the Soviet Union. She accepts.

Summer 1931: While Lenya is in Russia, Weill works full-time on a new opera, *Die Bürgschaft*, with librettist and designer Caspar Neher. At some point, he begins an affair with Neher's wife, Erika.

28 July 1931: The German cast and crew travel to Moscow; they remain in Russia for the next three months. Virtually no work is done on the film; in the end only a Russian version is made, in which Lenya does not appear.

18 October 1931: Weill tells Lenya that he has bought a new house, partly as a birthday present for her, at Wissmannstrasse 7 in Kleinmachnow (a suburb of Berlin). As far as can be determined, Lenya never actually lives with Weill in the house, but the deed is in her name.

8 November 1931: Returns from Russia and begins preparations for the Berlin run of *Aufstieg und Fall der Stadt Mahagonny*.

21 December 1931: Opens as Jenny in *Aufstieg und Fall der Stadt Mahagonny* at the Theater am Kurfürstendamm, directed and designed by Caspar Neher, conducted by Alexander von Zemlinsky. Weill has revised the score to accommodate non-operatic singers. It runs over fifty consecutive performances.

January 1932: Records "Querschnitt aus der Oper *Aufstieg und Fall der Stadt Mahagonny*," for Electrola (E.H. 736) with the Ensemble and Orchestra of the Theater am Kurfürstendamm, conducted by Hans Sommer.

26 April 1932: Opens as Jenny in an abridged version of *Aufstieg und Fall der Stadt Mahagonny* at the Raimund-Theater in Vienna, directed by Hans Heinsheimer. Meets Otto Pasetti (who sings the role of Jimmy) and soon after moves in with him. Lenya and Weill are now formally separated, although they remain in regular contact by letter.

Autumn 1932: Lenya's travels between 1932 and 1935 cannot be documented precisely, because the relevant pages from her passport for those years have been removed. At some point she and Pasetti travel to Monte Carlo, where they spend most of the next several months, at least until Spring 1933. They run up significant gambling debts.

11 December 1932: Appears as Jessie in *Mahagonny* (Songspiel) at the Salle Gaveau in Paris, with great critical acclaim. Lenya and Pasetti spend most of December in Paris and return to Vienna around the new year.

Early 1933: Begins divorce proceedings against Weill in Germany. The divorce may be partly tactical, as it will allow Lenya to recover some of Weill's assets which would otherwise be seized by the Nazis. Throughout 1933, Lenya and Pasetti attempt to liquidate assorted assets (including the house) and get the money out of Germany.

18 February 1933: Attends the premiere of *Der Silbersee*, a play with music by Weill and Georg Kaiser, in Leipzig. This is her first reunion with Weill since December 1932. (The play gets glowing reviews, but it is forced by the Nazis to close on 4 March.)

March 1933: Weill is now in some danger from the Nazis, who have taken power. Lenya and Louise Hartung (a Berlin photographer and friend) pack some of Weill's possessions at Wissmann-strasse 7 and drive him to Munich, where they check in to the Four Seasons Hotel. Lenya leaves Weill and proceeds to Vienna. Weill returns briefly to Berlin, but decides to flee a few days later. On 22 March, Caspar and Erika Neher drive Weill to the French border, and he leaves Germany for good, settling in Paris soon after.

5 April 1933: Meets Weill in Nancy. He offers her and Pasetti parts in his next work, a ballet with songs, with lyrics by Brecht. The piece, to be titled *Die sieben Todsünden*, is to open in Paris in June.

7 June 1933: Opens as Anna I in *Die sieben Todsünden* at the Théâtre des Champs-Élysées in Paris, choreographed and directed by George Balanchine. Although the engagement is relatively short, the company will also perform in London during July.

20 June 1933: Appears as Jessie in a concert version of *Mahagonny* (Songspiel) at La Sérénade in Paris.

30 June 1933: Opens as Anna I in *Die sieben Todsünden* (in an English version by Lenya and the impresario Edward James, entitled *Anna-Anna*) at the Savoy Theatre in London. The production runs until 15 July.

18 July 1933: Appears in a concert performance of *Mahagonny* (Songspiel) at the Aeolian Hall in London. Leaves England shortly thereafter and goes to Berlin, partly to take care of legal and financial business.

18 September 1933: Final divorce decree handed down in Potsdam.

November 1933: Finalizes the sale of the house in Kleinmachnow. Reunites with Pasetti in San Remo, Italy for more gambling.

29 December 1933: Appears with Pasetti in a concert performance of *Mahagonny* (Songspiel) at the Accademia di Santa Cecilia in Rome.

January-June 1934: Lives with Pasetti in San Remo, where they continue to gamble and try to get Weill's money and property out of Germany. Success at both efforts is limited.

16 August 1934: Opens as Pussy Angora in Walter Kollo's revue *Lieber reich aber glücklich* at the Corso Theater in Zurich, directed by Hans Curjel. Lenya stays in Zurich until October, when she moves into Weill's house in Louveciennes, a suburb of Paris. By this time she seems to have broken off entirely with Pasetti. Some time in late 1934 or early 1935, she has a brief affair with the painter Max Ernst.

7 February 1935: Has minor surgery to remove a vaginal polyp in Paris.

8 April 1935: Travels to London to stay with Weill. Lenya has been studying English on and off for two or three years; one of her reasons for going to London may be to continue her studies.

August 1935: Weill, in Salzburg working on the Biblical pageant *Der Weg der Verheissung* (text by Franz Werfel), informs Lenya that he will go to the United States early in September to supervise the music for a New York production. He invites her to sail with him and tells her how to arrange for the necessary visas.

2 September 1935: Lenya returns to Paris and obtains a temporary visa for travel in the U.S.

4 September 1935: Lenya and Weill sail from Cherbourg on the SS Majestic.

10 September 1935: Lenya and Weill arrive in New York and move into the St. Moritz Hotel on Central Park South.

1 December 1935: Max Reinhardt, director of *Der Weg der Verheissung*, announces that Lenya will take a role in the production, scheduled to open January 1936. The opening is postponed for a full year.

17 December 1935: Performs excerpts from *Aufstieg und Fall der Stadt Mahagonny* and the individual songs "Seeräuber-jenny," "Barbara-Song," (from *Die Dreigroschenoper*) and "J'attends un navire" from *Marie galante*. The occasion is "An Evening in Honor of Kurt Weill," held by the League of Composers, in New York at the Cosmopolitan Club. Other artists perform excerpts from Weill's works *Die Bürgschaft* and *A Kingdom for a Cow*. Neither Weill nor Lenya is received with enthusiasm.

Early 1936: Weill and Lenya move to the Hotel Park Crescent in New York.

June 1936: Weill and Lenya move to Connecticut for the summer to work with the Group Theatre on Weill's first American stage work, *Johnny Johnson* (book and lyrics by Paul Green). Weill spends most of his time teaching American actors to sing his way; Lenya has little to do. She has a brief affair with Green.

Autumn 1936: Lenya and Weill move into Cheryl Crawford's apartment on E. 51st Street in New York; preparations for *The Eternal Road* (English version of *Der Weg der Verheissung*) get underway again for a January opening.

7 January 1937: Opens as Miriam in *The Eternal Road* at the Manhattan Opera House in New York, directed by Max Reinhardt. The show is a *succès d'estime*, but runs out of money and closes after 153 performances.

19 January 1937: Lenya and Weill remarry in a civil ceremony in Westchester County, north of New York City.

Summer 1937: Lenya and Weill move into a new apartment on E. 62nd Street in New York.

27 August 1937: Lenya and Weill return from Canada, where they have obtained immigrant visas.

24 October 1937: Performs as The Suicide in Marc Blitzstein's radio-play *I've Got the Tune*, which is broadcast over CBS Radio.

13 December 1937: Lenya and Weill travel to Hollywood, where Weill has a contract to score a film *You and Me*. They stay until early February 1938.

April-May 1938: Takes a nightclub engagement at Le Ruban Bleu on W. 56th Street in New York. She performs several songs by Weill, as well as a song written especially for her by Marc Blitzstein called "Few Little English." The appearance helps to make her name and talent known among the sophisticated crowd in New York, but it does not lead to any immediate offers.

Late May 1938: Lenya and Weill rent a cottage in Suffern, NY, near Maxwell Anderson's house; Weill and Anderson begin work on their first show together, *Knickerbocker Holiday*.

Autumn 1938: Meets Walter Huston, star of *Knickerbocker Holiday*, and his wife Nan. Through them, she meets Mary Daniel, who will remain a close friend and regular visitor until her death in the late 1970's.

Christmas 1939: Weill sets a Brecht text, "Nannas Lied," as a Christmas present for Lenya. Apparently, she never performs the song in public. The lyric was part of Brecht's play, *Die Rundköpfe und die Spitzköpfe*, and had previously been set by Hanns Eisler.

28 May 1941: Lenya and Weill buy Brook House at 100 South Mountain Road in New City, NY, next door to the Andersons. They join a colony of artists in the area, including cartoonists Milton Caniff and Bill Mauldin, painter Henry Varnum Poor, and actor Burgess Meredith. Lenya, Mab Anderson, and Bunny Caniff quickly become inseparable card players.

Autumn 1941: Meets Howard Schwartz from New City with whom she has an on-and-off affair.

15 September 1941: Opens as Cissie in Maxwell Anderson's *Candle in the Wind* at the Colonial Theatre in Boston (out-of-town tryout). Anderson wrote the part especially for her.

22 October 1941: *Candle in the Wind* opens at the Shubert Theater in New York, directed by Alfred Lunt. Lenya gets good reviews, but the play is not so successful. It runs 95 performances, then goes on the road.

January 1942: *Candle in the Wind* begins its U.S. tour, which covers about forty cities and continues until the end of May. Lenya is able to see Schwartz occasionally while on tour.

June? 1942: Begins civil defense work in Rockland County, including looking for planes from a watchtower. This duty continues sporadically until the war is nearly over.

20 August 1942: Performs "Russian War Relief," a song by Weill and J.P. McEvoy, at a revue called *Rockland Riot*, a benefit for Rockland for Russia (a Russian war relief fund) at the Clarkstown Country Club in Nyack, NY.

1943: Records *Six Songs by Kurt Weill* for Bost Records (BA 8) in New York. The recording is supervised by Weill. Lenya sings "Surabaya-Johnny," "Denn wie man sich bettet," "J'attends un navire," "Complainte de la Seine," "Lost in the Stars," and "Lover Man" (later revised as "Trouble Man").

3 April 1943: Performs in a concert entitled "We Fight Back" at Hunter College in New York. The concert is produced and performed by European exiles. Lenya sings "Moritat," "Seeräuberjenny," "Surabaya-Johnny," and a new song, "Und was bekam des Soldaten Weib," which Weill composed a year earlier on a new text by Brecht. Weill accompanies her at the piano.

October? 1943: Learns that Howard Schwartz has been killed in a plane crash; she is devastated by his untimely death.

Spring 1944: Records two of Weill's songs for the U.S. Office of War Information for use in radio broadcasts to Germany. One is "Wie lange noch," with lyrics by Walter Mehring; the other is "Und was bekam des Soldaten Weib," which she performed the previous year. She also records "Lied einer deutschen Mutter," with lyrics by Brecht and music by Paul Dessau.

5 May 1944: Becomes an American citizen.

Summer (July-September?) 1944: Takes voice lessons with Eva Gauthier.

23 February 1945: Opens as The Duchess in the operetta *The Firebrand of Florence* by Weill, Ira Gershwin, and Edwin Justus Mayer at the Shubert Theatre in Boston (out-of-town tryout).

22 March 1945: *The Firebrand of Florence* opens at the Alvin Theatre in New York, directed by John Murray Anderson. The show flops, running only 45 performances, and Lenya's performance is harshly reviewed. The show's quick failure effectively dissuades Lenya from acting for several years.

27 March and 12 April 1945: Appears on two radio shows for CBS, interviewed by Mary Margaret McBride and Adelaide Hawley, respectively.

29 September 1948: Lenya's mother and sister arrive on a visit from Vienna, the first time Lenya has seen them since she left Europe. They stay at Brook House for almost two months.

17 March 1950: Weill has a heart attack and is taken to Flower Hospital in New York City.

3 April 1950: Weill dies of a heart attack at the hospital; the funeral is held near New City a few days later. For at least a month afterwards, Lenya is so distraught that neighbors are afraid to let her stay alone at night.

May 1950: Lenya renews her friendship with writer and editor George Davis, whom she and Weill had known since the late 1930s. In the following months, he becomes her preferred companion. With Davis's help, she resolves to "fight for [Weill's] music, to keep it alive, to do everything within my power for it." She maintains this goal with great tenacity until her death. Her voluminous legal and business correspondence, starting in 1950, attests to her perseverance.

4 July 1950: Gives a television interview to Kathi Norris (network unknown).

10 July 1950: Attends a Kurt Weill Memorial Concert at Lewisohn Stadium in New York, along with 10,000 other people. Maxwell Anderson delivers a eulogy, as he did at the funeral.

7 August 1950: Attends the opening of *Lost in the Stars* in San Francisco with Mab Anderson.

3 February 1951: Performs in a "Kurt Weill Concert" at Town Hall in New York. The program is repeated 17 February at Town Hall and 31 March at the 92nd Street Y. She participates in the second half of the program, a concert version of *Die Dreigroschenoper*. In the role of Polly, Lenya sings most of the female characters' musical numbers. This is her first public performance since *The Firebrand of Florence* (and since Weill's death).

6 February 1951: Lenya's mother dies in Vienna at the age of 85.

17 July 1951: Marries George Davis in a civil ceremony witnessed by Maxwell Anderson and Milton Caniff in Rockland County.

31 October 1951: Opens as Xantippe in Maxwell Anderson's *Barefoot in Athens* at the Martin Beck Theatre in New York, directed by Alan Anderson. Although Lenya was briefly replaced during out-of-town tryouts, her performance generally wins praise from reviewers. The play, however, does not, and runs only 30 performances.

23 February 1952: Performs in a "Kurt Weill Concert," at Town Hall in New York. Although the first half of the program is quite different from that of the previous year, the second half is the same.

14 June 1952: Appears as Jenny in a concert performance of Marc Blitzstein's English adaptation of *Die Dreigroschenoper* (*The Threepenny Opera*) at Brandeis University, conducted by Leonard Bernstein.

October 1953: Lenya and Blitzstein meet with two novice theater producers, Carmen Capalbo and Stanley Chase, who want to mount *The Threepenny Opera*. Their willingness to stick closely to the score and script (unlike other candidates) wins Lenya over. They also insist that she play Jenny.

Spring 1954?: With Marc Blitzstein, gives a television interview to publicize *The Threepenny Opera*. Lenya sings a verse of "Surabaya-Johnny" and "Mack the Knife" as Blitzstein accompanies her on the piano, and Blitzstein sings "Solomon Song."

10 March 1954: Opens as Jenny in *The Threepenny Opera* at the Theater de Lys in New York (off-Broadway), directed by Capalbo. The show is a hit, but closes after 96 performances because another play is contracted for the theater. The score is recorded by MGM Records (E3121) and released in July 1954 as the first off-Broadway cast recording.

20 July 1954: Opens as Mrs. Carroll in Martin Vale's play, *The Two Mrs. Carrolls*, at the Lakeside Summer Theatre in Lake Hopatcong, N.J., directed by Herbert Machiz. The show runs roughly ten performances.

3 April 1955: Lenya and Davis arrive in West Germany, her first visit since 1934. They are there to do research on Weill for a biography and to make recordings of Weill's music for Philips (which co-produces with Columbia Records in the U.S.). While in Berlin, Lenya crosses to East Berlin to visit Brecht. She and Davis remain in Europe until mid-July. In addition to making a recording herself, Lenya supervises the first recording of Weill's and Brecht's opera *Der Jasager* (1930) for MGM Records (E3270); recorded in Dusseldorf in late April, it is released in 1956.

5-7 July 1955: Records *Lotte Lenya singt Kurt Weill* in Hamburg for Philips (B 07 039); released in the U.S. by Columbia (ML 5056) in November 1955 as *Lotte Lenya Sings Berlin Theater Songs of Kurt Weill*.

20 September 1955: Re-opens as Jenny in *The Threepenny Opera* at the Theater de Lys, and remains in the cast (with a brief hiatus) until April 1956. She wins a Tony Award in 1956 as Outstanding Supporting or Featured Musical Actress, and the production wins a special Tony the same year. *The Threepenny Opera* runs 2,611 performances, finally closing 17 December 1961, having broken the record at that time for the longest-running musical.

22 September 1955: Records "Theme from The Threepenny Opera" ("Mack the Knife") with jazzman Turk Murphy on Columbia. The record is not released commercially in the U.S. (though available for radio play), but is released in February 1956 in Europe and becomes a hit in Germany.

28 September 1955: Attends recording session for "Mack the Knife" with Louis Armstrong and his All-Stars, in New York. Armstrong includes Lenya's name in the lyrics, an innovation other singers will take up. "Mack the Knife" has already been recorded as a popular song, and it will be recorded several more times in the 1950s, by Bobby Darin, Ella Fitzgerald, and Frank Sinatra, among others. At the same session, the band makes another recording of "Mack the Knife" with Lenya singing; this recording is not issued until 1982 on Book-of-the-Month (21-6547).

October 1955: Stays in Maurice Grosser's apartment on West 14th Street before leasing an apartment at 994 2nd Avenue in New York, as a *pied-à-terre* she shares with Davis.

November 1955: Returns to Germany with Davis to publicize the release of *Lotte Lenya singt Kurt Weill* and to attend the German premiere of Weill's "Broadway opera" *Street Scene* (*Die Strasse*) in Dusseldorf. On 21 November, she gives a concert at the Atlantic Hotel in Hamburg to launch *Lotte Lenya singt Kurt Weill*. They return to the U.S. 14 December 1955.

14 August 1956: Lenya and Davis return to Germany for more recordings. Brecht dies in East Berlin at the age of 58.

16 August 1956: Davis suffers a heart attack, from which he quickly recovers.

1-8 September 1956: Records *Die sieben Todsünden* for Philips (B 07 186) in Hamburg, conducted by Wilhelm Brückner-Rüggeberg; Columbia releases the recording in the U.S. (KL 5175) in March 1957.

7 October 1956: Broadcast of television program on Süddeutscher Rundfunk in Germany: "Lotte Lenya." Lenya sings, and the program features an interview conducted by Josef Müller-Marein.

3-11 November 1956: Records *Aufstieg und Fall der Stadt Mahagonny* for Philips (L 09 418-20) and Columbia (K3L 243) in Hamburg, conducted by Wilhelm Brückner-Rüggeberg. At some point during this trip, she and Davis meet Anna Krebs, who works for Philips, and who becomes one of Lenya's best friends.

February 1957: Release of *Johnny Johnson* on MGM Records (E3447). The recording, made in 1956, features Burgess Meredith and several members of the *Threepenny Opera* cast. Lenya supervises the recording and sings one song, "Mon Ami, My Friend."

August 1957: Records *September Song and Other American Theatre Songs of Kurt Weill* for Columbia (KL 5229), conducted by Maurice Levine; it is released in February 1958.

6 October 1957: Lenya and Davis attend the revival of *Die Bürgschaft*, in a version revised by director Carl Ebert and librettist Caspar Neher, in Berlin. Around this time, they meet David Drew, a young English musicologist who has expressed interest in writing a biography of Weill. He first made contact with Lenya in November 1956. Drew's extensive and varied research will help establish Weill as a major twentieth-century composer.

11 November 1957: Receives the Freiheitsglocke (Freedom Bell), the highest cultural award bestowed by the city of West Berlin.

25 November 1957: George Davis dies of a massive heart attack in Berlin, at the age of 51.

11-15 January 1958: Records *Die Dreigroschenoper* for Philips (L 09 421-22) and Columbia (O2L 257), conducted by Wilhelm Brückner-Rüggeberg. She is also contracted to record *Das Berliner Requiem*, but cancels the sessions after Davis's death. She returns to the U.S. in late March.

Spring 1958: Broadcast of "Night-Beat" on CBS Television. Lenya gives a brief interview and clips of pre-recorded songs are shown.

29 June 1958: Broadcast of "Camera Three" on CBS Television, an interview program in which Lenya also sings a few songs.

31 July 1958: Performs a "Kurt Weill Concert" at Lewisohn Stadium in New York.

August 1958: Records *Invitation to German Poetry* for Dover (IP-9892), reading a selection of 42 German lyric poems from Walther von der Vogelweide (13th century) to Brecht. The album is released in the autumn of 1959.

October 1958: Leases a small apartment at 316 E. 55th Street in New York, so that she does not have to stay alone at Brook House.

4 December 1958: Opens as Anna I in *Die sieben Todsünden*, in an English translation by W.H. Auden and Chester Kallman (*The Seven Deadly Sins*). The production, choreographed once again by George Balanchine, remains in repertory at the New York City Ballet through January 1960, traveling to Los Angeles during the last week of July 1959. Lenya's performance gets rave reviews; she is now well established as the definitive interpreter of Weill's music.

15 February 1959: Appears in concert at Carnegie Hall, performing a tribute to Kurt Weill. The first half features a wide-ranging selection of Weill songs; the second half is a concert performance of *Die Dreigroschenoper*, conducted by Maurice Levine.

Spring 1959: Takes a romantic interest in U.N. Secretary-General Dag Hammarskjöld. Over the next year or so, she sees Hammarskjöld two or three times in social and personal situations, but he apparently lacks interest. The relationship does not develop.

Summer 1959: Records *The Stories of Kafka* ("A Hunger Artist," "An Imperial Message," "A Fratricide," "The Cares of a Family Man," "Up in the Gallery," "A Dream," and "The Bucket Rider," all read in English) for Caedmon (TC 1114). The recording is released in November 1962.

11 November 1959: Reads for a "Schiller-Festabend" at Town Hall in New York, sponsored by Deutsches Theater in New York and Literarische Verein Wien. Lenya reads "Der Handschuh," "Die Hoffnung," "Grabschrift eines gewissen Physionomen," and "Der Wirtenberger."

7 February 1960: Performs in "A Kurt Weill Evening" at Carnegie Hall in New York, conducted by Maurice Levine. The supporting cast is nearly the same as in the previous year's Carnegie Hall concert, and the program ends once again with a concert rendition of *Die Dreigroschenoper*.

6 April 1960: Opens as Anna I in the German premiere of *Die sieben Todsünden* at the Städtische Bühnen in Frankfurt, choreographed by Tatjana Gsovsky. The production is accompanied by revivals of Weill's early one-act operas *Der Protagonist* and *Der Zar lässt sich photographieren*. The triple-bill remains in repertory during the summer.

6 May 1960: Performs in a Musica Viva subscription concert at the Herkules-Saal in Munich, conducted by Miltiades Caridis. The program includes *Mahagonny* (Songspiel), followed by Lenya's performances of Weill-Brecht songs and *Die sieben Todsünden*. Lenya repeats the program three days later in Darmstadt. The program is broadcast on Bayerischer Rundfunk on 5 September 1960.

Summer 1960: Appears on a Hessischer Rundfunk radio program, interviewed by Theodor W. Adorno.

9-10 July 1960: Records *Happy End* for Philips (B 47 080 L) in Hamburg, singing all the songs with choral backing, conducted by Wilhelm Brückner-Rüggeberg. The Columbia (OL 5630) issue is not released in the U.S. until August 1964.

August 1960: Returns to the U.S. and takes a new apartment, at 404 E. 55th Street. She keeps the lease for the rest of her life.

18 October 1960: Opens as Jenny in *The Threepenny Opera* at the Music Box Theatre in Los Angeles, directed by Carmen Capalbo, in a west-coast production featuring several of the actors who opened the show in New York in 1954. Lenya remains in the cast for about a month.

29 November 1960: Arrives in London to film *The Roman Spring of Mrs. Stone*, directed by José Quintero and distributed by Warner Brothers. Lenya plays Countess Magda Terribili-Gonzales, a procuress. She is nominated both for an Academy Award and a Golden Globe Award as best supporting actress, although she does not win either. Filming continues until March 1961. Lenya returns to the U.S. early in April, after a visit to Vienna.

Early 1961: Broadcast of a half-hour program in the "Monitor" series on BBC Television, directed by Ken Russell. The program includes performances of several Weill songs and an interview.

August-October 1961: Travels to England and Germany to do further research into Weill's life and work with David Drew. She intended to perform in Kenneth MacMillan's production of *The Seven Deadly Sins* at the Edinburgh Festival, but pulled out because of artistic differences. She is replaced by Cleo Laine.

14 November 1961: Appears in *Brecht on Brecht* (a revue of songs, poems, and excerpts from plays assembled by George Tabori) at the Theater de Lys in New York, directed by Gene Frankel. The performance, part of the ANTA matinee series, is repeated 20 November 1961.

3 January 1962: Opens in *Brecht on Brecht* at the Theater de Lys for a regular run, succeeding *The Threepenny Opera*. The original cast soundtrack is recorded by Columbia (O2S 203). Originally scheduled for a limited six-week run, the show logs over 200 performances.

Spring 1962: Meets the painter Russell Detwiler at a party given by W.H. Auden in New York. A courtship soon begins.

26 May 1962: Presents the Obie Awards in New York.

16 August 1962: Forms the Kurt Weill Foundation for Music as a non-profit corporation.

11 September 1962: Opens in *Brecht on Brecht* at the Royal Court Theatre in London for a four- week limited engagement. Detwiler travels to London separately for the opening.

2 November 1962: Marries Russell Detwiler in London. They take a honeymoon in Germany and return to New York on 29 November.

January 1963: Travels to London to attend the British premiere of *Aufstieg und Fall der Stadt Mahagonny*, translated into English by David Drew and Michael Geliot and conducted by Colin Davis.

April-July 1963: Films *From Russia with Love* in Europe, directed by Terence Young. Lenya's performance as Russian spymaster Rosa Klebb, including hand-to-hand (or foot-to-hand) combat with Sean Connery as James Bond at the end of the film, introduces her to the widest audience yet.

Autumn 1963: It is reported that Lenya will play Mother Courage at a production at the Theater de Lys, due to open in January 1964. The production does not materialize.

October 1963: Learns of a performance of "Das kleine Mahagonny" given by the Berliner Ensemble at the Theater am Schiffbauerdamm in Berlin from a report by David Drew, who writes Lenya that "Kurt is simply *annihilated*." Acting on Drew's outrage at the piece, which is a pastiche (with extensively altered music) of the original *Songspiel* and the later full-length opera, Lenya defends her interest in both works and forbids further performances of the new adaptation, acquiescing only to Helene Weigel's plea to allow the Berliner Ensemble to record it and keep it in repertory.

13 October-7 December 1963: Tours with *Brecht on Brecht*, to thirty or so colleges in the Northeast and Midwest. In Detroit, she meets a student named Ted Mitchell, who will become a close friend and frequent photographer.

28 October 1964: Broadcast of "Lotte Lenya: The Broadway Years of Kurt Weill" as part of the "Stage 2" series on CBS-TV. The program is directed by Jack Landau and co-stars Russell Nype.

1965: Tapes a segment for the television program, "Music in the Twenties," for WGBH-TV in Boston.

8 January 1965: Performs her third, and last, concert at Carnegie Hall, "A Kurt Weill Evening."

April-May 1965: Lenya and Detwiler travel to Germany for rehearsals of Brecht's *Mutter Courage und ihre Kinder*. Lenya, having increasing difficulty with Detwiler's drinking problem, first sends him to Anna Krebs (who has graciously agreed to look after him so Lenya can rehearse in peace), then is forced to send him back to the U.S.

12 June 1965: Opens as Mutter Courage in *Mutter Courage und ihre Kinder* at the Ruhrfestspiele in Recklinghausen, directed by Harry Buckwitz. The limited engagement runs about six weeks. For the first time in many years, Lenya gets predominantly negative reviews. The role is closely associated with Helene Weigel, Brecht's widow and Lenya's frequent sparring partner in Weill-Brecht disputes; the German critics prefer Weigel's famous interpretation of the role. The performance is televised 25 July 1965 on 2. Programm in Germany.

30-31 July 1965: Performs a concert of Weill songs at the Sporthalle in Cologne.

May 1966: Tapes a one-hour program with George Voskovec, "The World of Kurt Weill," for WGBH-TV (National Educational Television) in Boston. It is broadcast in February 1967.

Summer 1966: Harold Prince offers Lenya the part of Fräulein Schneider in the Kander-Ebb-Masteroff musical *Cabaret*, which she accepts.

30 August 1966: Broadcast of "Interregnum" on New York's WNDT (Channel 13). Lenya narrates the program about George Grosz and Germany between the wars. The program was made in 1960 in both English and German versions.

7 October 1966: Broadcast of *Ten Blocks on the Camino Real* on National Educational Television (WHYY in New York). Lenya plays the Gypsy in the drama based on Tennessee Williams's one-act play.

10 October 1966: Opens as Fräulein Schneider in the Boston tryout of *Cabaret*.

20 November 1966: *Cabaret* opens at the Broadhurst Theatre in New York, directed by Hal Prince. The show runs 1,165 performances, with Lenya in the cast the entire time except for a few brief hiatuses. The cast recording is made in December and is released on Columbia (KOL 6640). She is nominated for a 1967 Tony Award for best actress in a musical.

23 November 1966: Appears on the *Today Show* (CBS television) to plug *Cabaret*.

21 February 1967: Broadcast of *Das Berliner Requiem* on CBC-TV (CBC Showcase) in Canada. Lenya reads poetry between numbers.

March 1967: Detwiler is committed to Bellevue Hospital for treatment of alcoholism and is transferred in June to a sanatorium in Connecticut to continue treatment. He is released in July and succeeds in staying sober for about a year.

2 May 1967: Awarded a citation by the Aegis Theatre Club for achievement in theater, specifically her performance in *Cabaret*.

August-September 1967: Films "Lotte Lenya singt Kurt Weill" in New York for UFA. An English version is also made. The program is broadcast on Westdeutsches Werbefernsehen in 1969.

April-May 1968: Travels with Detwiler to Rome for filming of *The Appointment*, directed by Sidney Lumet for MGM.

Lenya plays another procuress, Emma Valadier. The film flops in its first screening in Cannes in 1969 and is never released in the U.S. Lenya returns to *Cabaret* in May.

27 September 1968: Signs a publishing agreement to transfer the American rights in Weill's music to The Richmond Organization and receives an advance of $250,000.

February 1969: Records "Welcome Home" and "Young Blood" by John Cacavas and Charles O. Wood (also known as Charles Osgood) for Metromedia Records (MM-165). The recording sells few copies due to its topical nature.

11 April 1969: Films "13 Stars for 13," for WNDT-TV (Educational Broadcasting Corporation) in New York.

27 June 1969: Awarded "Das grosse Verdienstkreuz" by the West German government in New York.

Late 1969: Declines the part of Coco Chanel in Alan Jay Lerner's musical, *Coco*. The role is taken by Katharine Hepburn.

30 October 1969: Detwiler dies from a fall caused by an alcoholic seizure. Lenya buries him near Kurt Weill in Mount Repose Cemetery. While trying to honor previous commitments, she goes into a period of inactivity and depression which lasts for about a year.

9 November 1969: Performs in "The Music of Kurt Weill," a concert at Philharmonic Hall (now Avery Fisher Hall) in New York. Lenya sings "Bilbao-Song" and "Surabaya-Johnny." Many other singers participate; the first half of the program is a selection of Weill's songs and the second half is a concert performance of *Lady in the Dark*.

Spring 1970: Attempts to stop an English adaptation of *Aufstieg und Fall der Stadt Mahagonny* at the Anderson Theatre in New York, directed by Carmen Capalbo. Lenya and Stefan Brecht (son of Bertolt) are appalled by the production before and during previews, but are unable to prevent it from opening. The show closes in May after only about five performances.

14 October 1970: Films an interview with Edwin Newman, which is broadcast later that month on NBC Television.

6-7 February 1971: Appears in a performance of *Brecht on Brecht* at the University of Cincinnati.

May 1971: Receives an award for achievement in theater from the Musical Theatre Society of Emerson College.

9 June 1971: Marries filmmaker Richard Siemanowski in a civil ceremony in Rockland County. They had met several months earlier when Lenya expressed interest in having a documentary about her and Weill made. Siemanowski does draft a script entitled *Lenya, and a Girl Named Jenny*, but it is never filmed. Lenya informs only two or three close friends that she has married again.

16 June 1971: Travels to Amsterdam to participate in the

Holland Festival performance of a concert adaptation of Weill's *Der Silbersee* by David Drew and Josef Heinzelmann (25-26 June 1971). She returns to the U.S. early in July. The performance is recorded on Unique Opera records (UORC—261-A), but it is not released commercially.

17 November-27 November 1971: Plays Mother Courage in a production of *Mother Courage and her Children* at the University of California, Irvine, directed by Herbert Machiz.

Early 1972: A pirated recording of Lenya's 1965 Carnegie Hall concert entitled "Kurt Weill Concert" is released on Rococo (4008).

14-22 April 1972: Performs as Jenny in *The Threepenny Opera* at Florida State University in Tallahassee. At the same time, the LeMoyne Art Foundation in Tallahassee holds an exhibit of Detwiler's paintings. This proves to be Lenya's last full-scale stage appearance.

Autumn 1972: Appears on the television program *What's My Line*, where a panelist guesses her identity within one minute.

10 February 1973: Performs in "Bertolt Brecht zum 75. Geburtstag" at the Schauspiel Frankfurt. First on the program, Lenya sings "Ballade vom ertrunkenen Mädchen," "Seeräuberjenny," and "Bilbao-Song." The retrospective features readings and songs from Brecht's plays, poetry, and journals. The program is broadcast the next day on Hessischer Rundfunk.

April 1973: Receives an award at the United Nations from the city of Vienna for improving cultural relations between Austria and the U.S.

20 May 1973: Commissions David Drew to act as "General Manager and European Administrator of the Kurt Weill Estate." Drew becomes Lenya's representative in dealings with European publishers, agents, media, and performers.

6 June 1973: Divorces Siemanowski on the grounds of abandonment. In fact, she and Siemanowski have never lived together.

1974: Begins to suffer from various health problems, including a hiatal hernia and arthritis.

12 February 1974: Broadcast of *Trio for Lovers*, part of the CBS Daytime 90 series. Lenya plays Rosa Harcourt, owner of a music shop.

1 January 1975: Broadcast of Lenya's appearance on the *Dick Cavett Show* on ABC Television. Cavett learned the German words to the "Bilbao-Song," and he sings with her on the program, which is also broadcast in Germany on 9 March 1976.

16 May 1975: Appears on the *Today Show*, NBC.

Summer 1975: Cancels concert appearance at a major Kurt Weill festival in Berlin because of the aftereffects of an auto accident. The festival saw the premieres of several of Weill's early works.

22 July 1975: Broadcast of *AM-NY* on WABC-TV, New York. Lenya sings "There's Nowhere to Go but Up" (from *Knickerbocker Holiday*) and gives a brief interview.

28 April 1976: Attends a concert entitled "The Musical Theater of Kurt Weill" at the Curtis Institute in Philadelphia. Lenya joins the chorus singing "Mack the Knife" as the encore.

28 May 1976: Broadcast of Lenya's contribution to the series of shorts, "Bicentennial Minutes," on CBS Television, which she recorded on 2 April.

15 November 1976: Opening of an exhibition at the Performing Arts Library at Lincoln Center, New York, entitled "Weill-Lenya." Lenya had spent a large part of 1976 combing her and Weill's possessions to gather material for the exhibition. The exhibition runs until 12 March 1977. On 4 April, Lenya donates Weill's autograph score of *Die sieben Todsünden* to the Library.

March 1977: Films a scene with Burt Reynolds in *Semi-Tough*, directed by Michael Ritchie and produced by United Artists. Lenya plays Clara Pelf, a masseuse with unorthodox technique. The film is released in November, and Lenya's scene, though brief, is memorable.

November 1977: Diagnosed with ovarian cancer.

4 April 1978: Receives Distinguished Service Award, at a dinner in her honor at the Rockland Country Club.

6 June 1978: Enters New York Hospital for bladder surgery.

18 October 1978: Celebrates her eightieth birthday by attending a concert of Weill's rarely-heard orchestral music performed by the Greenwich Philharmonia at Avery Fisher Hall. Though she does not perform, Lenya appears on stage in her bathrobe and accepts birthday greetings from the audience. (She had broken her wrist in September and wears the bathrobe to conceal the sling.)

12 November 1978: Sings "So What" and "The Pineapple Song" from *Cabaret* at a concert entitled "Sing Happy: The Work of John Kander and Fred Ebb" at Avery Fisher Hall. This is her last public performance.

December 1978: Tapes an interview with Schuyler Chapin for broadcast on PBS. The interview is divided into two parts (each half an hour)—"Lenya: The Berlin Years" and "Lenya: Paris-New York"—which are broadcast for the first time 30 January and 6 February 1979. Lenya gives a number of interviews for broadcast in the last years of her life; other notable ones are conducted by Peter Adam (broadcast on the BBC in May 1979), Beverly Sills, and Robert Jacobson (both shown on PBS as part of broadcasts of stage performances of Weill operas during the autumn of 1979).

Autumn 1979: Meets Teresa Stratas, who will sing the role of Jenny in the Metropolitan Opera's production of *Rise and Fall of the City of Mahagonny* (premiere: 16 November 1979). Lenya is deeply impressed with her and publicly passes to Stratas her mantle as the premiere interpreter of Weill's music.

and cast a sharp editorial eye on the text. I am also grateful to Tracy Carns and Hermann Lademann for sharing their publishing expertise from beginning to end. The final product was much enhanced by Bernard Schleifer's elegant design and his keen understanding of the subject matter.

A number of libraries and other repositories provided photos for this book. In 1980, Lenya placed on deposit at the Yale University Music Library all of Weill's musical scores that were in her possession (mostly for the American musicals) and a large collection of photographs, programs, correspondence, and documents. Special thanks go to Kendall Crilly, Music Librarian, for his continued cooperation, and Suzanne Eggleston, Public Services Librarian, who responded quickly and professionally to our request for almost one hundred photographs and provided detailed documentation for each. Other photos were provided by Bildarchiv Preussischer Kulturbesitz, Berlin; Bildarchiv und Porträtsammlung der Österreichischen Nationalbibliothek; Corbis-Bettmann; Harvard Theatre Collection, The Houghton Library; Museum of the City of New York; Paul Hindemith Institut; The Research Collections, New York Public Library; Stadtarchiv Zürich; Stiftung Deutsche Kinematik; Stiftung Archiv der Adakemie der Künste, Berlin; Theaterwissenschaftliche Sammlung, Institut für Theater-, Film- und Fernsehwissenschaft, Universität zu Köln; Ullstein Bilderdienst, Berlin; and the University of New Hampshire.

Artists and photographers also responded graciously with photographs and reproduction rights, including Richard Avedon, Arbit Blatas, Richard Ely, Neil Fujita, Martus Granirer, Al Hirschfeld (represented by Margo Feiden Galleries), Bill Madison, Ted Mitchell, Paul Moor, Lee Snider, Barron Storey, and Lys Symonette. George P. Lynes, II (Estate of George Platt Lynes) and Jerome S. Solomon (Estate of Carl Van Vechten) also granted reproduction rights. James Frasher granted permission to use the Lillian Gish letter, Stephen Davis allowed us to reprint the words to "Jimmy's Moll" by Marc Blitzstein, and Vincent Scarza loaned an original painting by Russell Detwiler. Thanks also go to the Artists Rights Society, Atlantic Records, Dover Records, European-American Music Corporation, HarperCollins, Opera News, PolyGram Records, Sony Records, Teldec, Universal Edition, and Warner-Chappell Music for permission to reproduce record covers and other documents.

Much of the text for this book would never have existed without the work of interviewers and journalists, including Peter Adam, David Beams, Schuyler Chapin, Edwin Newman, Alan Rich, Donald Spoto, George Tabori, Gottfried Wagner, and Robert Wennersten. The private side of Lenya comes into focus through her correspondence with friends such as Lucy Abravanel, Hesper Anderson, Saul Bolasni, Milton Caniff, Victor Carl, Bertha Case, Mary Daniel, Richard Ely, Ann Fall, Manfred George, Ruth Gikow, Felix Jackson, Ian Kemp, Anna Krebs, Gigi McGuire, Ted Mitchell, Paul Moor, Ann Ronell, and Lys Symonette. Institutions that hold various letters and interviews quoted in the text include the Bertolt-Brecht-Archiv, Akademie der Künste, Berlin; Columbia University Rare Book and Manuscript Library; Deutsche Literaturarchiv, Marbach; Hargrett Rare Book and Manuscript Library, University of Georgia; Houghton Library, Harvard University; Theatersammlung, Österreichische Nationalbibliothek; Yale University Music Library; and the Wilson Library, University of North Carolina, Chapel Hill.

It is impossible to list the number of colleagues, friends, and associates who over the years have either shared their knowledge of Lenya, donated valuable materials to the Weill-Lenya Research Center, or assisted in organizing and documenting Lenya's legacy. Taking the risk of omitting some names, I must share those of special importance: Maurice Abravanel, Hesper Anderson, John Andrus, Eric Bentley, Milton Caniff, David Drew, Richard Ely, Joseph Frazzetta, Neil Fujita, Felix Gerstman, Martus Granirer, Victor Carl Guarneri, Helen Harvey, Stephen Hinton, Hanne Holesovsky, David Hummel, Jane Klain, Maurice Levine, Elisabeth Lürzer von Zechenthall, Felix Jackson, Ronald Magliozzi, Eric Marinitsch, Henry Marx, Gigi McGuire, Mario Mercado, Burgess Meredith, Ted Mitchell, Paul Moor, Larry Moore, Michael Morley, Harriet Pinover, Harold Prince, Dennis Rooney, Ann Ronell, Jürgen Schebera, Peggy Sherry, Lee Snider, Donald Spoto, Guy Stern, Dolores Sutton, Lys Symonette, Gottfried Wagner, Robert Wennersten, and Murray Wortzel.

Personal thanks go to my partners Milton Chris Blazakis (in spirit) and David Gilbert, my parents, brothers and sister, and extended "family" in New York and elsewhere.

Finally, this book is dedicated to the memory of Henry Marx, the prominent German-American theater historian who organized the first major exhibition on Weill and Lenya at the New York Public Library in 1976 and one of the experts who answered Lenya's call in 1980 to serve the Kurt Weill Foundation as a trustee. Dr. Marx was a great friend of the Weill-Lenya Research Center, always passing along the gems of his discoveries from used bookstores the world over. I am deeply grateful to his widow, photographer Carin Drechsler-Marx, for sharing with me her extensive photo research on Lenya's life and career.

SOURCES

The location for each source is given in brackets at the end of the entry. WLRC=Weill-Lenya Research Center, New York. German translations are by Lys Symonette.

1 Letter to Lucy Abravanel, 26 July 1950 [WLRC Ser.43]

2 Oral history with conductor Maurice Abravanel [WLRC Ser.60]

3 Transcript of an interview with Peter Adam for "Lotte Lenya" broadcast on the Omnibus series for the BBC, 24 May 1979. [WLRC Ser.23/OM6/1979]

4 Letters to Hesper Anderson, 1972-1978 [WLRC Ser.43]

5 Anderson, Maxwell. Eulogy for Kurt Weill, 1950 [WLRC Ser.35]

6 Associated Press. "Age Bows to Love." *New York World Telegram and Sun* (1 November 1962)

7 Letter to Clive Barnes, 4 May 1970 [WLRC Ser.42/4/25]

8 Interview with David Beams, 15 & 28 February 1962, transcript of audiotape [WLRC Ser.60]

9 Belanger, Bill. "Actress Recalls 'That Magic Time.'" *Huntington (WV) Herald-Dispatch* [date unknown] [WLRC Ser.34/II/34]

10 Bergner, Elisabeth. *Bewundert viel und viel gescholten.* Munich: Wilhelm Goldmann, 1982. pp. 76-77. [Original in German; WLRC Ser.92]

11 "Jimmy's Moll," a draft of the lyrics for "Few Little English" by Marc Blitzstein. [WLRC Ser.26]

12 Letter to Saul Bolasni, 16 November 1954 [WLRC Ser.43]

13 Letters to Milton Caniff, 1973 [WLRC Ser.30/I/3]

14 Letter to Victor Carl, 19 September 1962 [WLRC Ser.30/1/15]

15 Letters to Bertha Case, 1965-1976 [WLRC Ser.30/11/8]

16 Transcription of Lenya's appearance on the Dick Cavett Show, CBS television, 1 January 1975. [WLRC Ser.114/22]

17 Transcription of an interview with Schuyler Chapin for the WNET/13 television program "Skyline," 7 December 1978. [Yale University Music Library, Weill/Lenya Papers, Box 73, Folder 4]

18 Corry, John. "Broadway: A Remembrance of Weill and Lenya at Lincoln Center." *New York Times* (12 November 1976) [WLRC Ser.53]

19 Dahl, Arlene. "Love Called Greatest Beauty Secret of All." [publication, date unknown] [WLRC Ser.53]

20 Dahlberg, Gertrude. "Lotte Lenya: Born and Bred in Defiance." *Journal-News* (4 February 1973) [WLRC Ser.53]

21 Letters to Mary Daniel, 1954-1959 [WLRC Ser.43]

22 Letter to George Davis, May 1955 [WLRC Ser.43]

23 Deutsch, Linda. "Lotte Lenya Shuns Thought of Retiring." *Long Island Press* (29 November 1971) [WLRC Ser.53]

24 Letters to music critic Olin Downes, 1950 [WLRC Ser.30/8/17. Original: Hargrett Rare Book and Manuscript Library, University of Georgia.]

25 Drosby, John. "Brecht Warning: Don't Catch Cult." *Sunday Tribune* (11 March 1962) [WLRC Ser.53]

26 Eckardt, Wolf von. "Keeper of the Flame." *International Herald Tribune* (8 January 1981) [WLRC Ser.53]

27 Letter to Richard Ely, 28 January 1976 [WLRC Ser.43]

28 Ephron, Nora. "Mrs. Kurt Weill." *New York Post* (8 January 1965) [WLRC Ser.53]

29 Letter from Max Ernst to Lenya, [1934?] [Original in German; WLRC Ser.43]

30 Letters to Ann Fall, 1970 [WLRC Ser.43. Original: Columbia Rare Book and Manuscript Library]

31 Foster, Maryan. "Just the Microphone and You." *Tallahassee Democrat* [date unknown] [WLRC Ser.53]

32 Gary, Beverly. "A Composer's Widow Keeps His Work Alive. *New York Post* (22 January 1962)

33 Letter to Manfred George, 11 May 1950 [WLRC Ser.43. Original in German: Deutsche Literaturarchiv, Marbach]

34 "Conversation Between Lotte Lenya and Ruth Gikow." Transcript, [1976?] [Yale University Music Library, Weill/Lenya Papers, Box 73, Folder 6]

35 Letter from Lillian Gish to Ted Mitchell, December 1981

36 Goldberg, Jeff. "Lenya Speaks." *SoHo Weekly News* (29 August 1974) [WLRC Ser.34/II/36]

37   Letter to Paul Green, [1938] [WLRC Ser.43. Original: University of North Carolina, Southern Historical Collection, Paul Green Papers]

38   Harrison, Jay. "*The Threepenny Opera* Opens in New Adaptation." *New York Herald Tribune* (11 March 1954) [WLRC Ser.51A]

39   Letters to Elisabeth Hauptmann, 1955 [WLRC Ser.30/1/2. Original: Bertolt-Brecht-Archiv, Akademie der Künste, Berlin]

40   Letter to Felix Jackson, 21 September 1957 [WLRC Ser.30/1/4]

41   Letter to Ian Kemp, 2 June 1970 [WLRC Ser.43]

42   Letter to Anna Krebs, 18 December 1956 [WLRC Ser.43]

43   Lambert, Constant. "Matters Musical." *Times* (London) (13 August 1933) [Transcript: WLRC Ser.50A. Original: Harvard University, Houghton Library, Bertolt Brecht Collection 385/72]

44   Letter to Floria Lasky, 29 March 1972 [WLRC Ser.42/4/38]

45   Autobiographical notes [WLRC Ser.34 and 37]. Lenya left behind a number of colorful recollections of her childhood and teenage years written in a first-person narrative in the form of sketchy autobiographical notes or stories told to others (mainly her second husband, George Davis, and British musicologist David Drew). The stories "as told to" Davis are infused with his own, somewhat romantic, literary flair and are probably generously fictionalized. The excerpts that appear here represent a different selection and ordering from the version that appeared in *Speak Low (When You Speak Love): The Letters of Kurt Weill and Lotte Lenya* (Berkeley: University of California, 1996).

46   *London Magazine*, May 1961 [Quoted in: Taylor, Ronald. *Kurt Weill: Composer in a Divided World*. Boston: Northeastern University, 1991. pp. 58-59.

47   Letters to Gigi McGuire, 1976-1977 [WLRC Ser.43]

48   Letters to Ted Mitchell, 1964-1978 [WLRC Ser.43]

49   Letters to Paul Moor, 1978-1981 [WLRC Ser.43]

50   Letters to Caspar Neher, 1953-1961 [Originals in German; WLRC Ser.43]

51   Norris, Ron. "When 64 Loves 37." *Daily Sketch* (1 November 1962): 5.

52   Transcript of an interview with Edwin Newman of NBC News for "Speaking Freely." 14 October 1970 [Yale University Music Library, Weill/Lenya Papers, Box 73, Folder 2]

53   Letter to Otto Pasetti, 20 October 1933 [Original in German; WLRC Ser.43]

54   Patureau, Alan. "Lotte Lenya Enjoys Being a Lively Legend." *Newsday* (5 November 1964): 3c [WLRC Ser.53]

55   Peper, William. "Song in Way of Her Action." [publication, date unknown, WLRC Ser.53]

56   Letter to Kurt Pinthus, 2 December 1959 [WLRC Ser.43]

57   Letter to music publisher T. Presser, 8 April 1970 [WLRC Ser.42/1/14]

58   Donald Spoto interviews Harold Prince. Transcript, date unknown. [WLRC Ser.60]

59   Alan Rich interviews Lotte Lenya. Transcript, date unknown. [WLRC Ser.60]

60   Letters to Ann Ronell, 1958 [WLRC Ser.43]

61   Thomson, Virgil. "Most Melodious Tears." *Modern Music* 11, no. 1 (November-December 1933): 13-14. [WLRC Ser.50A/S2]

62   Letter to Hans Heinsheimer at music publisher G. Schirmer, 7 June 1971 [WLRC Ser.42/1/18]

63   Scott-Maddocks, Daniel. "Keeping the Weill Flag Flying." *Records and Recording* (February 1961)

64   Southern, Terry. "The Beautiful-Ugly Art of Lotte Lenya." *Glamour* (September 1962) [WLRC Ser.53]

65   Spoto, Donald. *Lenya: A Life*. Boston: Little, Brown, 1989.

66   [Sturm, George] "Luncheon with Lenya." *EAM Accents* (Fall 1977) [WLRC Ser.34/II/39]

67   Letters to Lys Symonette, 1970-1971 [WLRC Symonette Collection]

68   George Tabori interviews Lotte Lenya. Transcript, date unknown. [Yale University Music Library, Weill/Lenya Papers, Box 73, Folder 5]

69   Letters to Universal Edition, Vienna, 1954-1977 [Originals in German; WLRC Ser.42]

70   Transcript of radio program with Lenya interviewed by Paul Vaughan. Broadcast on the BBC, 9 September 1981. [WLRC Ser.122/2]

71   Wadsworth, Stephen. "Zeitgeist: Lotte Lenya Breathes the Very Spirit of Berlin in the '20s When Kurt Weill Burst on the Scene." *Opera News* (1 December 1979) [WLRC Ser.34/II/40]

72   Gottfried Wagner interviews Lotte Lenya. Transcript, 28 May, 3 June, and 25 July 1978. [Original in German; WLRC Ser.60]

73   Wardle, Irving. "Brecht and Berlin as Lenya Knew Them." [publication unknown] August-September 1962. [WLRC Ser.34/II/33]

74   Weill, Kurt. "Meine Frau." *Münchner Illustrierte Presse* (14 April 1929): 487. [Original in German]

75   Robert Wennersten interviews Lotte Lenya. Transcript, 27 November 1971 [WLRC Ser.30/11/17]

76   Letter to John Wharton, 30 March 1950 [WLRC Ser.43]

77   Weill, Kurt and Lotte Lenya. *Speak Low (When You Speak Love): The Letters of Kurt Weill and Lotte Lenya*. Translated and edited by Lys Symonette and Kim H. Kowalke. Berkeley: University of California, 1996.

78   Letter to the Wuppertaler Bühnen, 2 November 1963 [Weill quote in German; WLRC Ser.42/7/8]

79   Transcript of unidentified interview. [Yale University Music Library. Weill/Lenya Papers, Box 73, Folder 3]

SELECTED BIBLIOGRAPHY

Lotte Lenya's papers are housed in the Weill/Lenya Archives of the Yale University Music Library (New Haven, CT) and the Weill-Lenya Research Center (7 East 20th Street, New York, NY). Finding aids for both collections have been published and are available from the respective institutions.

WORKS BY LENYA

LENYA, LOTTE. "That Was a Time!" *Theatre Arts* 40, no. 5 (May 1956): 78-80, 92-93.

Reprinted as the foreword to the Grove Press edition of Desmond Vesey and Eric Bentley's translation of *The Threepenny Opera* (1964). Written by George Davis based on interviews with Lenya and Elisabeth Hauptmann.

——. "I Remember Mahagonny." *Philips Music Herald* 4, no. 1 (Spring 1959): 6-9.

Also printed in the booklet accompanying the Philips recording of *Aufstieg und Fall der Stadt Mahagonny* in 1958 (both German and English releases).

——. "Kurt Weill's Universal Appeal." in *Music Journal* 17, no. 1 (January 1959): 48, 77-78.

——. "The Time Is Ripe." *Playbill* 6, no. 16 (April 16, 1962): 7-11, 43.

——. "Weill's Music Is Timeless." *New York Daily News* (January 28, 1973).

WEILL, KURT AND LOTTE LENYA. *Speak Low (When You Speak Love): The Letters of Kurt Weill and Lotte Lenya*, ed. & trans. Lys Symonette & Kim H. Kowalke. Berkeley: University of California Press, 1996.

WORKS ABOUT LENYA

BEAMS, DAVID. "Lotte Lenya." *Theatre Arts* 46, no. 6 (June 1962): 11-18, 66-72.

BORWICK, SUSAN. "Perspectives on Lenya: Through the Looking Glass." *Opera Quarterly* 5, no. 4 (Winter 1987-88): 21-36.

GAVIN, BARRIE AND KIM H. KOWALKE. *Lenya: ein erfundenes Leben* (Frankfurt: Hessischer Rundfunk, 1994) (video production).

LYNCH, RICHARD. "For the Record—Lotte Lenya." *Show Music* 5, no. 2 (November 1986): 32-35.

MARX, HENRY, ed. *Weill-Lenya*. New York: Goethe House, 1976 (catalogue of the "Weill-Lenya Exhibition" at New York Public Library in 1976).

NEMSER, CINDY, ed. "Lotte Lenya and Ruth Gikow on Art, Theater, Life . . .". *The Feminist Art Journal* 5, no. 4 (Winter 1976-77): 20-21.

PRASCHL, PETER. "Hoppla, Jenny!" *Stern* 42, no. 32 (16 August 1989): 66-74.

REED, REX. "Lotte Lenya." In *Do You Sleep in the Nude?* (New York: New American Library, 1968), pp. 82-94.

SPOTO, DONALD. *Lenya: A Life*. Boston: Little, Brown, 1989.

STERN, GUY. "Lotte Lenya's Creative Interpretation of Brecht." In *Brecht Unbound*, ed. James Lyon & Hans-Peter Breuer (Newark, DE: University of Delaware Press, 1995), pp. 101-118.

——. "Sporadische Heimkehr: Lotte Lenyas Besuche des Elternhauses und bei Wiener Verlegern." In *Eine Schwierige Heimkehr: Österreichische Literatur im Exil 1938-1945*, ed. Johan Holzner, Sigurd Scheichl & Wolfgang Wiesmueller (Innsbruck: Institut für Germanistik, 1991), pp. 314-321.

——. "Woman with a Mission." *The Theatre* (July 1959): 12-13, 44-45.

WADSWORTH, STEPHEN. "Zeitgeist." *Opera News* 44, no. 6 (1 December 1979): 16-20, 43.

WEAVER, NEAL. "'Lenya, Whatever You Do Is Epic Enough for Me!'—B. Brecht: An Interview with Lotte Lenya." *After Dark* 11, no. 3 (July 1969): 32-41.

Biographies of Kurt Weill necessarily also deal with aspects of Lenya's career. The most informative of these are Ronald Sanders, *The Days Grow Short* (1980), David Drew, *Kurt Weill: A Handbook* (1987), Stephen Hinton, ed., *The Threepenny Opera* (Cambridge Opera Handbooks, 1990), Ronald Taylor, *Kurt Weill: Composer in a Divided World* (1991), and Jürgen Schebera, *Kurt Weill: An Illustrated Life* (1995).

SELECTED RECORDINGS AND VIDEOTAPES

CENTENARY REISSUES

Lenya. Bear Family Records BCD 16019. A comprehensive collection featuring all of Lenya's commercial recordings (1929-1969, including spoken word recordings); a song from Marc Blitzstein's *I've Got the Tune* (1937); songs recorded for the Office of War Information (1943); previously unreleased recordings with Turk Murphy and Louis Armstrong; live recordings of Lenya's 1960 Munich concert and 1965 New York concert at Carnegie Hall; a previously unreleased reading of Brecht's "Kinderkreuzzug"; the soundtrack of a 1964 television program, *Lotte Lenya: The Broadway Years of Kurt Weill*; and two little-known songs by John Cacavas recorded in 1969.

Lotte Lenya Sings Kurt Weill, [volume 1]. Sony Masterworks Heritage MHK 63222. Includes: REISSUE OF *The Seven Deadly Sins* (1956, Columbia-Philips) and REISSUE OF "Lotte Lenya Sings Berlin Theatre Songs by Kurt Weill" (1955, Columbia-Philips): "Moritat vom Mackie Messer," "Barbarasong," "Seeräuberjenny," "Havana-Lied," "Alabama-Song," "Denn wie man sich bettet," "Bilbao-Song," "Surabaya-Johnny," "Was die Herren Matrosen sagen," "Vom ertrunkenen Mädchen," "Lied der Fennimore," "Cäsars Tod."

Lotte Lenya Sings Kurt Weill, [volume 2]. Sony Masterworks Heritage MHK 60647. Planned contents (at the time of this printing): REISSUE OF "September Song and Other American Theatre Songs by Kurt Weill" (1957, Columbia): "September Song," "It Never Was You," "Saga of Jenny," "Foolish Heart," "Speak Low," "Sing Me Not a Ballad," "Lonely House," "A Boy Like You," "Green-up Time," "Trouble Man," "Stay Well," "Lost in the Stars," and "Song of Ruth" (previously unreleased). FROM *Cabaret* (reissue of 1966 cast album): "So What?", "It Couldn't Please Me More," "Married," and "What Would You Do." FROM *Brecht on Brecht* (reissue of 1962 cast album): "Solomon Song," "Song from *Mutter Courage*" (Dessau), "Song of a German Mother" (Eisler). THREE VERSIONS OF "Mack the Knife": Turk Murphy with introduction by Lenya, duet with Turk Murphy, and duet with Louis Armstrong.

COLLECTIONS

The Collector's "Three Penny Opera" (Weill-Brecht), Mastersound DFCD1-110. Includes: FROM *Die Dreigroschenoper* (recorded 1930): "Seeräuberjenny," "Act I Finale," "Barbara Song," "Eifer-suchts-duett," "Moritat, Reprise." FROM *Aufstieg und Fall der Stadt Mahagonny* (recorded 1930): "Alabama-Song" and "Denn wie man sich bettet." FROM *Aufstieg und Fall der Stadt Mahagonny* (recorded 1932): Selections. FROM *Happy End* (recorded 1929): "Bilbao Song."

Die Dreigroschenoper/Berlin 1930 (Lotte Lenya/Marlene Dietrich), Teldec 9031-72025-2. Includes: FROM *Die Dreigroschenoper* (recorded 1930): "Seeräuberjenny," "Act I Finale," "Barbara Song," "Eifersuchtsduett," "Moritat, Reprise." FROM *Aufstieg und Fall der Stadt Mahagonny* (recorded 1930): "Alabama-Song" and "Denn wie man sich bettet."

Kurt Weill: From Berlin to Broadway [volume 1], Pearl GEMM CDS 9189. Includes: FROM *Die Dreigroschenoper* (recorded 1930): "Seeräuberjenny," "Act I Finale," "Barbara Song," "Eifersuchtsduett," "Moritat, Reprise." FROM *Happy End* (recorded 1929): "Bilbao Song." FROM *Aufstieg und Fall der Stadt Mahagonny* (recorded 1930): "Alabama-Song" FROM *Aufstieg und Fall der Stadt Mahagonny* (recorded 1932): Selections. REISSUE OF "Six songs by Kurt Weill" (Bost, 1943): "Lost in the Stars," "Lover Man," "J'attends un navire," "Complainte de la Seine," "Surabaya-Johnny," "Denn wie man sich bettet."

Kurt Weill: Berlin and American Theater Songs. CBS Records. MK 42658. REISSUE OF "Lotte Lenya sing Berlin Theatre Songs by Kurt Weill," omitting the last four songs (1955, Columbia-Philips): "Moritat vom Mackie Messer," "Barbarasong," "Seeräuberjenny," "Havana-Lied," "Alabama-Song," "Denn wie man sich bettet," "Bilbao-Song," "Surabaya-Johnny." REISSUE OF "September Song and Other American Theater Songs by Kurt Weill" (1957, Columbia): "September Song," "It Never Was You," "Saga of Jenny," "Foolish Heart," "Speak Low," "Sing Me Not a Ballad," "Lonely House," "A Boy Like You," "Green-up Time," "Trouble Man," "Stay Well," "Lost in the Stars."

Kurt Weill: From Berlin to Broadway: Volume 2, Pearl GEMM CDS 9294. Includes: FROM *Aufstieg und Fall der Stadt Mahagonny* (recorded 1930): "Alabama-Song" and "Denn wie man sich bettet."

Die sieben Todsünden/The Seven Deadly Sins and *Happy End*. CBS Records MPK 45886 [Reissue of the Columbia-Philips recordings, 1956 and 1960, respectively]

Weill: O Moon of Alabama (Historical original recordings (1928-1944). Capriccio 10 347. Includes: FROM *Happy End* (recorded 1929): "Surabaya-Johnny" and "Bilbao Song." FROM *Aufstieg und Fall der Stadt Mahagonny* (recorded 1930): "Alabama-Song" and "Denn wie man sich bettet." FROM *Aufstieg und Fall der Stadt Mahagonny* (recorded 1932): Selections. REISSUE OF "Six songs by Kurt Weill" (Bost, 1943): "Lost in the Stars," "Lover Man," "J'attends un navire," "Complainte de la Seine," "Surabaya-Johnny," "Denn wie man sich bettet." SONGS RECORDED for the U.S. Office of War Information, 1944: "Und was bekam des Soldaten Weib?" and "Wie lange noch?"

Weill: Die Dreigroschenoper (Historical original recordings (1928-1931). Capriccio 10 346. Includes: FROM *Die Dreigroschenoper* (recorded 1930): "Seeräuberjenny," "Barbara Song," and "Eifersuchtsduett."

SINGLE STAGE WORKS

Aufstieg und Fall der Stadt Mahagonny/Rise and Fall of the City of Mahagonny, CBS M2K 77341.
[Reissue of the 1956 Columbia-Philips recording]

Cabaret, Columbia CK 3040
[Reissue of the original 1966 cast album]

Die Dreigroschenoper/The Threepenny Opera, CBS MK 42637.
[Reissue of the 1958 Columbia-Philips recording]

Johnny Johnson. Polydor 831 384-2.
[Reissue of the 1956 MGM recording]

The Threepenny Opera, TER CDTER 1101.
[Reissue of the 1954 MGM original cast album (Blitzstein English adaptation)]

The Threepenny Opera, Polydor 820 260-2.
[Reissue of the 1954 MGM original cast album (Blitzstein English adaptation)]

VIDEOTAPES

Die Dreigroschenoper/The Threepenny Opera. Directed by G.W. Pabst. videotape: Embassy Home Entertainment, 1984; videodisc: *The 3 Penny Opera*, Criterion Collection (CC1139L), 1988.

From Russia With Love. videotape: Twentieth Century-Fox Video, 1982; videodisc: MGM/UA, 1988.

The Roman Spring of Mrs. Stone. Warner Home Video (11183), 1985.

Semi-Tough. Magnetic Video (a Twentieth Century-Fox Company), 1981.

INDEX

References to photographs and captions are printed in boldface. In general, Weill's collaborations with others are entered under Weill. However, works by Weill and/or Brecht that are closely associated with Lenya are entered under title. Works by other authors are entered under title. The chronology of Lenya's life and career (pages 233-243) is not indexed.